The Theory of Incidence of Sales Taxation

By JOHN F. DUE
Instructor in Economics, University of Utah

KINGS CROWN PRESS
MORNINGSIDE HEIGHTS · NEW YORK
1942

PRINTED IN THE UNITED STATES OF AMERICA

Z14-staff, staff-500

King's Crown Press is a division of Columbia University Press organized for the purpose of making certain scholarly material available at minimum cost. Toward that end, the publishers have adopted every reasonable economy except such as would interfere with a legible format. The work is presented substantially as submitted by the author, without the usual editorial and typographical attention of Columbia University Press.

FOREWORD

A disturbing gap exists between the economic world and the doctrines of tax shifting and incidence that are relied upon by those who formulate tax policy. The gap has become more evident in the past decade or so, its details clearer. The doctrines generally assume conditions of perfect or nearly perfect competition, with an occasional excursion into the unusual case of monopoly. Actually, the more important tax measures commonly affect business sectors where competition approaching the atomistic extreme is almost entirely absent, and where monopoly analysis gives a highly restricted view. What does exist, especially in the fields of heavy excise taxation and general retail sales taxation, is apparently something in between, something on the order of the monopolistic competition analyzed by Professor Chamberlin (including the case where the number of competitors in the group is large), or the various types of "modified, intermediate or hybrid competition" listed by Professor J. M. Clark.

Professor Due's book is the first, and so far the only, detailed and extensive development of the theory of shifting and incidence that is based on these in-between situations. It throws open a new field in tax analysis and may easily prove a major influence in guiding the course of subsequent studies in shifting and incidence. It will disturb and perhaps alter opinions commonly expressed, based loosely on older analyses, concerning the extent and direction of the shifting of various types of sales taxation. The high level of its analysis, set against a realistic description of the economic forces in wholesale and retail distribution, make it directly useful in the formulation of tax policy.

One word as to the publication of this volume: it is an experiment in low-cost publication and distribution, made possible by the newly created facilities of the King's Crown Press. It is based on the assumption that important scholarly works in economics for which the market is somewhat limited will be just as useful in offset reproduction as in the letterpress form, which is unavailable because of expense. Dr. Due's book was submitted in typescript to the University of California in the

Spring of 1939 as his doctoral dissertation. It has been my privilege to urge, and assist in arranging, its publication.

Carl Shoup

Columbia University
September 1, 1941

P R E F A C E

The last ten years have brought such revolutionary changes in value and distribution theory, and analysis of the level of national income, that many applications of economic theory to particular problems, as to that of tax incidence, have not been kept up-to-date with the changes in the theory itself. The need for reorientation of the theory of incidence of sales taxation in light of these developments became so apparent to the author during graduate study that the subject was chosen for his doctor's dissertation, which served as the basis for this book. The analysis was completed during the spring of 1939; since that time some writers have begun to give attention to the problem, especially in journal articles; mention of these is made in subsequent chapters.

The author has tried so far as possible to use terms in such a way as to conform with most common usage, but in some cases deviation from this principle has seemed desirable for purposes of clearer exposition. An important example of the latter is the use of the term sales tax to refer to specific as well as ad valorem levies. Although the treatment is essentially non-mathematical, charts have been included in order to attempt to aid those who wish to take the trouble to work through them to understand the conclusions. The charts are not in all cases mathematically accurate, except so far as is necessary for accuracy of the conclusions. Apology must be made for the complexity of some of the charts and parts of the context itself, but the subject matter does not lend itself to simple explanation. The review of monopolistic competition analysis in the first chapter may well be passed over quickly by those familiar with recent value theory; it was included because many students of public finance are not specialists in value analysis. Chapters II and III deal with situations of not great importance in themselves, but were necessary as a basis for the sections following. In Appendix II to Chapter VII will be found an analysis of chain store tax incidence; although this levy is not a sales tax, the similarity of its incidence to that of the retail sales tax seemed to warrant its inclusion.

The author wishes to express appreciation to the editors of the Quarterly Journal of Economics for permission to use material included in the Note entitled "Ad Valorem and Specific Taxes," published in the August, 1940 issue of the Quarterly Journal, to the editors of the Southern Economic Journal for permission to use the material in the article entitled "A Theory of Retail Price Determination," published in the January, 1941 issue of the Southern Economic Journal, to the editors of the National Tax Association Bulletin for permission to use the material of the article entitled "The Incidence of Retail Sales Taxes," published in the May, 1940 issue of the Bulletin, and to the editors of the Journal of Marketing to use the material of the article entitled "The Incidence of Chain Store Taxation," published in the October, 1940 issue of the Journal.

I wish also to express appreciation to those whose suggestions have been very useful in the development of the analysis. Credit is due especially to Dr. M. M. Davisson of the University of California, under whose direction the original study was undertaken and completed, and to Dr. Carl Shoup of Columbia University, whose suggestions have been particularly helpful, and through whose efforts publication has been made possible. In addition, I want to express gratitude to Miss Carol Ford of Cogswell Polytechnic College in San Francisco, and to Mr. Ralph Robinson of the University of Utah for aid in physical construction of the study and the index.

Salt Lake City, Utah
June 27, 1941

TABLE OF CONTENTS

FOREWORD . . . v

PREFACE . . . vii

CHAPTER I. INTRODUCTION . . . 1
I. The Inadequacy of the Theory of Incidence of Sales Taxation . 1
II. Definitions . . . 2
III. The Theory of Monopolistic Competition . . . 3
Analysis of Cost . . . 5
Short Period . . . 5
Long Period . . . 5
Supply Curves . . . 6
Pure Competition . . . 6
Monopolistic Competition . . . 7
Pure Competition . . . 7
Price Determination . . . 7
Monopolistic Competition . . . 8
Introduction . . . 8
Price Determination . . . 10
Equilibrium of the Individual Firm in Monopolistic Competition . . . 10
Equilibrium of the Industry . . . 11
Sales Policy . . . 12
Pricing Practices . . . 14

CHAPTER II. THE INCIDENCE OF SPECIAL SALES TAXES UNDER CONDITIONS OF PURE COMPETITION . . . 17
I. Short Run Incidence . . . 17
II. The Process of Readjustment Toward a New Stable Equilibrium . 20
III. The Incidence of the Tax After Long Run Adjustments Have Been Made . . . 21
The Effect on Incidence of Different Degrees of Demand Elasticity . . . 23
The Effect of the Tax on Other Factors Influencing Price . 23
Changes in Demand Produced by Taxation . . . 23
The Effect of the Tax on Production Functions . . . 25
The Effect of the Tax on Prices of the Factors of Production . . . 25
The Significance of Dynamic Conditions for Incidence . . 28
The Significance of Limited Jurisdiction of Political Units Imposing the Tax Levy . . . 28
Multiple Line Enterprises . . . 30
IV. Conclusion . . . 31

CHAPTER III. THE INCIDENCE OF SPECIAL SALES TAXES UNDER CONDITIONS OF MONOPOLY . . . 34
I. Long Run Incidence . . . 34
Constant Cost . . . 34
Decreasing Cost . . . 38
Increasing Cost . . . 41
II. Short Run Incidence . . . 43
III. Modifying Factors . . . 44
Imperfect Knowledge . . . 44
Regulation of Prices . . . 44
Fear of Control . . . 45
Price Discrimination . . . 45
IV. Variations in Constants . . . 46
V. Summary . . . 48

CHAPTER IV. MONOPOLISTIC COMPETITION AND THE INCIDENCE OF SPECIAL SALES TAXES . . . 51
I. Introduction . . . 51
II. The Process of Readjustment . . . 52
III. The Amount of Price Rise . . . 53
General Statement of Incidence . . . 53
The Significance of Oligopoly Elements . . . 54
Possibility of Shift in Elasticity of Demand . . . 55
Selling Costs . . . 57
The Significance of the Existence of Monopoly Profits . . . 61
Modifying Factors . . . 64
Diversity of Cost Curves and Demand Curves . . . 64
Product Variation . . . 65
Multiple Lines . . . 66
Average-Cost Pricing . . . 73
Variations in Constants . . . 75
IV. Conclusion . . . 76

APPENDIX TO CHAPTER IV. THE PROCESSING TAXES OF THE AGRICULTURAL ADJUSTMENT ACT . . . 83

CHAPTER V. SPECIAL AD VALOREM AND GROSS RECEIPTS TAXES . . . 88
I. Pure Competition . . . 88
Constant Cost . . . 89
Decreasing Cost . . . 90
Increasing Cost . . . 92
II. Monopoly . . . 93
Price Discrimination . . . 95
III. Monopolistic Competition . . . 96
Absence of Monopoly Profits . . . 96
Limited Entry and Excess Profits . . . 97
Modifying Factors . . . 99
Selling Costs . . . 99
Average Cost Pricing . . . 100
IV. Summary . . . 102

CHAPTER VI. GENERAL PRODUCERS SALES TAXES 104
I. Initial Price Increases: Variations Among Lines . . . 104
II. Modifying Factors 105
Reductions in the Rate of Interest 105
Reductions in Wages 110
Shifts in Demand Curves 111
III. The Significance of the Exemption of Certain Lines . . 113
IV. Summary 114

CHAPTER VII. RETAIL SALES TAXES 116
I. Taxes on Sales of Single Line Retailers 116
Retail Price Determination 116
The Effect of the Imposition of a Tax 119
II. Taxes on Sales of Multiple Line Retail Enterprises . . 122
The Theory of Retail Pricing with Multiple Lines . . 122
The Incidence of a Tax on Retail Sales: Multiple Line Enterprises 130
Special Sales Taxes 130
On Lines Not Contributing to Overhead Cost . . . 130
On Lines Contributing to Overhead 132
General Retail Sales Taxes 137
The Initial Reaction of Individual Firms . . . 137
Separate-Charge Provisions 138
Modifying Phenomena 139
Retail Pricing Practices 139
Failure of Certain Firms to Raise Prices . . . 141
Differences in Elasticity of Demand 143
Secondary Readjustments 144
Exodus of Firms 144
Shifts in Cost 146
Fall in Employment and Changes in the Rate of Interest 148
Variations in Quality of Service 149
Shifts in Demand 160
The Exemption of Certain Lines from the Tax . . . 161
III. Conclusion 162

APPENDIX I TO CHAPTER VII. EMPIRICAL STUDIES OF RETAIL SALES TAX INCIDENCE 166

APPENDIX II TO CHAPTER VII. CHAIN STORE TAXES 168
Initial Price Increases 168
The Effect of Competition of the Independents 169
The Significance of Chain Store Excess Profits 170
Differences in Number of Units in Various Chains . . . 171
Differences in Average Volume of Sales Per Store . . . 174
Price Increases by Independents 176
Conclusion 177

CHAPTER VIII. GENERAL SALES TAXATION 180
I. The Concept of a General Sales Tax 180
II. The Theory of Incidence 180
Initial Reactions 180
Secondary Reactions 181
The Production Stages 181
The Retail Level 183
Interest Rate Reduction 185
III. Comparison with Retail Sales Tax 186
Taxation by Limited Jurisdictions 191
IV. The Effect of the General Sales Tax on Integration . . 192
V. Summary 194

CHARTS 199

NOTES 207

BIBLIOGRAPHY 245

INDEX 251

I

I N T R O D U C T I O N

THE INADEQUACY OF THE THEORY OF INCIDENCE OF SALES TAXATION:

The theory of incidence of taxation has occupied a place in the study of political economy since the days of the Mercantilists, and, from the writing of the Wealth of Nations, has been an integral part of the general system of economic theory.[1] In the last half century, the number of treatises dealing with incidence alone is small, but virtually every general work in the field of Public Finance, as well as many in economic theory, have devoted attention to the problem. General agreement, with variations only in detail, is to be found among practically all of the writers as to the final resting place of various types of government levies. However the analyses suffer from serious deficiencies which greatly interfere with the significance of the results. In the case of the sales tax, assumptions on which the analysis is founded are so far removed from actual conditions as to render the results of little practical importance. In addition, in many cases actual confusion exists in the analysis because of failure to adhere closely to the assumptions which have been made. In the first place, the analysis, based on orthodox value theory, accepts the traditional competition-monopoly dichotomy, and treats the two cases in isolation, giving nothing more than incidental attention to the intervening territory. Furthermore, unfortunately, many of the writers either are not sure just what they mean by competition, or "their common sense occasionally gets the best of their bad theory," and, as will be shown below, they attempt to introduce into an analysis of incidence under supposedly pure competition elements which are incompatible with the analysis, but which are essential phenomena of a world characterized by widespread monopolistic elements. Thus, to provide a more significant statement of the theory of incidence it is necessary first to reexamine the latter under pure competition, and under pure monopoly in the traditional sense of the term, with a definite realization of the exact nature of the conditions of those situations, as well as to consider the implications for tax incidence of semi-monopolistic conditions, with the various accompanying phenomena.

A further deficiency is the failure to consider adequately the significance of the application of the more general types of sales taxes to a number of commodities. Except for a few scattered references, the chief of which appeared only in very recent years, it is implicitly assumed that the incidence of a general manufacturers' sales tax can be determined simply by considering the incidence of the various parts of the levy. In particular, the effect of such levies upon unemployment and interest rate changes must be introduced in order to determine the final resting place of the tax. Furthermore, in regard to interest rates, the recent work of J. M. Keynes and others has raised considerable doubt as to the adequacy and even correctness of the orthodox theory of interest and capital upon which traditional incidence theory is based.

Finally the few references to retail sales taxes which have been made are not based upon any adequate theory of retail pricing or any satisfactory explanation of vertical price relationships: the relation between prices at various levels in the process of production and distribution. Unfortunately, economic theory can supply little aid along these lines, as only recently have such problems received any attention in the latter field. Accordingly the analysis of retail sales levies in subsequent chapters must suffer from lack of an adequate theoretical basis, but an effort is made to give some consideration at least to the problems involved.

DEFINITIONS:

Before proceeding farther, it is necessary to define certain concepts used in subsequent sections. By <u>incidence</u> is meant the pattern of the final distribution -- in the sense of form, not of process[2] -- of the burden of a tax among the various economic groups; that is, the extent to which the real incomes of various groups are reduced as a result of the tax. By the term "various economic groups" is meant the four factors of production, specific groups of persons within these factor groups, and consumers as such. The reduction in real income may occur through reduction in money incomes, increases in prices of goods consumed, reductions in quality of goods consumed, and declines in the value of property held occurring as a result of the tax. Not only immediate changes in the prices of the commodity must be considered, but also any secondary reactions such as changes in prices of the factors of production which may influence location of burden. Thus the concept is defined as to include a portion of that which is called effects in the Colwyn Report,[3] Silverman,[4] and other works; the term effects is confined to reactions to the tax other than those affecting final distribution of the burden.

The term producer is used in the narrow sense to include only those engaged in creation of form utility: farmers, manufacturers, processors, etc., excluding those engaged in the distribution of goods to final consumers. The latter activities are of course a part of production in the economic sense; the term is narrowly confined simply for lack of a more widely accepted name for this type of activity. By firm is meant an enterprise engaged in economic activity; by industry is meant the group of firms engaged in the production of the same or substantially similar products.

By the term "sales tax" is meant any levy upon physical units sold or revenue received from the sale of goods.[5] The gasoline tax is an example of the former type; the usual retail sales tax, of the latter type. The simplest form, the special sales tax, is a levy upon the sales of the firms in a single industry; in the case of the producers sales tax, sales of all or nearly all producers, as defined above, are included. The retail sales tax is levied only upon sales at retail. The most inclusive type to be considered is the general sales tax, including sales at all stages in the production and distribution process. Other definitions will be given as required in the course of the analysis.

THE THEORY OF MONOPOLISTIC COMPETITION:

Before beginning the analysis of incidence itself, it seems advisable to provide as a background a brief review of the theory of monopolistic competition, which must serve as a basis for the analysis to follow. The theory could more logically be called the theory of the individual firm, since it deals with conditions of pure competition as well as of pure monopoly and monopolistic competition. However, since the other term has found widest acceptance, in the United States at least, it will be retained, despite the fact that the name applies more logically to only a portion of the analysis.[6]

The theory of monopolistic competition represents a reorientation of particular equilibrium value analysis, taking into account the blending of competitive and monopolistic elements, as well as the traditional cases of both elements in isolation, and making use of a technique of analysis which deals with all situations in a similar manner, to provide what may be called a general theory of value on the particular equilibrium level.[7]

The theory provides in the first place redefinition of the theory of value under pure competition in terms of the individual firm. Rather than considering the industry as a whole directly, or through the fiction of the "representative" firm, the analysis deals with the position of the individual firms in relation to the general situation of the industry. The relative unimportance of conditions of pure competition in present-day economic society is stressed, and emphasis is given to the futility of attempting to explain certain seemingly competitive phenomena by means of an analysis that denies their existence.

In the second place the usual monopoly concept is extended to take into consideration elements of competition, not only in price, but also in selling activity and quality-service variation, among producers of close substitutes, each producer having exclusive control over a narrow line of goods, but being subject to more or less intense rivalry by firms in closely related lines.

Finally, the theory makes extensive use of the recently developed marginal analysis as applied to revenue of individual firms.[8] This technique replaces the so-called "areas" technique of Alfred Marshall, providing an easier method of showing the point at which an individual firm will operate, and the price it will charge.

The traditional dichotomy in value theory between monopoly and competition, the price determining forces being analyzed in the two cases in different terms, is replaced by a unified technique which subordinates orthodox monopoly to the status of special case in monopolistic competition, and which, while differentiating sharply between the latter and pure competition, applies the same type of analysis to both situations.[9] The differentiating criterion between the two contrasting cases lies in the nature of the demand curves confronting the individual firms. The firms react in the same manner to the environment, but the environmental conditions, as to demand, are different.

ANALYSIS OF COST: Prior to a summary statement of price determination under the two sets of conditions, attention will be given to the nature of cost curves of individual producers and industries. The Marshallian distinction between long and short run will be accepted, the criterion being as to whether or not sufficient time has elapsed to allow adaptation of fixed plant rather than mere change in degree of utilization of existing plant.[10]

Short Period: In the short period, costs can be separated into two types, direct or prime, and fixed or supplementary. The former includes those elements which are incurred only because certain amounts of output are produced. The latter consists of the items of expense which go on regardless of whether the plant is operated or not, and independent of the volume of output. The fixed cost obviously declines per unit at larger volumes of output; the variable cost per unit is ordinarily relatively constant within usual ranges of output, increasing sharply when plant becomes fully utilized. Accordingly total cost declines per unit so long as the fall in fixed cost caused by spreading of the given total over larger volumes of output offsets any increase in variable cost per unit. After plant reaches full utilization, the latter will more than offset the former, and total cost per unit will rise. The total cost curve is therefore U-shaped; it is intersected at the lowest point by the marginal cost curve indicating the additions to cost necessary to turn out successively larger volumes of output.[11] (Note SRAC and SRMC on Chart 1.)

Long Period: In a period of time sufficiently long to allow full readjustment of capital equipment through extension or amortization and non-replacement, all costs are variable, as all items can be readjusted to the optimum sizes for different volumes of output. The long period average cost curve is the envelope of all the short period curves; that is, for each volume of output, the cost is that with the plant capacity adjusted to the optimum size for the output in question.[12] The long run curve, just as the short run curve, is U-shaped, as unit costs are high for a small volume of output as the most efficient scale of production cannot be attained; at larger volumes costs fall from economies of division of labor and specialization;[13] eventually they rise again as the organization of the producing unit becomes cumbersome and difficult to coördinate, and in some cases also because of increases in prices of specialized resources.[14] There is a long run marginal cost curve formally comparable to the short run marginal curve. There is likewise a cost curve for the industry, in the sense of a curve showing the location (as to level on the cost axis) of the low points of the average cost curves of the individual firms, with different amounts of total output for the whole industry.[15] In a constant cost industry, the cost curves of the firms are unaffected by changes in total output, and the industry cost curve is a straight horizontal line. In an increasing cost industry, the individual curves rise as output increases, and the industry curve slopes up; the reverse is true in a decreasing cost industry.[16]

SUPPLY CURVES - Pure Competition: Under conditions of pure competition,[17] there are supply schedules, represented by supply curves, for both firm and industry. At any one time the market supply curve of each firm depends on the estimates of future prices, and the stock on hand; more will be sold at higher prices than at lower. The curve for the industry is the summation of those for all the firms.

In the short run period, for each firm, the portion of the short run marginal cost curve above its intersection with the average variable cost curve is the firm's supply curve, since the firm will operate at the level of output at which price equals marginal cost. The curve for the industry is the summation of the curves for the firms, and slopes up from left to right.

In the long run period, the supply curve for the firm is the portion of the long run marginal cost curve above its intersection with the average cost curve. For the industry, however, the curve is not merely the summation of the curves of the existing number of individual firms, as the number of firms may be readjusted. Rather, the curve indicates the total amount that will be supplied at each price, with the number of firms which will enter and remain in the industry if the price stays at the particular level. The actual nature of the curve depends upon the cost conditions of the industry. Under constant cost, an unlimited amount will be supplied at the price equal to average cost for each firm, and none will be supplied below this. With increasing cost, the industry cost curve indicates the total supply curve; at each price, the number of firms will adjust to the level that such an amount will be supplied that average cost of each firm is equal to the price. The same is true with decreasing cost.[18]

Monopolistic Competition: For conditions of monopolistic competition, it is impossible to draw an industry supply curve, inasmuch as the supply forthcoming at any price depends on the way in which the total demand is distributed as between individual firms. Nevertheless, the industry cost curve, considered above, is of significance in price analysis in regard to monopolistic competition, as the location of the cost curves of the firms, and thus the price, depends upon the output of the entire industry, except in a constant cost industry.

PURE COMPETITION - Price Determination: The essential distinguishing characteristic of pure competition is the infinite elasticity of the demand curve for each producer. Every firm considers its market unlimited, in the sense that any amount, within ranges of possible output, can be sold at the market price.[19] Likewise, price cannot be increased without complete cessation of sales; the individual firm has no control over price, which depends on total supply and demand schedules. Each firm will sell at the market price; at any one time the latter depends on the relation of the total market supply and demand schedules, and bears no relation to cost. In a short run period, the price comes to the level as determined by the short run supply and demand schedules; it must at least cover average variable cost, but may exceed or be less than average cost. The firms will operate at the level of output at which price equals short run marginal cost.

In the long period, the long run industry supply curve and the demand curve determine price; firms will operate at the level of output at which price equals long run marginal cost; price must also equal average cost or firms will enter or leave the field.[20] Since average cost and marginal cost are equal to each other only at the point of lowest average cost, each firm must operate under optimum conditions.

Thus, permanent equilibrium exists for the industry only when, for each firm, long run and short run marginal cost and long run and short run average cost are all equal to price, short run marginal cost being above short run average variable cost by an amount equal to average fixed cost. Any other situation will lead to readjustment either of each firm, or the number of firms, or both.

It should be emphasized that the cost conditions of the industry as a whole are independent of those of the firm; the industry as a whole may be in conditions of decreasing cost in an equilibrium situation. Such a condition does not make expansion of present firms, or the creation of new ones, profitable because no one firm, by expansion, can gain benefit of external economies.

MONOPOLISTIC COMPETITION - Introduction: The essential requisite of monopolistic competition is the absence of completely infinite elasticity of demand for the firm. Additional amounts of output can be disposed of only at lower prices; the firm cannot sell an unlimited amount at the market price. Such a situation arises either when any producer has complete control of the supply of an article which cannot be duplicated exactly in the eyes of the consumer by any other firm, or when the number of sellers is so small that each realizes that his own price policy will so strongly affect the sales of other firms as to lead to a readjustment of the policies of the latter. The former situation arises always when products of the various firms in an industry are differentiated by physical changes or branding. The second situation is known as oligopoly.[21] When both factors which may produce a situation of monopolistic competition -- differentiation and oligopoly -- are found together, the demand will appear very much more inelastic, cet. par., than with either alone. If each seller realizes that his own price reduction will injure other sellers in such a manner as to cause them to reduce their own prices, obviously the sales to be added by a given price reduction will be very much less than otherwise. If each is certain that the other firms will act exactly as he does, the demand curve will appear to each firm to be of the same elasticity as that for the industry as a whole. Actually, however, there will be considerable uncertainty as to the action of competitors; in general, the greater the number of competing firms the greater is the uncertainty. This factor, of course, will make the demand appear more elastic than otherwise.

The analysis of monopolistic competition differs from the traditional monopoly analysis in that the former considers the relationships between firms having monopoly over their own particular products, but being in close competition with other firms producing similar but not identical products, whereas the traditional monopoly analysis dealt with one single firm, assuming the demand schedule for that firm to be independent of the profits made by the firm, and ignoring the relation between the firm and any other firm. Under monopolistic competition analysis, it is recognized that in some cases a situation of complete monopoly exists, in the sense that a firm sometimes enjoys such complete absence of competition that the demand schedule of the firm may be considered to be independent of the rate of profits that the firm may make and unaffected by price changes by the firm,[22] and thus analysis of the firm does not have to consider relationships with other firms.[23] But for monopolistic competition analysis this is a special and relatively rare case, in a broader field in which most firms enjoying some monopoly power have more or less serious competition and in which the relationships between the firms must be considered in explaining the determination of equilibrium. It should be indicated that the concept of an industry, that is, the group of producers turning out the same product, is no longer clear when the products are differentiated;[24] nevertheless it seems useful to retain the term, redefining it as consisting of the group of firms turning out products so substantially similar that profits made by one in the group will influence the action of other actual or potential producers in the same group so as to affect the demand curve of the first producer.[25] While it is true that Camels and Chesterfields do not appear as identical products to the consumers, nevertheless there is a very much sharper break between cigarettes and the nearest substitute than there is between different brands of cigarettes. Large profits in cigarette production will lead to the creation of new brands of this commodity, not of cigars or snuff. Thus, the analysis of monopolistic competition gives attention to the problem of equilibrium within an industry thus defined, where each producer has monopoly over his own product.

Price Determination - Equilibrium of the Individual Firm in Monopolistic Competition:

Under conditions of monopolistic competition, each firm has the power to set its own price; in order to maximize net receipts, it will expand output until marginal revenue equals marginal cost; the price will be set at the level at which the output thus determined can be sold. The average revenue curve slopes downward to the right, as additional units can be sold only at lower prices. Thus, the marginal revenue curve must be below the average revenue curve, as each additional unit adds less to the total revenue than is received directly for it, because the other units must be sold at lower price. Thus, when marginal revenue equals marginal cost, price must be above marginal cost, since it is necessarily above marginal revenue. Accordingly, if the firm is operating at the point of lowest cost, price will be above average cost, since at this point marginal revenue will equal both marginal cost and average cost, and marginal revenue is necessarily below average revenue. If price equals average cost, the firm cannot be operating at the point of minimum cost.[26] When, further, the number of firms is so small that each firm considers the effect of its own action on that of its competitors, the demand curve will appear very much less elastic; the marginal revenue curve will be much steeper and, other conditions being the same, will intersect the marginal cost curve at a point of much lower output. If each producer fully realizes that any price change will be followed by a similar change by competitors, the price will be the same as if one producer controlled the entire output.[27] To the extent that producers are uncertain about the policy of the others, the demand will be more elastic and the price lower.

Equilibrium of the Industry:

If free entry into the field exists -- in the sense that no firm has been able to build up such a reputation monopoly that other firms are unable to take away sufficient business to lower its profits to normal -- firms will flow into or out of the field until average cost equals average revenue and thus price.[28] As the average revenue curve is sloping, it must come to tangency with the average cost curve above the minimum of the latter. (F on Chart 13.) Thus operation is not carried on at the optimum point. Marginal cost and marginal revenue will be equal, as will average cost and average receipts, but marginal cost does not equal average cost, nor does marginal revenue equal average revenue. The same result will occur whether oligopoly prevails or not; the point of tangency of average cost and average receipts will be higher to the extent that the reactions of other firms is considered.

If, in the short run, marginal revenue, while equaling short run marginal cost, does not equal long run marginal cost, a readjustment of plant capacity will occur until marginal revenue equals both long and short run marginal cost. If average revenue covers average variable cost but not average total cost, some firms will gradually retire; if average revenue exceeds average variable cost by an amount greater than average fixed cost, new firms will enter the industry. In many cases, however, excess profits will remain.[29] When the sloping nature of the demand curve is due to the existence of only a small number of producers in the field, without differentiation, elimination of excess profits will fail to occur only when the optimum size of the firms is so large that the difference between the number allowing excess profits and the additional one to eliminate them would plunge all into loss. Where the sloping nature of the curve is due to differentiation, there is much greater likelihood of excess profits remaining. It is difficult to duplicate closely the product of the competing firm; if by particularly skillful advertising a large permanent clientele is built up by the older firm, newcomers may find it impossible to gain sufficient business to eliminate all excess profits from the old firms. Nevertheless, there would be a constant tendency for these profits to disappear, in contrast to the situation envisaged by the traditional monopoly concept, where the producer was assumed to be protected by law, control of raw material resources, etc., against competition, which otherwise, attracted by the excess profits, would affect his demand schedule and his profits.

Sales Policy:

It has been assumed in the preceding analysis that each producer accepts the demand schedule as given, impossible of being influenced by his own effort. Under conditions of pure competition, this is necessarily the case; selling effort is useless as a means of increasing demand when all output can be disposed of at the market price, nothing can be sold above this price, and the price cannot be affected by any action of an individual firm. But in the case in which the demand curve for the firm is no longer horizontal, there is a possibility for the firm to exert further influence on it. Under conditions of oligopoly with identical products, advertising may be of aid by increasing the total demand for the product, but the total increases must be shared with the other firms in the industry. But when products are differentiated, there are far greater possibilities of increasing sales at given prices by means of selling effort. Not only is business taken from competitors, but a large part of the new business turned to the industry comes to the firm in question.

As a result of the existence of selling costs, the previous analysis of the nature of equilibrium under conditions of monopolistic competition must be reformulated. No longer can the assumption be made that demand curves for the firm exist independent of the activities of the firm, but the relationship between selling cost and demand must be taken into consideration. With a given cost situation, for each possible price there is an optimum selling expenditure: an expenditure of such an amount that the marginal cost thereof will just equal the marginal revenue of the expenditure. The advertising cost curve -- that is, the curve of the cost per unit necessary to sell successive additional amounts, price remaining constant -- is probably of the same nature as the production cost curve. Up to a certain point costs decrease because of the cumulative effect of advertising and the more complete utilization of specialized technique; after this point, increasing cost will prevail, as less accessible markets are sought and old markets are exploited more intensively. Thus, beyond some point further advertising expenditures would fail to bring a net gain, and will not be made.[30]

Thus, for each firm, at each price there is a new total sales volume, representing the actual sales with optimum selling expenditure at that price. These volumes for the various possible prices make up a new average gross receipts curve. (TR on Chart 14.) A net revenue curve (ANR on Chart 14) can now be determined by subtracting, for each price, the selling costs (the optimum for that price) from the gross receipts. New marginal revenue curves likewise can be determined from the average curves. The marginal net receipts curve, in conjunction with the marginal cost (production) curve, determines the point to which volume of output is extended; the gross receipts curve indicates the price received for that amount of output.[31] Under conditions of free entry into the field, the average net receipts curve will be tangent to the average production cost curve. (At X on Chart 14.) But the price is not at the point of tangency, but at the point on the gross receipts curve directly above the point of tangency. Equilibrium exists only when no firm can gain by further expenditure on selling cost or further price change, and all firms are making only such a rate of profit as to cause neither inflow nor exodus from the industry.

However, the preceding analysis rests upon an assumption which greatly lessens the significance; namely, that the producer can determine the net gain from various amounts of advertising at different price levels. Not only are returns from selling expenditures to a considerable degree unpredictable in advance, partly because of the importance of novelty, partly because, despite continued research, of the inability to predict accurately the reaction of buyers to a particular advertising plan; but even after the expenditures have been made, it is extremely difficult to tell just what effect the expenditures have had upon sales. Many firms simply spend a certain percentage of past or expected sales, or profits, on advertising; others modify the appropriation on the basis of trends in sales, in competitors' selling expenditures, or on the basis of what the officials feel to be necessary to accomplish certain tasks. Thus the gross and net revenue curves will in many cases bear very definite relationships to each other. If the amount of advertising expenditure is determined as a percentage of expected sales, whether or not advertising costs per unit increase at lower prices depends on the expected elasticity of the demand curve; if the amount is determined independently of sales volume or prices, the selling cost per unit must diminish at lower prices, unless the demand is perfectly inelastic. In the long run, however, these factors are modified on the basis of experience as to results of the advertising campaign. Nevertheless, even over a long period it is doubtful if in most cases anything more than a very rough approximation to optimum selling expenditures is realized.[32]

Pricing Practices:

A further result of monopolistic competition is the changed method of market price determination, and the development of certain resulting pricing practices. Under conditions of pure competition, each seller brings his output (determined on the basis of expected prices) to the market and sells it at the going market price, which varies constantly with contemporary supply and demand conditions. The individual seller has no control over the price at which he sells. A change in cost will be reflected in price change only in so far as it causes a readjustment in the supply coming onto the market.

Under monopolistic competition each seller takes the initiative in setting his own price, the buyers taking what they want at the set price. A shift in cost will ordinarily cause the producers to readjust price directly, although in many cases increase or decrease in the number of firms will be necessary for final equilibrium. But demand changes will be less likely to cause price readjustment. As one result, price fluctuations are necessarily less frequent than under pure competition, in part simply from inertia on the part of the seller. This tendency is strengthened by definite gains expected from a stable price policy.[33]

A second result is the tendency for price discrimination to occur. Under pure competition, with free entry, discrimination is obviously impossible, as no one would buy at a price higher than the market price, and there would be no gain from selling below. Even if parts of the market can be separated, the price level would quickly come to the same level in each. But when one producer or a group acting in unison controls the entire market, it is possible to discriminate between parts of the market (i.e., parts on a geographical basis, or on the basis of classes of buyers according to income, use made of product, etc.). Even where nothing more than differentiation exists, discrimination becomes possible, though less likely because of the relatively great elasticity of demand curves.[34] However, no matter how widely parts of the market can be separated, no price discrimination will occur unless the different parts are characterized by different elasticities of demand. When the latter exists, prices will be higher in the markets of relatively inelastic demand than in those of high elasticity. The total sales in each market will be adjusted so that marginal revenue is the same in each market, and equal to marginal cost.[35] Different inelasticity may result from different income levels or tastes in the various markets, or differences in extent of competition.

An additional phenomenon of pricing under monopolistic competition is the tendency to price on an average cost or cost-plus basis. It is impossible in most cases to determine accurately either marginal revenue or marginal cost at various possible prices. The difficulty is furthered by the presence of a large amount of overhead costs, which makes marginal cost for any one product virtually indeterminate. Accordingly a producer ascertains as well as he can the direct cost attributable to each unit, allocates overhead on some more or less arbitrary basis, and adds a certain percentage for profit.[36]

A final pricing feature is the tendency for producers of identified merchandise to extend their control over price beyond the point at which the goods leave their possession. It is essential that producers keep the goodwill which they have built up, both on the part of the final consumer and the dealers. The use of branded products by some dealers as "loss leaders" to draw business to their stores may cause the consumer to lose faith in the quality of the product or the propriety of the regular price; of greater importance is the fact that other dealers will cease to push those products widely used as leaders. Accordingly producers, urged on by those retailers injured by the loss leader practices, have sought to control the price at which the retailer sells the product, and thus have come to control the margins of the retailers on the goods in question.

With completion of this brief summary of the theory of the determination of value in light of the analysis made by those who have dealt with the problems of the individual firm under varying conditions of competition, attention will now be turned to the central problem of this study, that of the determination of the incidence of various types of sales taxes. The problem of incidence is essentially one of readjustments in price resulting from changes in cost and demand produced by the tax, and accordingly the theory of value was necessary as a basis for that which is to follow. The first levy to be considered is the simplest type of a sales tax, a tax per unit of output of the firms in a particular industry.

II

THE INCIDENCE OF SPECIAL SALES TAXES UNDER CONDITIONS OF PURE COMPETITION

The incidence of a levy per unit of output imposed upon all firms in a particular industry will be considered first under conditions of pure competition, as described in the previous chapter. The traditional analysis of the problem has been entirely in terms of the industry as a whole;[1] the development of the theory of monopolistic competition allows consideration of the reactions of the individual firms and thus facilitates greater precision.[2] It is assumed that the industry is in equilibrium when the tax is imposed, since the purpose is to consider the relation of the new equilibrium to the old, whether the latter was actually attained at the moment or not.

SHORT RUN INCIDENCE:

The first effect of the tax will be to raise the cost curves -- average and marginal, long run and short run -- of the individual firms.[3] All the curves are raised uniformly by the amount of the tax; when they are plotted, the new curves become closer (horizontally) to the old curves in the steeper portions of the latter. (Note Chart 1.) Thus the new and old marginal curves are closer (in this sense) than the new and old average curves.

Since price must remain unchanged until supply is reduced, marginal cost will exceed price. Accordingly, the firms must reduce output until these two are again equal. As the marginal cost curve for the firm (SRMC' on Chart 1) slopes upward, for the range of output immediately less than the original equilibrium level, there will be a point of intersection (H) of the revenue curve and the new marginal cost curve, provided that the tax is not too great. If, however, the tax is so great that the price is less than the new marginal cost at all levels of output, production will cease; the same is true if price does not cover average variable cost.[4]

This reduction in supply, from OR to OH on Chart 1, which will take place as soon as output can be readjusted, will cause an increase in price. The amount thereof can be determined by reference to the industry supply[5] and demand curves. (See Chart 2.) The short run supply curve for the industry, ISS, is of great inelasticity, necessarily so for all ranges above the old equilibrium point down to the levels of price at which the average variable cost of a considerable number of firms is not covered.[6] Thus, the new cost curve, after the tax, will be above, but only slightly to the left, of the old curve, except to the extent that significant exodus of firms occurs immediately due to failure to cover variable cost. On Chart 2, price will rise to N.

After this short run adjustment has taken place, each firm will find the demand curve confronting it at a somewhat higher level (AR' on Chart 1), but, as shown by the industry cost and demand curves, not tangent to its new average cost curve (i.e., cost including tax). That is, even the new demand price is below long run supply price, indicating that firms are failing to cover all costs. (On Chart 1, the firm operates at the point J). The demand curve for the firm will have risen not because of the efforts of the producers to boost prices, since the latter is impossible in pure competition, but rather from the immediate reduction in output.[7] The latter will be greater to the extent that a number of firms no longer cover average variable cost after the tax and thus immediately close down. It must be noted, however, that, if the tax is small, in the absence of careful marginal cost calculation, the need for cutting output will not appear to the individual firm, and there will be no immediate price rise.[8]

In some industries -- certain lines of agriculture in particular -- there is no possibility of any immediate readjustment in the total supply of goods. Where the commodities are perishable, there is no conceivable way for any immediate price increase to occur regardless of how much producers would like to get rid of the tax, unless the latter is so great that the return net of the tax no longer covers the cost of placing the goods on the market. When goods can be stored, however, there may be an immediate price increase, if producers, aware that the tax will cause a future price increase, hold a part of their supply. This tendency may be supported by an increase in demand caused by the action of speculators who anticipate the rise. To the extent, however, that prices do increase at once, the final adjustment will be delayed, as the average small producer, reacting primarily to present prices, will not cut his output of this crop as he otherwise would.

It will be noted that the firms are no longer producing at the optimum point, long run or short run. It is not profitable to expand output (beyond OJ on the chart), even though average cost would fall, as to do so would raise marginal cost above price; any expansion would involve further losses. With departure from the optimum, long run average cost is now below short run average cost; it might seem that readjustment of capacity would take place. If the latter requires investment of new funds, the readjustment will not occur, because average cost exceeds price, and no capital will be invested under the circumstances. If plant capacity can be lowered without expense, this will be done as a transitory step toward new long run equilibrium.[9]

In the period of readjustment, the firms will not be covering all costs of production; if all factors were equally immobile, the reward to each would be reduced in like manner, apart from differences in bargaining strength or contractual position.[10] Actually, some factors will be more mobile than others; the return to the completely mobile factors must not fall or the industry will lose its supply.[11] Thus the burden falls on the owners of the immobile factors; in particular on the receivers of the residual return to the extent that they are unable to pass it off on to others -- onto the suppliers of skilled labor, the bondholders, or the owners of land which cannot find employment of equal importance to entrepreneurs in other lines. The reduction in return going to the last two groups is often delayed by the existence of contractual obligations; reorganization, however, may occur to reduce bond interest charges. Some readjustment in the relative quantities of different factors used will be made if possible, some of the more expensive (i.e., the mobile) factors being replaced by greater use of the immobile.[12]

THE PROCESS OF READJUSTMENT TOWARD A NEW STABLE EQUILIBRIUM:

As longer periods of time are considered, the variable cost curve moves toward the average total cost curve, becoming, in the long period, identical with the latter. That is, on Chart 2, ISS' moves until it becomes identical with ILS'; when the time is reached at which the entire plant must be rebuilt, all costs are variable. In the process of migration, the average variable cost curves for some firms eventually pass the price curves, and the firms discontinue business. That is, as time passes, it will become necessary to make large reinvestments if operation is to continue; the knowledge that an average return will not be earned on the investment will prevent the latter being made, and operations will stop. This may be delayed very long, however, in certain lines of enterprise, where replacements must be made gradually, in small amounts, if the plant is to be kept running. If the owners of the enterprise are making some return over that which they could get by investing the salvage value in other lines of endeavor, the minor replacements will be made to forego complete loss of the investment and of the return being made, however far it may be below the average rate of profits. In this case the long period supply curve, once the plants are built, does not include average profits on the total sum invested, but merely average profits on the amount of the salvage value of the enterprise plus average profits on the capital going into replacements. There is thus a wide margin between the price level which will bring new capital into the industry, and that which will keep in the existing capital.

There are two problems which must be considered in regard to the exodus of firms. One question concerns the factors determining which of the firms must go out first; the other involves the number which must leave before equilibrium is reëstablished. As to the first, the problem is one of defining the marginal firms -- the firms whose average variable cost curves, in their upward movement,[13] first reached the price line. One group to be included consists of those firms making use of a relatively high percentage of factors whose remuneration cannot be reduced -- labor particularly -- if the firm is to retain them. Further, those firms whose capital equipment is nearest the point of requiring extensive reconstruction will go out before those whose plants have been more recently built.[14] Finally, in terms of Marshallian analysis, there are at any time new firms entering, old ones on the down-grade, for various reasons of an individual character. The increase in cost speeds along the collapse of those that are already decaying.[15]

The second problem concerns the number of firms that must withdraw before a new equilibrium, with tangency of average cost and price curves, is reached. Given the optimum size of the firms, this depends in part upon the elasticity of demand; the greater the falling off in sales as price increases, the greater must be the exodus before a new equilibrium is reached. In terms of the industry curves, the less steep the slope of the demand, the farther to the left of the old intersection will it meet the new cost curve. In addition, the reduction in output necessary depends on the cost conditions of the industry as a whole. As firms leave, the locations of the cost curves of the remaining firms may be affected.[16] The greater the extent that cost curves are lowered by exodus of firms, the smaller will the reduction in output be before the new stable position is reached.

It is entirely possible that a tax may force all firms in an industry out of operation. If the demand is very elastic because of the existence of a close substitute which is not taxed, any price increase will cause almost complete loss of sales. Unless the industry is of sufficiently great increasing cost nature, the price line for each remaining firm will not rise above the average cost curve for the firm before all have been eliminated. The commodity will thus no longer be produced.

THE INCIDENCE OF THE TAX AFTER LONG RUN ADJUSTMENTS HAVE BEEN MADE:

As yet, the final long-term incidence of the tax has not been indicated. In general, firms will continue to leave the field until price is again equal to average cost of production, including the tax, as reinvestments will not be made as long as an average rate of return is not earned.[17] Thus seemingly the entire amount of the tax will pass onto the consumer.[18] However, as previously indicated, the departure of firms from the industry may affect the location of the cost curves of the remaining firms. If the industry is one of constant costs, as on Chart 2, this will not occur, and, since the average production cost will be the same as before, the price will rise by the amount of the tax. On Chart 2, price will have risen from M to P, or by the exact amount of the tax; for each firm, the average revenue curve will be at the level of AR" on Chart 1, and average cost will again equal price.

If the industry is one of decreasing cost, the reduced output will result in failure of subsidiary industries, the abandonment of transportation lines, and an upward movement of the cost curves of the individual firms. Thus the final result will be an increase in price by more than the amount of the tax.[19] On Chart 2, ILS would slope downward from left to right, passing through M; thus the intersection of ILS' and DD would be to the left of P, and the price rise will be greater. The additional burden on the consumer is caused by higher cost of production as reduced volume prevents the use of more efficient means.

When cost per unit is greater at large volumes, as is typical for example in agriculture, the reduction in output, by relieving the necessity of using less efficient resources, whether they be land, management, or some other element,[20] or by causing a price fall in the case of specialized, non-adaptable permanent factors, will lower the cost curves. When raw materials used are produced under monopoly or semi-monopoly conditions, the fall in cost will be intensified by the reduction in monopoly profit in the raw materials field as demand falls. Thus somewhat less than the amount of the tax will be shifted because of the reduction in cost as output is lowered.[21] The remainder of the burden rests upon the owners of the factors the supply of which is not reduced for the industry by the falling return. In agriculture, for example, the burden would rest upon landowners. The marginal land would be withdrawn from cultivation, and the differential return on the better land would be reduced. On Chart 2, ILS would slope upward from left to right, passing through M; thus the intersection of ILS' and DD would be to the right of P, and the price rise would accordingly be less.[22]

THE EFFECT ON INCIDENCE OF DIFFERENT DEGREES OF DEMAND ELASTICITY: One aspect of incidence, as yet unconsidered in this study, concerns the significance of different elasticities of demand for price changes resulting from the tax.[23] Under conditions of constant cost, there is obviously no effect, since price must increase by the exact amount of the tax regardless of the nature of the demand. With increasing cost, greater output reduction occurring when demand is elastic will increase the amount of cost reduction and thus lessen the price increase necessary. On Chart 3, price will rise from M to N with the more elastic demand, from M to P with the less elastic. Under decreasing cost conditions, the reverse is true; the greater output reduction with more elastic demand will force greater increase in production cost before equilibrium is reached, and produce greater price rise. On Chart 4, price will rise to R with the more elastic demand, to S with the less elastic one. Thus the rule of traditional incidence theory, that the more elastic the demand, the less the price increase, is not valid as a general statement.[24]

THE EFFECT OF THE TAX ON OTHER FACTORS INFLUENCING PRICE: The analysis to this point has been based on the assumptions of constant demand for the commodity, constant technological conditions, and constant prices of the factors of production. The first of these assumptions requires the conditions of unchanging tastes, incomes, and prices of other commodities. Inquiry must be made as to the significance of these assumptions, taking into consideration whether or not the elements in question are influenced by the tax, and whether or not the assumption that they remain unchanged, apart from the effects of the tax, during the period in which shifting takes place, is essential to the validity of the theory of incidence.

Changes in Demand Produced by Taxation: First, as to possible effect of the tax on demand, the orthodox analysis assumes implicitly that the government, or the recipients of the government funds, spend the tax money in the same way that the individuals who would have received the money if it had not been paid in taxes would have, or that the total amount of the tax money spent on the commodity on which the levy is imposed is too small to influence its demand. In many cases, this assumption is satisfactory; for example, it is unlikely that a tax on cigarettes supplying revenue for general government expenditures will cause a shift in the demand schedule for cigarettes. It is possible, however, that the receipts of a levy may be used in such a manner as to modify significantly the purchases of the goods in question and influence incidence. A tax on gasoline, the revenue from which is used to construct highways, may increase greatly the demand for this product. If this were an industry of pure competition and increasing cost, for example, the price rise would be greater than that produced by the tax considered only as an element influencing cost. In the case of a decreasing cost industry, price will rise less than otherwise and may even fall as a result of the demand increase. Or, if the tax money is paid out to a different income group from that which would have received it if the tax had not been levied, modifications in purchases may result.[25] Demand for the commodity will also be influenced by any change in total volume of income resulting from the levying of the tax and the expenditure of the receipts. There will be a tendency to a decline in total output as marginal productivity of capital is reduced in the taxed industry. This may, however, be offset by reduction in interest rates, or by changes in propensity to consume or investment opportunities in untaxed fields coming about as a result of the tax.[26]

Finally, demand for the commodity will be influenced by changes in prices of other goods. Some changes in the latter are inevitable because of the alterations in sales as changes in price in the taxed line cause more or less to be expended on non-taxed goods according to the different elasticities of demand for the various commodities. As these other prices change, in the manner determined by the cost conditions in the fields concerned, the demand schedule of the product subject to the tax will in turn be altered, and further changes in price will occur. With increasing costs in the industry gaining sales, a part of the burden of the tax on one industry is passed on to consumers of other goods because of increase in cost of producing the latter; with decreasing costs, consumers in the untaxed industry benefit as a result of the levy imposed on the field. In all cases in which demand shifts, subsequent effects on incidence depend upon cost conditions in the taxed industry.

Throughout the analysis to follow, except where specifically mentioned, the possibilities of changes in demand will be ignored. It is, in general, impossible to make further generalizations on the problem than those indicated above, and to avoid constant repetition of these, the assumption of given demand schedules will be made, and, except in a few cases, attention is devoted solely to the effect of taxes upon cost. The possibilities of shifts in demand must not be forgotten, however, and in the case of practical application of the theory of incidence to particular levies, the effect on demand must be taken into consideration.[27]

The Effect of the Tax on Production Functions: The second assumption mentioned was that of given production functions. A tax cannot influence methods of production in an industry which enjoys pure competition both before and after the tax. Each firm will operate at the point of lowest cost, and with the same volume of output after the readjustment of equilibrium as before the levying of the tax. Accordingly, there is no interference with the use of available technological equipment.[28] Nor can a tax be expected to facilitate the invention of new methods. From a short run standpoint, a tax might check installation of new techniques if average cost would exceed price regardless of the change; the tax would stimulate replacement if the latter would bring cost to the price level. But the former would be the case only until exodus of firms occurred; in the latter the change would not be made any more profitable because of the levy. Thus, over longer periods there would be no influence along these lines.

The Effect of the Tax on Prices of the Factors of Production: The third assumption is that of constant prices of those factors of production for which the industry must compete with other lines of activity.[29] If the tax produces any change in these prices, the location of the cost curves of the individual firms will be affected. In terms of the classical theory of value and distribution, the reduction in investment and employment caused by the curtailment of output[30] will cause sufficient decline in interest rates and wages to restore the original level of employment. One result of this would be a lowering of the cost curves of the firms subject to the tax; accordingly the price rise in this field will be somewhat less than otherwise. The prices of all other goods would fall slightly because of the reduction in cost; the burden resting on consumers of the taxed article would be offset in general by a slight reduction in price of other goods, and the tax would be borne by the various groups engaged in production. The only injury to consumers as a whole arises out of the reallocation of productive resources in a manner unfavorable to their interests.[31]

However, if the traditional explanation of the determination of the prices of the factors, based on the assumption of a given level of income, is abandoned in light of the analysis in recent years by J. M. Keynes and others, the possibilities of modification of incidence along these lines becomes less certain. The rigidifying influences of labor unions tend to check money wage reductions; furthermore, it is not by any means certain that a reduction in money wages will lead to a fall in real wages and an increase in employment.[32] In the case of unskilled labor, substantial wage reductions may occur, which may reduce the unemployment of this group, but for labor as a whole, the likelihood of elimination of unemployment from wage reductions does not appear great. Likewise, in regard to interest rates, in light of the criticisms of the classical theory developed by J. M. Keynes and others,[33] it would seem that interest rates cannot be explained satisfactorily in terms of supply of and demand for savings, and accordingly it is not at all obvious that the reduction in employment of capital, by making the supply of savings greater than the demand for them at the old interest rate level, would lower the rate and restore the old level of investment. The theory of interest stands in a rather unsatisfactory state at present, but the Keynesian analysis, explaining the interest rate in terms of the relation of the demand for money to hold for liquidity purposes, and the supply of money in existence, provides a more satisfactory approach than the classical theory, and will be used in subsequent analysis. It must be recognized, however, that the Keynesian theory as it is today is by no means a completely developed explanation. In terms of this approach, fall in interest rates can come only from an increased supply of, or reduced demand for, money.[34] The former is unlikely since the volume of unemployment created by the tax burden in one industry is not likely to be sufficiently great to affect government effort to reduce unemployment. Some reduction in demand for money will occur because of the smaller volume of business transactions; again, when only one industry is affected, this can have little influence on the interest rate. In general, in terms of the Keynesian analysis, the tax reduces the marginal efficiency of capital in one industry, and tends to reduce total output and employment accordingly. The burden of the tax thus rests on the consumer of the product; there is a further indirect burden of the levy borne by those losing employment as a result.

To the extent that interest rates do fall, a portion of the burden initially resting on consumers will pass on to the class supplying money capital. The subsequent effect upon wages depends upon changes in marginal productivity of labor as output expands at the lower rates of interest. It would appear that changes in productivity of labor are not likely to be great, since the expansion in the labor force is accompanied by an expansion in the amount of capital; change in marginal product depends on the relative reaction of these two forces. Incidental injury is suffered by those permanently unemployed; this is not compensated for by any gain to the state, and represents a net loss in addition to that borne directly by consumers. In the case of those workers, especially in unskilled groups, whose wages are cut, a portion of the tax burden rests directly on them, but these groups will suffer from less unemployment than the other groups. If the demand for labor of the types concerned is not elastic, there will be a net loss in purchasing power for the group, which will reduce employment in other lines, and to a large extent offset the gain in employment in the groups in which wages decrease.[35]

THE SIGNIFICANCE OF DYNAMIC CONDITIONS FOR TAX INCIDENCE: The second problem regarding the assumptions is that of inquiry as to the significance for the theory of incidence of variations in the elements assumed constant caused by forces other than the imposition of the tax. During the period of readjustment to the new equilibrium, tastes, incomes, techniques of production, and supplies of the factors are constantly changing, and producing modifications in price. But, at least from a long run standpoint, these changes will not affect the theory of incidence of the tax. The latter seeks to explain the influences of the tax alone upon price, to explain the modifications caused by the levy in the equilibrium prices of goods and factors. The other forces which are varying during the period are themselves changing the level of the equilibrium price, but the change produced in the latter by the tax is something entirely distinct from these other variations, and is not influenced, except temporarily, by the latter. As far as short run incidence and the time interval until final equilibrium is realized are concerned, the nature of changes in other factors: the trend of demand, secular or seasonal, and the trend of technological development and of factor supplies, are of importance. For example, in a rapidly expanding industry, a tax will be passed on to the full extent much faster than in one of declining demand. In the latter case actual abandonment of plant, which will not occur immediately, is necessary for shifting; in the former, shifting occurs merely from a reduction in the rate of expansion.

However, statistical analysis of the incidence of a tax is rendered difficult by the fact that the "constants" are shifting. Actual measurements of price changes following the imposition of a tax often will show very little about incidence, because of the operation at the same time as the tax of these other forces which also affect price. It is impossible to determine the relative extent to which changes found are caused by the tax and by other factors producing a shift in equilibrium.

THE SIGNIFICANCE OF LIMITED JURISDICTION OF POLITICAL UNITS IMPOSING THE TAX LEVY: The entire preceding analysis is based on the assumption that the tax is levied on all firms competing in the production of a particular commodity.[36] In certain cases, however, levies are imposed by political jurisdictions of area less than that occupied by the competing producers, and limited in power in such manner as to be unable to levy import duties. The cost curves of the producers in the area subject to the tax will be raised, whereas those in other areas will not.[37] In the short period the untaxed firms will at first not be affected significantly; the taxed firms will continue in business if price still exceeds average variable cost, and reduction in output will be of little importance. As time passes, however, and average variable cost rises, firms in the taxed area will cease operations; this process will continue until prices have risen sufficiently to allow average cost to be covered. However, the firms in the untaxed area will be enjoying excess profit, and the increase in production in these areas will check the price rise. If there are no transportation costs, and if factor prices are the same in both areas, all production in the taxed area will cease; prices will return to the original level. There will have been no shifting of the tax, but rather a relocation of production into other producing areas.[38] If the taxed firms make use of specialized immobile factors, e.g., mineral deposits, the gains from which are sufficiently great to offset the effect of the tax, the producers will not shift out of the area, but will experience lower production costs as the burden is passed back to the owners of these specialized factors. To the extent that movement must take place, if the income to the specialized factors is insufficient to absorb all the tax, there will be an increased cost of production and price in the non-taxed areas as output increases. This will allow more of the taxed firms to continue in business than otherwise. Thus, part of the tax will be shifted in the form of higher prices, not only to home consumers, but to those of other jurisdictions. An incidental result will be a clear gain to owners of the specialized immobile factors in the non-taxed areas. If all of the specialized factor is in the area taxed, the general analysis of the chapter applies. It is interesting to note, however, that a part of the burden is shifted to persons outside the taxing jurisdiction, to the extent that the entire burden is not borne by the owners of the specialized, immobile, permanent factors.[39]

MULTIPLE LINE ENTERPRISES: The preceding analysis has been based on the assumption that each firm is turning out only a single product. When this is not the case, certain modifications are necessary. With joint products, where one product cannot be produced without the other, as in the case of meat products and hides, the value of each good is to a certain extent indeterminate. The total price of both must cover the total cost, but it is impossible to make any definite statement as to the price of each, except that the special cost for which either one is directly responsible must be covered by the price of the goods in question. When a tax is levied on one of the products, the reduction in output will cause a rise in the price of both. The price increases will cease when total costs are again covered; part of the tax burden will be passed onto the consumers of the untaxed article, and the consumers of the other will escape part of the burden. If the special costs of the taxed line are not covered, the price of the other article will rise until it covers that part of joint costs formerly borne by the taxed good. There is no compensation to the government.

When, however, several products are carried by the firms as a means of spreading risk, or utilizing more fully certain resources,[40] rather than because of physical necessity, the results are quite different. The first reaction will ordinarily be an increase in the output of the untaxed lines produced by those also turning out the one subject to the levy, as resources are diverted from the latter. This may occur in a short period of time if the factors in use are not too specialized. The price of the taxed article will rise, perhaps almost immediately by the full amount of the tax if the multiple line enterprises dominate the field. However, prices of the other products will fall, and exodus of firms will occur until costs are again covered. The prices of these lines will tend to rise to the original level; any increase beyond this point will be checked if the products can be produced independently of the taxed line as cheaply as along with this article. In contrast to the original situation, these other goods will be produced by a smaller number of firms, each turning out a greater amount of output. The additional output in these lines covers that part of the common costs formerly borne by the taxed line. In the case of the latter, the original price increase, equal to the amount of the tax as modified by changes in cost conditions, will remain. Either fewer firms will be producing this article, or each firm will be producing less than before; the total number of enterprises in this and the allied fields is necessarily less. If there are certain definite advantages of combining the taxed line with the others, the prices of the latter must rise slightly above the old level so as to compensate for the lower net return from the use of factors on these lines formerly used to produce units of the taxed line. The price of the latter will fall slightly. But, in general, the tax cannot be passed off onto consumers of the other lines, so long as they can be produced separately of the taxed lines almost as cheaply as with the latter. The prices of the non-taxed lines would remain below their old levels only if reduced output of the taxed article lowered prices of semi-specialized factors which could be utilized in the production of the other goods.

CONCLUSION:

The initial effect of a sales tax levied per unit of output on a single industry under pure competition will be a slight reduction in output, as marginal cost is readjusted to again equal price. A slight price increase will be produced by this change.[41] The latter does not come about from any attempt on the part of producers to raise prices because of the tax, as the latter is impossible under pure competition. The tax is borne by the owners of those factors which cannot easily move out of the field, and in particular, so far as is possible, by the groups receiving the residual return; namely, proprietors or the common stockholders. The relative bargaining strength of the parties concerned, based on relative legal and tactical position, is a further element in determining the resting place of the burden.

However, the firms will not be covering average total cost; the firms whose average variable costs first rise above price will withdraw from the field, and prices will rise until each firm is again covering average cost. During the process of withdrawal, the cost curves of the firms will shift, in a manner determined by the nature of cost of the industry as a whole, and modify price increase. However, if the industry is one of constant cost, the curves will not move, and the price will rise by the exact amount of the tax. Under decreasing cost conditions, the price will rise by more than the tax; if increasing cost prevails, price will rise by less than the tax. The actual price increase depends not only on the severity with which increasing cost or decreasing cost operates, but also on the elasticity of demand. With increasing cost, the more inelastic the demand the greater the price increase; with decreasing cost the opposite is true. Where increasing cost operates, the part of the tax which is not shifted rests on the factor or factors of a specialized nature which are no longer used as intensively as before the levy.

There are further possible influences on incidence to consider. A tax will not ordinarily affect significantly the demand schedule for the commodity, but may do so in certain cases where the money is spent in such a way as to influence the sale of the object taxed. There is no reason to believe that a tax will affect the production functions of the industry burdened. Finally, while a tax on a single commodity may seriously affect the price of specialized immobile factors, and thus the location of the cost curves of the firms, it seems unlikely that there will be significant effect on the price of general mobile factors. The exact result in this regard depends on the influence of the tax on the general determinants of the level of economic activity, and through this on the rewards to the factors. Some fall in the prices of the factors may occur; this will check the price increase of the commodity in question and reduce the prices of other goods. If factor prices fall sufficiently to restore the original volume of employment, as would occur in terms of the traditional theory of distribution, the only burden on consumers as a whole will arise from the fact that a reallocation of resources less desirable from the point of view of the consumers has occurred. The burden of the tax will rest upon the groups engaged in production.

In conclusion, the question of whether or not other types of increase in cost will produce similar reactions as the tax under consideration deserves attention. In general, any cost increase tends to pass on to consumers over a period of time, as modified by changes in cost caused by the reduction in output. The original number of firms will be unable to cover cost at the old price, and exodus will continue until average cost is again covered. However, unlike a tax per unit of output, other types of cost increase may not represent an addition to cost varying directly with volume of output. An increase in wages, for example, may not act in this manner if the number of employees does not vary proportionately with output; the same is true as to interest rate changes, or alterations in raw material prices. The latter could be expected to produce the same effect as a tax more closely than changes in any of the other costs. In the other cases, the shape of the cost curves of the firms will be altered, the location of the minimum point shifted, and the elasticity of the supply curve of the industry as a whole affected. Price changes and incidence will be altered accordingly. The exact nature of the change cannot be indicated without more extensive analysis. Additional differences would be produced by the fact that the effect of other types of cost increase on demand, on the use of different methods of production, and on the prices of factors will not be the same as that of the tax. But, in general, the same type of analysis can be applied to the effect of other cost increases on price as is applicable in the case of a tax.

III

THE INCIDENCE OF SPECIAL SALES TAXES UNDER CONDITIONS OF MONOPOLY

As indicated in the first chapter, only a small part of the contemporary economic system operates under conditions approaching those of pure competition. Monopoly elements of widely varying strength dominate extensive spheres of the economy. Rarely is the control in any sense absolute; the semi-monopolists, whether owing their positions to differentiated product or oligopoly, are subject to more or less intensive competition from other firms also enjoying similar positions. But as a preliminary step to consideration of incidence of sales taxation in such circumstances, attention will be given to the situation of pure monopoly in the traditional sense of the term. The concept involves control of the entire output of a product by a single firm, so protected from competition that the demand schedule for the product of the firm will not shift when the firm changes its prices,[1] and will not be affected by any reaction dependent on the rate of profit of the firm. Thus, the demand schedule can be assumed as given, not subject to change as a result of readjustments of prices charged or changes in profits earned by the enterprise. The theory of incidence under monopoly has received considerable attention, but restatement in terms of the recently developed marginal revenue technique allows greater precision, and serves as a basis for the analysis of incidence under monopolistic competition in the chapter to follow. The discussion is based in part on the very brief treatment in Chapter 5 of Joan Robinson's Economics of Imperfect Competition.[2]

LONG RUN INCIDENCE:

CONSTANT COST: When a tax per unit of output is levied on a monopolist, the incidence will be different according to the period of time considered. The analysis will be made first of final long run adjustment, after sufficient time has elapsed for complete readjustment of capacity to have been made. As a starting point, it is convenient to consider conditions of constant cost, with straight line demand curves. The new cost curve after the tax will be higher than the old by the amount of the tax, intersecting the marginal revenue curve farther to the left than previously, and thus producing a price increase. This is indicated on Chart 5; the new cost curve CMC' cuts the MR curve at a point of lower output (S'N') than the old (SN), and price rises from P to P'. Further, the exact amount of the price increase can be determined. With a straight line demand curve, the marginal receipts curve falls at a rate twice that of the curve of average receipts.[3] As output is reduced following the imposition of the tax, marginal receipts per unit rise; the reduction in output is continued (to S'N') until MR again equals MC. As MC has increased by the amount of the tax (S to S'), output will be reduced until MR has risen by the amount of the tax (from S to S'); as AR rises one-half as fast as MR, price will have risen by exactly one-half the tax (from HP to H'P').[4] The other half of the tax is absorbed in monopoly profits. Note that this result is independent of the slope of the demand curve as long as the latter is a straight line.[5] If the demand curve is steeper, output reduction will not be as great, as MR will be steeper; but AR is also steeper; the smaller amount by which output is reduced (as compared with a less steep demand) will just be offset by the greater rise in price, per unit of output reduction. This result must occur, since the reasoning of the first part of the paragraph applies equally well to any straight line demand curve regardless of the steepness.[6] However, when a situation is considered in which the demand curve becomes more or less steep for prices above the old price, the incidence is altered. When the demand curve becomes steeper above the old price,[7] the marginal curve will be farther to the left and of steeper slope than if the average curve had retained the slope of its original position throughout its entire length. At the point at which the steepness of the demand curve increases, the marginal curve will fall sharply (see Chart 6); thus the output range through which it is declining at levels of greater output, the range in which it must intersect the cost curve if equilibrium is to be established, is farther to the left, and thus the marginal revenue curve cuts the marginal cost curve farther to the left -- at N_2, instead of N' on Chart 6. Thus, price will be higher than it would have been if the same slope had continued (P_2 instead of P') for two reasons: the output reduction will be greater, since the MR curve is farther to the left, and a given output reduction will cause a greater rise in price because of the steeper demand curve.[8] Price not only rises by more than half the tax, but may easily rise more than the tax, as is the case on Chart 6. Expressed in other words, when the demand is less elastic above the old price than would be the case if the original slope were retained, a given output reduction will not cause as great a falling off in sales as otherwise; in the case considered, it was profitable before the tax to keep prices sufficiently low to sell to those buyers who would purchase only at relatively low prices; after the tax it is no longer profitable to reach this group at all. Once sales must be confined anyway to that portion of the market in which the demand is relatively less elastic, a considerable price increase is profitable.[9]

Where the demand curve becomes more nearly horizontal above the old price, where at slightly higher prices a large number of buyers would drop out of the market, the marginal revenue curve rises sharply just above the old price, and then at successively smaller levels of output becomes more nearly horizontal than the original curve. Thus, ordinarily the MR curve of this type of demand curve will cut the MC curve farther to the right than if the original slope had been maintained -- at N_2 on Chart 7 -- and the price rise will not be as great (from P to P_2 instead of to P'). However, MR' eventually crosses MR; if the tax is sufficiently large that the new cost curve does not intersect the marginal revenue curve till the latter is to the left of the level at which it would have been if the average revenue curve had continued straight, then the output reduction will be greater with this curve than with the straight line demand curve. But apparently this would usually be more than offset by the smaller price increase from a given output reduction. Thus, in general, if the demand curve becomes less steep above the old price, marginal revenue per unit will rise very quickly as output is reduced, and thus will again equal marginal cost with only a small output reduction. If the increase is not great enough to carry MR over the MC line in the range of rapid rise, the output reduction may be greater than if the demand curve had remained straight. But a given output reduction will cause less price increase. It appears practically certain that this will more than offset the difference in output reduction; less of the tax will be added to the price than if the demand curve had continued straight.

With a demand curve which becomes less steep above the old price, it is possible that a situation may arise in which there will be no price increase at all following the imposition of the tax. If the change in slope is substantial, there will be a portion of the MR curve which will be vertical. If cost conditions are such that both the old and new MC curves intersect MR in the vertical part of the latter, there will be no output reduction or price rise. (Thus on Chart 7 MR' would intersect CMC' at N^x instead of at N^2). The monopolist would experience such a great fall in sales from any price increase that MR would be carried above MC, and possible profits foregone; price remains unchanged. With a vertical section in MR, MC and MC' can both equal MR' at the same level of output.[10]

In general, under constant cost conditions, cet. par., there will be less price increase as a result of a tax on a monopolist than on the firms in a competitive industry. Under pure competition, marginal cost equals price rather than marginal revenue for the industry as whole, the latter being considerably below price. Thus, when MC is raised by the amount of the tax, output must fall until price has risen by the same amount. Under monopoly conditions, marginal cost equals marginal revenue and is less than price. Output will be reduced until MR has been raised by the amount of the tax; when this has occurred, price will have risen considerably less. The fact that average cost is less than price allows part of the tax to be absorbed by the firm. It should be noted that even when price increases by an amount greater than the tax, some burden will remain on the monopolist, as any output readjustment, which must occur if price is to change, results in a reduction in profits. Otherwise, the readjustment would have been made before the tax was imposed.

DECREASING COST: In the few cases in which relatively pure monopoly does exist, decreasing cost conditions are typical.[11] One chief factor leading to monopoly control is the existence of internal economies of such great magnitude that before one of the firms has obtained full advantage of increase in output, all competitors will have been driven out of business. Likewise, one of the factors responsible for government regulation and guarantee of monopoly status is the desire to prevent useless duplication of equipment in fields in which one firm alone can provide service most cheaply. Monopoly may, of course, arise with other cost conditions through financial concentration or government control, but will not come about from the operation of strictly economic forces,[12] except with decreasing cost.

Under such conditions, as output is reduced following the imposition of the tax, marginal cost rises; at each successively lower level of output, marginal cost is greater than the old equilibrium marginal cost, not only by the amount of the tax, but by an additional amount, because of the rise in production cost per unit. Because the marginal curve slopes in this manner, it must intersect the marginal revenue curve, regardless of the elasticity of the latter, farther to the left than if cost were constant: at N^2 instead of N' on Chart 8. Thus the price increase will be greater than in the case of constant cost (to P^2 instead of to P'), and accordingly will be equal to more than one-half the amount of the tax. Thus with decreasing cost, as marginal revenue rises as output is reduced, marginal cost rises also; since the former must rise above the marginal cost (excluding the tax) by the amount of the tax, it must rise farther to achieve this result, cet. par., than if marginal cost did not increase.[13]

If the slope of the AC curve is such that MC will have risen by twice the amount of the tax, when the new equilibrium is reached, price will increase by just the amount of the tax. Such an increase in MC will occur when its slope is the same as the slope of the demand curve. Under such conditions, for each unit of output reduction, marginal cost rises one-half as far as marginal revenue; thus the reduction in the latter must be just twice as great as would be the case under conditions of constant cost, when marginal cost and marginal revenue are again equal. If output is reduced twice as far, with a straight line demand curve, price will increase twice as much and thus by just the amount of the tax.[14] If the MC curve slopes more steeply than the AR curve, the price will rise by more than the amount of the tax (as is always true under pure competition with decreasing cost), as output will be reduced more than twice as much as under constant cost. As the slope of the MC curve approaches the slope of the MR curve, the increase becomes extremely great. The limiting case is the position just before MC is parallel to MR; where MC is steeper than MR there can have been no equilibrium before the tax.[15]

As indicated above, under conditions of constant cost, incidence is the same regardless of the slope of the demand curve so long as the demand curve is a straight line. Where decreasing cost conditions prevail, however, incidence is affected. Before undertaking explanation of this, it is necessary first of all to be certain of the basis of comparison. Ideally the latter should be made between incidence under two demand curves of different slope, intersecting at the point to which price, with a given cost curve, would tend under either demand curve. This is, of course, impossible, because with different degrees of steepness of the demand curves, the marginal revenue curves would not have the same slopes and would not intersect the marginal cost curves at the same points. Accordingly, it is necessary to compare two demand curves which cross at the equilibrium price established with one of them, it being recognized that the initial price with the other is different; the problem then is to compare the relative changes in prices under the two conditions.

The proposition that under constant cost conditions always the same per cent of the tax must be shifted (with regular demand curves) regardless of slope requires that under such conditions the MR curve of the less steep demand curve (MR on Chart 9) must cut the new cost curve (CMC') just sufficiently farther to the left from the intersection with the old cost curve (CMC) -- as compared to the output reduction in the case of the steeper demand curve (the marginal of which is MR^1) -- that is, SR as compared with ST -- to offset exactly the extent to which for the steeper demand curve a given output reduction causes a greater price rise. Under decreasing cost conditions, the output reduction and the price increase are greater than under constant cost regardless of the slope of the demand curve. But the price rise will be the same in the two cases of demand only if the reductions in output in the two cases remain in the same proportion as under constant cost. That is, if with a given decreasing cost curve, the output reduction in the case of the less steep demand curve is twice that under constant cost, the reduction in the case of the steeper demand curve must also be twice as great as that under constant cost if differences in output reduction are to offset each other in the same manner as under constant cost.

Actually, however, this cannot be the case. With the sloping marginal cost curve, the excess in output reduction over that under constant cost, in the case of the less steep demand curve, must be proportionately greater than in the case of the steeper demand curve. Thus on Chart 9, output reduction in the case of MR, with decreasing cost, is from OS to OF, or twice that with the constant cost (OS to OR); in the case of MR^1, the reduction is from OS to OK, only slightly more than with constant cost (^{O}S to ^{O}T). Thus the price increase, in contrast to that under constant cost, is greater in the case of the demand curve with less slope than in the case of that with greater slope (P to P" instead of to P' in contrast to p^1 to $p^{1''}$ instead of p^1 to $p^{1'}$). Since price rises by the same amount in each under constant cost, price will rise by a larger per cent of the tax, with a less steep demand curve, under decreasing cost conditions. Thus price in the case of demand curve AR rises from P to P", or by exactly the amount of the tax (DMC' is parallel to AR'); in the case of the demand curve AR^1, price rises from p^1 to $P^{1''}$, or about three-fourths the amount of the tax. Under decreasing cost, with a relatively horizontal demand curve, output reduction must go so much farther than in the case in which the curve is relatively steep, before marginal recéipts and marginal cost are again equal, that the difference in price rise from a given output reduction cannot offset it, and the price rise is greater.

The significance of changes in the slope of the demand curves is similar to that under constant cost. If the demand becomes steeper above the old price, the price rises more than if demand had continued straight; the increase in either case is greater than if costs were constant. If the demand becomes less steep, price will rise less than if the curve had not changed slope.

INCREASING COST: The final possible cost condition is that in which cost per unit rises as output expands. A monopoly may be found in such a situation if one firm gains control of all the raw material supply, or if demand is sufficiently great that all forces leading to decreasing cost have been fully exploited, yet there is not sufficient demand to support a second enterprise. Or the monopoly may be guaranteed its position by legal or other non-economic means. With increasing cost, the marginal cost curve slopes upward from left to right; thus when it is raised as a result of the tax, the intersection with the marginal revenue curve will be farther to the right than if the curve were horizontal. On Chart 10, output (with demand curve AR^1) is reduced from OH to OL rather than from OF to OS. Thus the price increase will be less than under constant cost -- from P^1 to $P^{1'}$ instead of from $P_1{}^1$ to $P_1{}^{1'}$ -- and accordingly is less than one-half the amount of the tax. In other words, in all cases marginal revenue must rise until it again equals marginal cost. Since marginal cost is less than in the case of constant cost, for successively lower outputs, because of the fall in production cost, the increase in marginal revenue is not as great by the time the latter again equals marginal cost as in the other case.

As to the significance of different slopes of demand curves, the problem is again to compare the relative price increase for a given tax under two situations in which the slope of demand is not the same, the demand curve being a straight line in each case. As compared with constant cost, regardless of the slope, the price increase will be somewhat less for any given demand curve. The difference will be the same in the case of the two slopes only if the output reductions as a result of the tax are in the same relation to each other as under constant cost; if there is any difference, the relative price change will be different. That is, if with constant cost, output falls four times as much with the less steep demand curve to give the same price rise as with the other curve, and if under increasing cost conditions output falls three times as far in the one case as in the other, price will have risen more in the case of the steeper demand curve. Greater output reduction with the former curve will not have been sufficient to overcome the effect on price of the steeper slope of the latter. The actual situation under increasing cost is of this nature. As output is reduced, production cost per unit falls; as output reduction is greater in the case of the less steep demand than in the case of the steeper curve, the effect of the production cost decline in requiring less output reduction than would occur with constant cost is of greater significance for the former than for the latter; thus the difference in output reduction will not be as great relatively to the constant cost condition. The fall in output, as compared with constant cost, is relatively greater for the steeper demand curve; thus the price increase will be greater in the case of the steeper demand curve than in the case of the less steep curve. On Chart 10, with cost curve CMC (constant cost), with demand curve AR, output falls from OF to OM; with demand AR^1 the reduction is from OF to OS; the reduction is approximately 30% as great in the latter case. With cost curve IAC (increasing), in the case of AR^1, output falls from OH to OL, and with AR from OE to OM, the relation now being about 10 to 5 instead of 10 to 3. Price in the case of AR and IAC rises from P to P_1 instead of from P' to P_1 as under CMC, or about one-half as far; with AR^1 the increase is from P^1 to $P^{1'}$ instead of Pl^1 to $Pl^{1'}$, about 4/5 as far. The total price rise is about 40% of the tax in the case of the steeper demand, and 30% in the other. In general, the possibility of significant differences is much less than in the case of decreasing cost. The possible range in the latter is between slightly over one-half of the tax and almost infinite increase, in the former between slightly under one-half and zero.

The significance of differing slope for incidence is thus the same under monopoly as under competition. In either case, with straight line demand curves, under constant cost, slope does not affect incidence; with increasing cost more of the tax will be passed on with a steep demand curve; with decreasing cost the reverse is true. It is surprising that there is such widespread acceptance of the maxim that the more inelastic the demand, the more that will be shifted, and vice versa. The rule does not apply generally, but only, with regular demand curves, under increasing cost conditions (which are certainly not typical of monopoly conditions), and regardless of the cost condition, with demand curves which become steeper above the old price when compared with those which do not.

SHORT RUN INCIDENCE:

Up to this point attention has been given solely to long run incidence after all adjustments have been made. Except in lines in which demand is increasing, final readjustment can be made only as existing plant wears out; in the meantime incidence may be very different from that in the long run.

When the tax is first imposed, the firm is free to raise its prices as it sees fit; the price increase does not have to wait for a reduction in supply as in the case of competition. The reduction in supply comes immediately, as less can be sold at the higher prices. The extent of price increase depends on the nature of the short run marginal cost curve. The latter is typically increasing (at larger outputs) for amounts less than the old equilibrium, regardless of the long run cost situation. Once the equipment has been installed, its cost does not enter into marginal cost of producing; as output is reduced, in the short run, the equipment will still be available for use, and marginal cost will not rise. Furthermore, if size of the plant has been properly adjusted to demand, near the point of operation prior to the tax, marginal cost may be rising very rapidly as the plant comes near to optimum utilization. Thus, provided the monopolist acts intelligently, only a small amount of the tax will be added to the price. In fact, if the marginal cost curve is almost vertical near the old equilibrium, there will be virtually no increase in price at all.

On Chart 11, MR intersects the new marginal short run cost curve (SRMC') only a relatively short distance to the left of the intersection with SRMC; the price increase, from P to P_s, is only about one-fourth the amount of the tax. However, the plant will eventually wear out; in longer periods of time, the portion of the short run marginal cost curve to the left of its intersection with SRAC' rises to the long run marginal level; as it rises, it intersects marginal revenue farther to the left, and the price rise from the tax becomes greater until it reaches Pl -- the long run equilibrium figure. The new plant will be considerably smaller than the old, and costs will be much higher.

MODIFYING FACTORS:

The analysis above is based on rigid assumptions that the monopolist has full knowledge of cost and market conditions and always acts in such a way as to maximize net revenue. These assumptions lessen severely the significance of the conclusions reached.

IMPERFECT KNOWLEDGE: In the first place, the firm does not have full knowledge either of the demand curve or of the cost curve. It is impossible to know in advance the exact loss in demand a given price increase will cause, or to ascertain definitely the marginal cost with different volumes of output. This problem of imperfect knowledge renders almost all economic analysis less significant, and nothing more can be said beyond the statement that not only is it unlikely that the original monopoly price is the real optimum one, but likewise that the price readjustment from the tax may be far removed from that which would yield optimum returns. Where the optimum price adjustment is small, there may be no change at all; where comparison is made between incidence under two different conditions, and the results are almost the same, in actual practice there is likely to be no difference at all.[16]

REGULATION OF PRICE: Furthermore, there are several other cases in which monopoly price will not have been at the optimum prior to the tax. Where the monopoly is regulated, as in the case of a public utility, price will supposedly equal average cost of production,[17] production being carried beyond the point at which marginal revenue equals marginal cost. Under constant cost conditions, as average cost will be raised by the full amount of the tax, price will also rise by the full tax, if public regulatory bodies recognize the tax as a part of cost. This increase will occur, however, only if the new price will not exceed that which will yield maximum monopoly revenue. If the old price charged was close to the optimum price, and the tax were relatively large, price would not, except under extreme decreasing cost conditions, rise by the amount of the tax. But if regulation had forced the old price far below the optimum, and the tax were not too great, the entire tax, under constant cost conditions, would be passed on.

FEAR OF CONTROL: Furthermore, fear of possible competition or regulation, or expropriation, may check the collection of maximum monopoly price. In this case, the price may be raised by the full amount of the tax, or even more, as the levy provides a good excuse to justify a price increase nearer to monopoly levels. On the other hand, the company may feel that any price increase will cause serious popular opposition, and thus will be forced to bear all of the burden.

PRICE DISCRIMINATION: A further assumption has been that of a single price to all buyers. Actually a monopolist may find it profitable to discriminate as between groups of buyers when elasticity of demand is not uniform. As previously indicated, higher prices will be charged in markets where the demand curves are steeper. However, the same amount of the tax will be shifted in either case, if the demand curves are straight lines. When the tax is imposed, total output will be cut until marginal revenue is equal to marginal cost, output going into each market being reduced till marginal revenue has risen to the new marginal cost. The marginal revenue in each market must be equal both before and after the tax (since each equals the same marginal cost); thus the increase in marginal revenue will be the same in each market. Since with straight line demand curves a given reduction in marginal revenue will always cause one-half as great a reduction in average revenue, the price increase will be the same in each case. This result is independent of the cost conditions in the industry.

On Chart 12, the total output before the tax is ON, the intersection of MC and AMR, the total marginal revenue curve for both markets.[18] The price is P' in the market of which AR' is the demand curve, P" in the market of curve AR". After the tax, output is reduced to N'; price rises to P'^t and P''^t respectively, increasing by the same amount in each, inasmuch as in each marginal revenue is increased from S to T, and a given increase in marginal revenue will give the same increase in price, as long as demand curves are straight. ST is greater than the tax because the firm is operating under decreasing cost.

When one demand curve changes slope relative to the slope in the other, above the equilibrium price, then the price increase in the two cases will be different. Where the demand curve in one is becoming more steep than that in the other, there will be a greater price increase in the former, as a given increase in marginal revenue will be accompanied by a greater price rise than in the case of the latter. The reverse is true when the former is becoming less steep.

Where the taxes are imposed by minor political jurisdictions, it is likely that some of the markets, if they are divided on a geographical basis, will be taxed, and others will not. In general, there will be no price change in the jurisdictions where there is no tax, and appropriate increases where there are. However, the change in output in the taxed areas may affect the marginal cost for the remaining areas, and produce price increases or decreases, as determined by the general cost nature of the industry.

VARIATIONS IN CONSTANTS:

It is necessary at this point to consider variations in the "constants": demand schedules, production functions, and factor prices. In general, the same considerations apply as in the case of pure competition; certain differences between the two cases must however be pointed out. As far as demand is concerned, the fact that the tax reduces monopoly profits is likely to produce some differences in shifts in demand in contrast to that which would take place with pure competition. Not only does a redistribution of purchasing power in favor of the poorer classes directly affect the demand for various commodities, but this is likely to influence propensity to consume, with subsequent changes in total demand for all goods. Furthermore, the effects of changes in demand upon price will be different in monopoly in contrast to pure competition, and, since the increase of monopoly profit when demand increases and the fall when demand declines has no counterpart in pure competition, secondary reactions on income distribution will not be the same in the two cases.

In regard to production functions, the reduction of output caused by the tax may lessen the ability to utilize most economical methods of production, since the most profitable volume of output subsequent to the tax may be too small to allow utilization of certain types of capital equipment. However, the tax does not affect the availability of methods of production; the fact that more efficient methods cannot be used profitably at lower volumes of output is taken into consideration in the cost curve, and requires no particular attention.

The final possible source of variation relates to changes in factor prices. The chief difference in contrast to pure competition arises out of the change in propensity to consume resulting from the reduction of monopoly profits. The latter is an inevitable result unless the firm failed to set prices at the optimum level before the tax. This change, in theory at least, will affect the total volume of income and the prices of the factors. In general, however, it is impossible, when only one industry is subject to such a levy, that significant changes along these lines will occur. The total profit earned in any one industry is too small a part of total profit as to influence substantially the propensity to consume for the economy as a whole. Thus, in general, it is unlikely that the effect on factor prices will differ greatly from that with pure competition. However, to the extent that factor prices do change as a result of the tax, the reactions on the price of the commodity will not be the same as with pure competition, the differences in the two cases being similar to those of immediate price changes caused by the tax in the two cases.

SUMMARY:

This chapter has been concerned solely with the effect of a tax per unit of output on a single monopolist in the usual sense of the term, the demand curve for the firm being assumed as given, independent of any action on the part of the monopolist himself or of any other firms motivated by the action or situation of the firm in question. Over a period of time sufficiently long for all readjustments to be made, under constant cost conditions, with a straight line demand curve, price will rise by exactly one-half the tax. Since marginal cost rises by the full amount of the tax, marginal revenue must also; a given rise in the latter is accompanied by an increase in average revenue, and thus price, one-half as great. Under conditions of decreasing cost, somewhat more than one-half the tax will be added to price, as marginal cost rises as output is reduced, and marginal revenue must be increased farther than under constant cost. Where average revenue and marginal cost curves are parallel, price will rise by exactly the amount of the tax; when marginal cost is steeper than average revenue, price will rise by more than the tax. Under increasing cost conditions, price will rise by less than one-half the tax, because the decline in marginal cost necessitates smaller increase in marginal revenue. Thus, cet. par., the imposition of a sales tax will cause less burden to the buyer with monopoly conditions than with competition. The portion of the tax not passing forward is absorbed in monopoly profits. Under competition, if all factors are mobile, and if the prices of the factors are unaffected by changes in the industry in question, there is no source from which any of the tax on a single industry can come except from the buyer of the product.

Under constant cost, so long as demand curves are straight, the degree of slope of demand has no significance for incidence, although the amount of output reduction necessary is, of course, affected. However, under decreasing cost, the amount of price increase varies directly with the slope of demand, as in this case the greater slope of demand intensifies the operation of the decreasing cost conditions which require greater output reduction. Under increasing cost, the reverse is true; the less steep the demand, the greater will be the significance of the reduction in cost at smaller volumes of output in lessening the curtailment of supply necessary. Thus difference in slope affects incidence in the same manner as under conditions of pure competition. When the steepness increases above the old price, the price rise will be less, as a given output reduction will cause less price increase. While output reduction may be less than if the demand had continued straight, it does not appear that this can be of sufficient importance to offset the other tendency. When the demand curve becomes steeper, the price rise will ordinarily be greater not only because output reduction is greater, but because a given output reduction will cause a greater price increase.

The short run incidence is likely to be different than that in the long run; it is very likely that short run marginal cost will be rising near the old equilibrium; where this is the case the initial price increase will be relatively small regardless of the long run cost conditions. As short run marginal cost is normally below long run marginal, immediate price rise will be less than that in the long run. The method by which the immediate increase takes place is different from that of competition; the decrease in "supply" comes very quickly, depending only on the action of the firm in raising its price.

The fact that the assumptions on which the analysis is based do not represent actual conditions lessens the significance of the conclusions; the monopolist lacks perfect knowledge of cost and revenue conditions; his price may be subject to regulation, or he may fear possible interference with the conduct of his business if he raises price. Where different prices are charged in different markets, there will be no difference in incidence in the various markets so long as the demand curves are straight lines, as marginal revenue must rise the same amount in each. Where, however, there is a difference in change of slope of the market demand curves above the old prices, the price changes will not be the same in the two cases. The significance of changes in demand and factor prices is similar to that under pure competition. The chief possible sources of variation arise out of the different manner in which a monopolist reacts to changes in costs and demand in contrast to that of the firms in competition and out of the effect of the tax on monopoly profits and thus on the propensity to consume. Significant variations from these sources are unlikely.

IV

MONOPOLISTIC COMPETITION AND THE INCIDENCE OF SPECIAL SALES TAXES

INTRODUCTION:

The discussion in the previous chapter was based upon the assumption that the demand curves for the firms were not subject to modification as a result of any action taken by the latter. As pointed out in the introductory chapter, however, in practically all cases in which firms do possess some control over price, they are subject to varying degrees of competition from other firms having similar power. In these cases, changes in price and in profits earned will produce reactions on the part of these competitors in such a manner as to affect the demand curve of the first firm. It is necessary, therefore, to extend the analysis of incidence to take into consideration this intermediate sector characterized by the presence of elements of both competition and monopoly.[1]

The method of approach to the problem involves consideration of two general cases. The first concerns the situation in which elimination of all excess profits through perfectly free entry of firms has brought average revenue and average cost curves of all firms in the field to tangency. In the second case, limitation of entry and excess profits are assumed. In subsequent sections, the significance of selling costs, oligopoly, non-uniform demand and cost curves, multiple lines, average cost pricing, and other phenomena of monopolistic competition are introduced.

The situation characterized by tangency of the average revenue and average cost curves is commonly considered as the typical feature of the condition of monopolistic competition. Only under such circumstances are the elements usually regarded as fundamental attributes of monopolistic competition, excess capacity and improper utilization of resources, inevitable. It must be emphasized, however, that completely free entry is necessary for realization of this position; with various consumer preferences established, it will commonly be possible for firms to maintain a sheltered position, with excess profits, over a long period of time

Nevertheless, the condition provides a suitable basis for introduction of the analysis, and also is of significance in itself, as it represents the equilibrium position in cases in which preferences as between firms are relatively weak. It is assumed at first that demand and cost curves are uniform, that selling activities and oligopoly are absent, and that each firm produces only one product. Modifications of these assumptions will be introduced at later stages in the analysis.

THE PROCESS OF READJUSTMENT:

When a tax per unit of output is first imposed, each firm raises its price (and thus lessens its output) to the extent that marginal revenue will equal the new and higher marginal cost. The short run marginal cost curve after the tax will be lower than the new long run marginal, and the curve is not necessarily of decreasing cost nature; thus the price rise will be less than that which would occur if adjustment were made at once on the basis of long run marginal cost. On Chart 13, short run cost curves are eliminated for purposes of simplification; it is assumed that the long and short run curves are identical. The difference is only one of degree. On this chart, each firm will raise its price to PN, the demand price of that level of output at which MR again intersects MC (MC'). However, the AR curve is drawn on the assumption that the other firms keep their prices constant. Actually, each firm finds that when it raises its price to PN it loses much less in unit sales than it would have supposed, judging from its own individual demand curve AR; this result arises from the fact that all other firms are raising their prices likewise, at the same time. The individual firm's sales drop, not to OS, but only to Oy, as shown by the slope of DD.[2] In the face of this slight decline in sales, which calls for a recomputation of AR, the individual firm is induced to put the price still higher in its striving for minimizing losses. This will continue until the point is reached where the output actually sold after the price change will be such that MC and MR are again equal.[3] Price will come to P^2, the increase being an amount approximately three-fourth as great as the tax.[4]

However, AR' remains below AC'. Seemingly, by proper output reduction, tangency of these two curves could be obtained. But, when the point is reached that MR' equals MC', no firm will reduce output so long as each acts independently of the others, since to do so would apparently involve increase in losses. Actually, all would gain if they acted in unison in making the price increase, but this will not occur in the absence of oligopoly. DD and AR' cannot intersect at the tangency of the latter with AC', so long as AR' does not change its slope as it moves; thus, when AR' is tangent to AC, the actual revenue will not be that expected; average costs will not actually be covered.[5] If each firm produced temporarily just the output which would allow all to cover average costs, it would be profitable for each to lower prices slightly, as AR' would be slightly above AC' to the right of the intersection of DD and AC'. Thus all will be pulled down into a situation of loss.

The only escape is through exodus of firms. As time passes, average variable cost of some firms will rise above the average revenue line, and the firms will cease to operate. As this process continues, the DD curve for the remaining firms will shift to the right; this must continue until the DD curve (DD') intersects the AR' curve for each firm at the point of tangency of AR (AR_2) and AC' (at P_3 on Chart 13). Only when this has happened will MR equal MC' at such a point that average cost is just covered by average revenue.

THE AMOUNT OF PRICE RISE:

GENERAL STATEMENT OF INCIDENCE: If the demand curve does not change slope in the process of output reduction, the individual average revenue curve will move up by the exact amount of the increase in the average cost curve (from P' to P_3 on Chart 13), as the new point of tangency is necessarily, under the conditions, directly above the old. Thus, if the cost curve of the firm does not shift as a result of the exodus of firms, the price will rise by exactly the amount of the tax; the incidence is the same as under pure competition. If the industry as a whole is one of increasing or decreasing cost, the cost curves of the firm will shift, and price will rise by less or more than the amount of the tax. There seems to be no reason why, cet. par., the existence of monopolistic competition should significantly affect the degree of decreasing or increasing cost from external economies; thus, the long run incidence is the same under monopolistic competition as under pure competition, so long as there is complete free entry and no monopoly profits in the former.

After the complete readjustment has taken place, each firm remaining will be producing the same volume as before the tax, as with the given slopes of cost and demand curves, and the assumption of tangency, only at the old output level can losses be avoided. The temporary output reductions, necessary to reduce losses so long as the number of firms in the field remains too great, are no longer profitable. If any readjustments in capacity -- temporarily advantageous -- were made, it will be profitable to return to the old capacity as final equilibrium is attained. Thus under the conditions assumed, the fact that the individual firms operate under decreasing cost conditions has no significance whatsoever for incidence.

When the difference between short run and long run considerations is introduced into the analysis, it must be noted that short run marginal cost is lower than that over the longer period for ranges of output below the old optimum, once the plant is constructed. Thus the price rise will not be as great in the short run; as time passes it will be profitable to make further price increases, as more elements enter into marginal cost. This process accompanies the exodus of firms; the rise in price from the increase in marginal cost over time lessens the need for exodus of firms, and brings the final equilibrium to that indicated above.

THE SIGNIFICANCE OF OLIGOPOLY ELEMENTS: Where oligopoly exists as well as differentiation, but firms are free to enter the field, average receipts and average cost will come to tangency, but at a very much higher price level than when firms ignore the reactions of their competitors to their own action. When the tax is imposed, the slope of the marginal revenue curve for each firm approaches that for the industry as a whole,[6] since it is realized that competitors will make price increases provided the firm in question does also. The curve is much steeper than in the preceding case. The initial price increase will differ according to the nature of the marginal cost curve. If the latter is increasing, there will be more price increase than in the absence of oligopoly; the reverse is true if cost is decreasing unless the slope of the curve increases in steepness above the old price in sufficient degree.[7] However, if tangency prevailed before the tax, no firm will be able to cover average cost by any sort of price adjustment which it is profitable to make. If other firms would hold prices constant, any one firm could restore its profits by reducing price, since its average revenue curve under these conditions[8] would pass above the AC curve at greater volumes of output. But each producer realizes that others will cut prices also if he does, that his average revenue curve is not of this nature, but very much steeper (DD on Chart 13). Accordingly, action of this nature will not be taken. Exodus of firms is necessary; this must go on until the individual demand curves are again tangent to average cost. When this has occurred, the price will have risen by the amount of the tax, provided industry costs are constant. Long run incidence is thus the same as if the oligopolistic elements were not present.

POSSIBILITY OF SHIFT IN ELASTICITY OF DEMAND: The assumption has been made to this point that the demand curve confronting the individual firm does not change slope as firms leave the field. There are, however, several different possibilities of change along these lines. If the customers of the firms leaving business do not become closely attached to any of the remaining firms, the elasticity of demand for the products of the latter will be increased, the slope of the curve lessened, and the price rise will be less than otherwise; AR_2 on Chart 13 will come to tangency with AC' at a lower point. It is interesting to note that the exodus of firms must be greater; DD' must shift farther to the right to intersect AR_2 at tangency. The reduced elasticity lessens the number of firms and the amount of excess capacity. This eliminates the need for as great a price increase as otherwise, as the point of equilibrium for each firm stands at a lower cost level than before.

On the other hand, the demand curve may become more steep. The number of firms may fall sufficiently that a feeling of mutual dependence will arise among the remaining firms, or an existing oligopoly situation will be strengthened. The AR curve will appear to the firm as of the slope of the DD curve (Chart 13), and a great price increase will be made. Each firm will avoid cutting prices along the new and higher revenue curve parallel to the old AR curve because it is realized that this is not the real average curve and that the competitors would cut also if any one takes the initiative. Under such conditions there may be an inflow of firms into the field, and a price increase very much greater than the amount of the tax.[9] Thus there is possibility of a price increase of magnitude impossible under monopoly or pure competition[10] with similar cost conditions.

No oligopoly situation is absolute; uncertainties of various types prevent the realization of positions which would be optimum from the point of view of the firms concerned. When a tax is imposed, the oligopolistic elements are likely strengthened as far as the part of cost consisting of the tax is concerned; the latter is a definite cost which each firm knows will be imposed on all others. With more or less uniform accounting methods which encourage treatment of the tax as an element by which to increase price in full amount, each firm is likely to feel that others will act in this manner and accordingly can do so itself without significant loss in volume. However, once the price has been raised so as to eliminate all tax burden, there is no assurance that some price cutting will not take place. However, if all firms are now operating at a profit, it is entirely possible that they may not cut, even though, before the imposition of the tax, they would have taken advantage of such a situation, to some degree at least, to better themselves at the expense of their competitors. If after the imposition of the tax, despite readjustment, each firm is operating at a loss, the oligopoly may be strengthened, if each firm fears to cut prices for fear of precipitating a violent price war. On the other hand, some of the firms, struggling desperately to avoid bankruptcy, may start price cutting to gain volume, and by causing general collapse of the oligopoly elements in the situation, precipitate a very severe price decline. It is conceivable that the low levels may remain over a considerable period of time. The tax can be credited with having lowered price, a phenomenon impossible under pure competition or pure monopoly. The burden of the tax in a sense rests on those entrepreneurs who have gone out of business[11] and thus have been deprived of their returns; as a result of the process, the consumer actually benefits from lowered prices. In one sense the burden still rests upon the consumer, since the revenue which goes to the government is part of that obtained from the consumer, and of which no factor now actually engaged in production is deprived. Nevertheless, since this is more than offset by the lowered production cost, the burden may be considered to rest on those groups losing their incomes as a result of the tax.

SELLING COSTS: It is now necessary to consider the significance of selling costs. The location of the demand curve for the product of a firm depends not only upon prices charged by the firm's competitors, but also upon the advertising activities of the firm in question and of the other firms in the field. For each price there is an optimum expenditure on selling, given the prices and selling activities of other firms; with this there is a certain possible total sales volume. The curve connecting the points designating these latter amounts for the various prices[12] is indicated by TR on Chart 14. For each volume of sales, the price minus the selling cost gives a certain average net revenue figure; there is an average net revenue curve (ANR on Chart 14) designating these amounts for the different possible prices. When equilibrium is reached, with free entry of firms, the average cost curve, exclusive of selling costs, of the firm is tangent, not to the demand curve, but rather to the average net revenue curve; the price is that indicated on the total revenue curve for the equilibrium output. Also, through this point of tangency must pass the curve of average net revenue, formally comparable to DD on Chart 13, which indicates the amounts that can be sold at the various prices under the assumption that other firms also make the same adjustments in price and selling activities as the firm in question. (ND on Chart 14.) This curve is, of course, very much steeper than the ANR curve.

When a tax per unit of output is levied, marginal cost will intersect marginal revenue (the marginal of the net revenue curve) at a point of lower output, and price will be raised. The output fall will be less than anticipated; further price adjustment will be made in the same manner as indicated in the previous section, until losses are minimized. There is one essential difference between the adjustment in this case and that in the preceding section; the relationship between output reduction and price rise is different, since price is determined on the basis of the total revenue curve, which is not necessarily parallel to the average net revenue curve. The output adjustment will be made on the basis of the marginal curve of the latter, but the price rise coming about from the output reduction depends on the slope of the gross revenue curve. The analysis of the relation between the slopes of the original demand curve without advertising, the net revenue curve, and the gross receipts curve has not been developed, and it is impossible to deviate in this study to consider the problem.[13] Thus nothing more can be said than to indicate the possibility that this factor may affect incidence. It is impossible to say whether there will be more or less temporary price increase, cet. par., with a situation with selling activities than in one without.

This adjustment is, however, only temporary. Each firm cannot avoid losses, as indicated in the previous section, until some of the firms leave the field, since when ANR is tangent to AC', ND will pass to the left of the point of tangency. Thus the position cannot be maintained, as with the price at the level of tangency, sales will be less than anticipated, and loss will be incurred. The exodus of firms will occur as previously indicated; the new equilibrium will be reached at the point at which ANR' is tangent to the new average cost curve (AC'), and ND (now ND') passes through the point of tangency. But price is determined on the basis of the total revenue curve rather than of the average revenue curve. So long as the ANR and TR curves remain in the same relation to each other, price will increase by the same amount as average net revenue increases, and thus by the same amount as if there were no selling cost. If one rises by a certain amount, the other must rise, at the same levels of output, by the same amount if the two curves are to remain the same distance apart. Thus, on Chart 14, the final output will be OP, being determined by the point of tangency between ANR' and AC'; ANR will have risen by the same amount as AC (assuming that the industry is one of constant cost), and price from P to P', or by the same amount.

But there is good reason to believe that the relationship between ANR and TR will shift as firms leave the field. Both the optimum amount of advertising at each price and the net return per unit of advertising expenditure are likely to shift. The reduction in the number of firms seeking the business may make it desirable to spend less to sell various volumes of output; if this is the case, the average total revenue and average net revenue curves will draw closer together, and less price increase will accompany the movement of average revenue to the new tangency with average cost. In terms of Chart 14, when ANR has reached tangency with AC', TR will not have moved up as far as ANR has moved, and the price increase will be less. This is advanced as a possibility rather than as a certain tendency; the likelihood of a shift in the TR-ANR relationship must certainly be recognized. A further potential cause of difference in incidence as compared to the condition in which there are no selling costs is the possibility of a shift in the elasticity of the average revenue curve resulting from the exodus of firms. The nature and amount of such a shift will be influenced by a number of factors, such as the buying habits of the purchasers of the firms leaving business, and cannot be analyzed in detail at this point.

As indicated in the first chapter, it is very difficult to find exactly optimum amounts of advertising expenditure. There are several practices common in determining advertising budgets which may involve probable deviation from optimum outlay for this purpose, but which make the relation between ANR and TR more definite than otherwise.[14] When selling expenditures are determined as a percentage of expected dollar sales, the selling expenditure will be greater per unit at higher price levels; thus the average net revenue curve will be less steep than the average total revenue curve, and a given output reduction will cause a greater price rise than otherwise. The same result will come about if advertising costs are determined independently of expected sales, as a fixed customary sum, etc. The divergence will be greater in the case of the latter than in the case of the former, cet. par., the steeper the demand curve.

Another factor which often influences the determination of the size of the budget is the amount of profits being made, or the amount of cash on hand. Accordingly, when taxes are imposed, and losses made, there will be a tendency to reduce advertising expenditures, a tendency which will be furthered greatly if all firms do the same thing, as the losses from failure to advertise will be less. Thus, reduction of advertising expenditure may allow each firm to return to a position of profitable operation with no exodus of firms whatsoever. If all the firms act in this manner, the total revenue curves may not fall back to any extent, yet the ANR curve, shifting to the right as selling costs are cut, may come to tangency with AC without any firms leaving. The ND curve will have shifted to the right along with the shift in ANR and thus will intersect at tangency. The position is not necessarily stable, since any one firm can gain by advertising if the others do not. Yet, if oligopoly elements are present this may not be done. Thus final equilibrium may be attained without exodus of firms even though there were no monopoly profits to start with. The entire tax will be paid by the firm, not from monopoly profits, but from that part of income formerly spent in advertising. The more that demand for the product as a whole falls as advertising is reduced, the greater is the likelihood of exodus. The burden falls in part on those formerly engaged in the production of advertising service.[15]

In summary, the existence of advertising costs allows new possibility of variations in incidence. From a short run standpoint, the reduction of output by the firm may cause a different degree of price rise than if there were no selling costs, since the average gross revenue and net average revenue curves may not be parallel. As to long run incidence there is the possibility that the gross revenue and net average revenue curves may shift in relation to each other, and that net average revenue may change slope and so affect price rise. And the existence of advertising expenditures, which are not a necessary cost of turning out the product, provides a possible outlet for absorption of the tax, under certain pricing and advertising policies. But in general selling activities apparently do not introduce significant changes in the theory of incidence. In the remaining parts of the analysis, except where otherwise indicated, it will be assumed, for simplification, that the cost curve includes optimum selling expenditure for each price, and that the demand curve indicates the demand with optimum selling expenditures at each price.

THE SIGNIFICANCE OF THE EXISTENCE OF MONOPOLY PROFITS: When the possibility of the absence of tangency of average revenue and average cost is introduced,[16] a new problem for incidence arises. Under such circumstances there is a certain equilibrium output for each firm which allows equilibrium in the industry. This output must be such that at the level of output at which marginal revenue is equal to marginal cost, expected price is equal to realized price; in other words, DD must intersect AR directly above the MR-MC intersection.[17] Thus on Chart 15, MR intersects MC at N, directly below the intersection of AR and DD at P. Price stands at P; output is ON. Any other position will cause readjustment; unless each firm is in the situation indicated, there can be no equilibrium. For each possible higher cost curve, there is a different point of equilibrium farther to the left and higher than the previous. Thus there is a series of equilibrium volumes of output for different levels of cost, other factors, except cost, remaining the same. The curve KK, on Chart 15, indicates the location of these equilibrium points for various cost curves. For each possible cost curve, output must be less than would be the case with pure competition (curves of the industry in the latter being compared to curves of the firm in the case in question), as output in competition is determined by the intersection of average cost and average revenue (DD in this case) curves; each firm in the present case does not expand to this point, as MR would cross MC while AR is still above the latter, and thus above AC. On the other hand, output must, for each cost curve, be greater than if the case were one of pure monopoly. In the latter, output is determined by the intersection of the marginal revenue curve of the firm (MDD on Chart 15) and MC; under the case here considered, the marginal revenue curve (MR) is more elastic than in the previous case; thus the average revenue curve (AR) must also be more elastic than if the case were one of pure monopoly (DD); thus the average revenue curve is lower than that with monopoly (DD) at the point at which the marginal curve with monopoly (MDD) intersects MC. If the firm tried to operate at this level of output, realized price would exceed expected price, and an output increase would occur until an equilibrium is reached in the manner previously discussed. This same reasoning applies for any cost curve of the same slope. Thus a line connecting these levels of equilibrium output must be of less slope than MDD, and of steeper slope than DD, and thus approach each at successively lower levels of output. (Note line KK on Chart 15.)

When a tax is imposed, the new permanent output will be determined by the intersection of the new marginal cost curve and the equilibrium line KK. Only at this level of output will marginal cost and marginal revenue be equal at the level of output at which actual and expected sales are the same. As this line is of less slope than the marginal revenue curve, and is steeper than the average revenue curve, the price rise resulting from the tax will be somewhat less than under pure competition and somewhat more than under monopoly.[18] In the example shown on Chart 15, the price increase is from P to P', or 80%, almost as much as would occur under pure competition.

When the firm is one of decreasing cost, when the tax is imposed, a greater output reduction is necessary for the new optimum, regardless of the nature of competition in the industry. The line of equilibrium for different cost levels is the same, however, as under constant cost, as is indicated in Chart 16, as the same reasoning which applies to constant cost in this matter applies also under other cost conditions. When a tax is imposed, the new AR curve will intersect the equilibrium line farther to the left, but the change, as compared to the previous situation, is exactly the same, so long as the old and new AR curves are parallel, as in the case of competition or monopoly; the relative price change in the three remain the same. Exactly similar reasoning can be applies to increasing cost conditions, except that there will be less output reduction in all three cases of competition.

Where oligopoly exists with limited entry, each firm realizes that the demand curve for the product of the industry -- DD on the charts -- is its own real demand curve, and adjusts output so that the marginal of this curve is equal to its marginal cost. The price is determined in the same way as monopoly price, apart from uncertainties, differing only if the division of business among several firms instead of concentration in one affects cost at the optimum level of output. Under such conditions, a tax per unit of output will cause the same price increase as in the case of monopoly. The significance of uncertainty can be summarized briefly. To the extent that each firm is uncertain as to the policy of the others, the original price will be lower than the monopoly level. When the tax is imposed, uncertainty as to the reaction of other firms may prevent any price increase. Or, more likely, since a tax is a definitely known cost, affecting all alike, each may be certain that the others will pass on the entire tax, and thus price will rise by more than under pure monopoly, to a point nearer optimum monopoly price. It is impossible to generalize more specifically than this. Other causes of uncertainty indicated by Chamberlin[19] appear to have no particular significance for incidence theory. If the price before the tax was the optimum, it is entirely possible that the price rise from the tax will be greater than is profitable. If each firm feels that the other firms will raise price by the full amount of the tax, each may raise in this manner in the fear that not to do so would precipitate a price war.[20]

MODIFYING FACTORS - Diversity of Cost Curves and Demand Curves: Several other factors must be given attention. In the first place, because of differences in cost curves and demand curves among individual firms, in most lines some firms merely cover costs, while others enjoy monopoly profits. It is difficult to generalize as to incidence under such conditions as compared to the situations previously discussed. The output reductions and price increases by the non-marginal[21] firms will increase the demand for the products of the marginal firms; this will aid them in covering cost (since all marginal firms in monopolistic competition must be in conditions of decreasing cost), and will allow more to stay in business than if all firms in the industry were marginal. Tangency between the average revenue curve and the new average cost curve can be brought about by price increases by the non-marginal firms as well as by exodus of marginal. If there is a large number of the latter compared to the non-marginal, it is unlikely that a new equilibrium can be brought about by this means, and some exodus of firms must come about. If any of the old marginal firms remain in business, the price increase in the case of the products of the marginal firms must be just the same as if there were no supra-marginal ones; the final increase in the case of the latter will ordinarily be greater than if no marginal firms were forced out of business, since they will operate farther from the point of lowest cost. There is no assurance that the final price rise will be the same in the cases of the marginal and non-marginal firms. Elasticity and location of demand curves and the nature of the cost curves differ among firms. Not only are the original prices different, but the amount of price rise from the tax is not the same in the various cases. The problem of different cost and demand curves introduces no particular difficulties for the theory of incidence, since the theoretical analysis developed by the latter applies equally well to each individual firm regardless of variations as between firms. Care must be taken, however, in applying the analysis to incidence in an actual industry. A particular tax will cause the various firms in the industry to react differently, and readjustment of relative output by the various firms will occur as a result.

Product Variation: It has been assumed thus far that the product is determined, independent of the action of the firm; actually, however, a firm may vary the quality of the product offered. At any one time each firm chooses the optimum product, the product for which net revenue, with price and advertising expenditure for that price at the most profitable levels, is the greatest. When the effect of a tax is considered, the analysis, as always when product differentiation is concerned, is difficult. Where the price for one reason or another -- law, custom, etc. -- cannot be changed, the increased cost may render a reduction in quality of product profitable. In fact, unless the industry is one of increasing cost, or the individual firms enjoy sufficiently great decreasing costs when no excess profits exist to start with, production must cease entirely under a fixed price condition if quality cannot be reduced. Further, even when a price rise is possible, a quality reduction may be made instead. It is very difficult for buyers to judge quality in many cases, and a poorer grade may be substituted for the better grade without realization thereof by many buyers. Of course, the tax does not render this any more profitable than before; where such is possible, the firm had not reached optimum before. But the tax may be an incentive to attempt to reach the optimum more closely. Finally, even where price adjustments are possible and are made, it may be profitable to readjust quality; this will in turn lead to further price readjustments until a final equilibrium is reached. The direction and amount of change depends on the particular circumstances, and any generalizations are impossible.[22]

When any change in quality takes place, the concept of incidence becomes less clear. If in one case price increases by a certain amount, and in another, similar in all other respects, quality changes in such degree as to allow the firms to restore similar positions of profit as in the first case, it is impossible to compare the relative burden resulting from the two changes. From the point of view of loss in satisfaction suffered by the consumer, it is impossible to compare a given price increase with a given quality reduction. Further, where the latter occurs, it is impossible to say how much of the burden is passed to consumers, as it is impossible to measure relative amounts of utility gained from two different products. However, to the extent that producers escape part of the burden by this means, it is reasonable to maintain that part of the tax is borne by the consumers, when a cheaper, poorer product is substituted for one of higher cost. Yet, if the consumer never becomes aware of the difference, this is not exactly accurate. The utility of an article is determined by personal reaction to the good, and actual physical qualities are of significance only in so far as they affect this reaction.

Where products which are considered by the consumers to be of substantially different desirability are taxed at the same rate per unit of output, the tax will influence the relative desirability of the various lines. If the original prices were in proportion to the marginal utilities of the different grades to the consumer, an addition of a fixed amount to the price of each will make the cheaper grades poorer bargains, and lead to a transference of purchases as between grades, further affecting price changes according to cost conditions.[23]

Multiple Lines: Up to this point in the discussion of incidence, the possibility of the production of more than one product by a firm has been ignored. This phenomenon is, of course, possible under pure competition, but is not of particular significance under such conditions. The limit to profit making by an individual firm is the eventual increase in cost per unit when production is carried beyond a certain point, and combining of lines is profitable only if management costs per unit are thus reduced, or, in a world of uncertainty, risk is spread more widely. Under monopolistic competition, with expansion of profits checked by limited markets, and with excess capacity, which may be reduced by taking on side lines, a common phenomenon, there is a special incentive to produce more than one type of product. In some cases the establishment of an enterprise may be profitable in the first place only if several lines are carried. Such a large investment in factory, skilled personnel, distribution system, and advertising may be necessary that no one line of goods can provide sufficient excess over direct cost of production to cover the "overhead" cost, and the sum of profits in several lines is necessary to cover this overhead, which will be little greater for a series of goods than it would be for one line. Even if one line would be profitable, despite the high fixed cost per unit, the latter can be reduced and profit per unit increased by adding other lines. Further, once the enterprise is established, if part of the establishment is not fully utilized, the average cost and marginal cost of additional lines may be extremely low, as there is no overhead necessarily attributable to these lines, either in the short or long periods. If anything in excess of the special cost of producing these lines is received, it will be profitable to add them.

The total enterprise in which several lines are carried will be started and will remain in business over a period of time only if average total revenue from all lines covers average total cost. If completely free entry into the field exists, average revenue will equal average cost; if not, it may exceed the latter. As far as any one line is concerned, output will be expanded until marginal revenue equals marginal cost; in the short run it is profitable to keep the line if average revenue covers the average cost immediately attributable to the production of units of this good. In the long run any line will be taken on and kept only if average revenue covers direct costs attributable to this product plus the fixed costs which would not be incurred if this particular line were not produced. Even if the line contributes nothing at all to common costs,[24] there will be no reason to discontinue it so long as it pays for itself.

However, in some lines average revenue must exceed average special cost;[25] in the short run the total of such excess in the entire enterprise must be sufficiently great to equal the sum of common variable costs or operations will cease; in the long run average revenue must exceed average total special costs by the amount of common costs, fixed and variable, or the enterprise will be junked. If there is not free entry, the former may exceed the latter.

Unfortunately for purposes of analysis the situation is very unstable. There will be variations as between firms as to lines carried and profit made on various lines; one group of firms which depend upon certain lines to cover their overhead will find it profitable to extend operations to other lines which will provide some average revenue in excess of average special costs. Some of these latter will be lines which provide chief basis for support for other firms, which in turn will retaliate. The net result will be general chaos, departure of firms, and reëstablishment of some sort of a temporary equilibrium which will in turn tend to break down in the same manner. The fundamental difficulty lies in the fact that a part of the cost of any good of a group produced together is indeterminate,[26] and accordingly there is no accurate guide to the flow of capital and the determination of the direction of production. Production will be increased in certain fields, and existing firms will be forced out, by firms which are not necessarily more efficient but enjoy lower cost in this line because their common costs are borne by other goods.

The only escape from this tendency to disequilibrium is through the development of elements of oligopoly in the situation involving the failure of firms to take advantage of immediate profit opportunities in order to avoid retaliation by the firms depending for their support on the lines in which the opportunities appear. The chief means is apparently through the use of some basis for pricing which does not necessarily lead to equating marginal revenue and marginal cost: some sort of average cost pricing which involves arbitrary allocation of a certain percentage of overhead to each line.[27] If the same basis is used by all firms in the field, the tendency to destruction will be avoided. Nevertheless, the situation is not very stable; different firms will calculate and allocate costs on different bases, and there will be constant incentive for firms to expand till marginal revenue equals marginal cost. Much trade association activity has been directed toward standardization of cost calculation and allocation to avoid "destructive" price cutting.[28]

For analysis of incidence when several lines are carried, it is necessary to assume first that an equilibrium exists at the time the tax is levied, in which certain lines yield nothing toward overhead, while other lines yield sufficient excess so that the entire enterprise covers total average cost. Complications for incidence arising out of average-cost pricing will be indicated later.

The effect of a tax per unit of output levied on a single line of such an industry will differ according to the conditions of profit on the line concerned. If the line is marginal, that is, if average special revenue just covers average direct cost, the firm will drop the line at once, if, after the tax, average revenue no longer covers average direct special costs. If the latter is covered, but not average fixed special costs, the line may be dropped at once if the specialized factors can be used for some other product on which better returns can be made, or, if not, at a later period, when the specialized fixed plant wears out. The price change can come very much more quickly than if the product were turned out by a single enterprise; not only is the percentage of fixed cost attributable to the product in relation to the total cost less, but there will be less friction in departing. When entire firms must leave, the hopes of the owners, especially if they are also salaried officers, for better times, often delays exodus. When a firm is merely dropping one line, one that contributed little or nothing to net profit anyway, and one which likely can be added again with little trouble if demand increases, the action will be taken more quickly, if the firm calculates costs at all carefully.

As some of the firms drop the line, other firms will experience demand increases; a sufficient number of firms must drop the line that those remaining will again be able to cover special costs on the product. Since the average cost of the product will have risen by the amount of the tax, price must increase until average revenue also has risen by this amount. Thus, price will rise by the amount of the tax, unless the dropping of the line by some firms affects the costs of the other firms. Where the latter occurs, price increase will be modified, along lines previously indicated. In general, the price increase is the same, cet.

par., as if pure competition prevailed. But the significant feature is that complete shifting of the tax occurs with no exodus of firms whatsoever.

In the case of the products for which average revenue exceeds average cost, if after the tax average revenue still covers average special cost, no firm will drop the line. But the firm, if enjoying no excess profits before, will no longer be covering total cost. However, there are several sources of relief apart from exodus of firms. As this line becomes less profitable, marginal cost for the other lines falls off (part of the non-specialized "overhead" formerly required for this product is now available for others), and total profits in the other lines may increase despite the price fall. Likewise, as marginal cost rises because of the tax in the line subject, reduction of output by other firms will allow each firm to raise its price more than otherwise. Nevertheless, these adjustments cannot allow full restoration of profits, or the firms would not have been operating at the optimum before the tax. But if the product is a relatively minor source of profits for the firms, it seems unlikely that any firms will actually be forced out of business because of the levy. It is difficult to define exactly the amount of price increase; apparently, however, the rise will be similar to that in the case in which the number of firms in a field is limited and monopoly profits exist. Marginal cost rises by the amount of the tax; the firms raise price until marginal revenue equals the new marginal cost; as they do so, the output does not fall off as much as they expect because other firms have also raised prices. A final equilibrium will be reached in which the rise will have been somewhat greater than one-half the tax and somewhat less than the tax (with constant cost conditions in the industry and straight line demand). When the firms are enjoying excess profits, or even where they are not, and the product taxed is a minor source of profits, this will be the final price rise.[29]

Where, however, a tax of considerable size is imposed on a line which supplies a large part of the support of the overhead, there can be no solution until some of the firms disappear from the field.[30] This will occur at once if total variable cost is no longer covered, or over a period of time if variable costs, but not fixed costs, are covered at first. Seemingly this process must continue until average revenue returns to its old excess over average cost, or by the amount of the tax if cost is constant. Actually, however, such will not be the case. As firms go out of business, output in the non-taxed lines falls; for the remaining firms, sales, and possibly prices, increase; profits made from these lines rise. This will lessen the need for exodus of firms, and the price rise will be less than if the good had been separately produced, simply because departure of firms from business involves reduction of output in other lines and increases profits of the firms remaining.[31] The firms which depend most heavily on the good in question will likely be the first to go out of business, but other factors, such as age of equipment, are significant also.

One further possibility must be considered. If after the tax, average direct cost of a product formerly yielding a profit is not covered, the firms will drop the line. But this will not relieve them of their difficulty, as they will be unable to meet total common cost, under the assumptions. The price rise will have come about more quickly than in the previous case; price will have risen by an amount equal to the difference between the full amount of the tax and the excess of average revenue over average special cost, except as modified by changing cost conditions as output falls, as only then will firms again be willing to carry the line at all. But the firms are not yet covering all costs; thus exodus of firms must occur also, and the final price rise will be similar to that in the preceding case, but more of the rise will be independent of the exodus and can thus come more quickly. As this is the case, there will be less chance of check on price increase through increased output in non-taxed lines contributing more toward common cost.

One factor has been neglected as yet -- namely, the significance of shifts in demand as between taxed and untaxed lines carried by the same firms. The various lines may be fairly close substitutes, and a price increase in one will lead to a shift in demand schedules in the other.

This will increase profits in these other lines; the prices in the latter may fall under certain cost conditions. The increase in profits will lessen the necessity for so great an exodus of firms as would otherwise be necessary. The price increase in the taxed line may thus be less than otherwise.[32]

The significance of multiple lines for incidence can be summarized briefly. Where the products taxed are unimportant in the total profit of the firm, or yield no profit, the price adjustment will be made very much more quickly than if the product is turned out by single line firms, as firms will drop lines of unprofitable goods much faster than they will cease operation. Where no profit was earned on the line, complete shifting will occur without any exodus of firms, even though there were no excess profits in the field, an occurrence impossible under any condition previously mentioned. The amount of price increase will be the same, cet. par., as under pure competition.

Where lines are important sources of profits, the short run incidence will be similar to that of the situation in which monopolistic competition, excess profits, and limited entry exist. If excess profits exist in this case, the long run incidence will, in general, remain the same. If such is not the case, however, firms will not cover all costs after the tax; exodus will be necessary, and the final incidence will be somewhat different than in any of the cases previously mentioned. The amount of price increase tends to the same level as under pure competition, but the exodus of firms and price rise is prematurely checked by the increased profits on non-taxed lines as firms leave the field, and the final increase is somewhat less. Thus there is a clear case of a part of a tax being passed onto the consumers of untaxed goods. A further factor which may lead in the same direction is the tendency for demand for non-taxed lines to increase. The resulting price increases in the latter may, however, be in part offset by other forces. As output is reduced in the taxed line, marginal cost of production for the other lines falls, and output increase is encouraged. And, if decreasing marginal cost conditions prevail in the untaxed line, a price decline will result from the demand increase.

But, as previously indicated, a multiple line industry tends to instability; it is questionable whether generalizations based on the assumption of an equilibrium which is not stable, except on the basis of rather rigid assumptions that the lines carried by the different firms in the industry are substantially similar, and that no raiding of chief profit sources of other firms occurs, are very significant. As mentioned above, one of the chief means of escaping from this instability is the development of some sort of average cost pricing.

Average-Cost Pricing: As pointed out in the first chapter, price determination is often carried out on the basis of average cost of production, including "overhead," plus an additional percentage of cost depending in amount on some rate of profit which the firm feels that it can get. The implications of this for incidence must now be considered with reference first to single line and then to multiple line industries. With the former, when average revenue equals average cost before the tax, the immediate effect of average-cost pricing will be to raise price by the full amount of the tax (except as modified by a shift in average cost as output is changed), since average cost rises by the amount of the tax. This cannot, however, restore profitable operation. Exodus of firms may occur as losses are experienced; in this case the final incidence will be the same as with marginal pricing methods. The price increase in the period of readjustment, which is often quite long, will have been greater. The exodus, however, is not inevitable. The reduction in output increases average cost per unit; each firm may simply raise prices again, to such a level as to restore profitable operation.[33] If all firms act in this manner, exodus will be avoided. The consumers of the product will be burdened not only with the tax, but with an additional sum necessary to allow continued payment of returns to the owners of the original number of enterprises in the face of reduced volume of output. As indicated previously, under pure competition, with constant cost, not only does the consumer bear the entire amount of the tax, but in addition the owners of the resources forced out of the field suffer loss of incomes. In the case under consideration, the consumer is forced to carry the second burden as well as the first.

Where excess profits exist, average cost pricing will lead to a permanently greater price increase. Average cost will be raised by the amount of the tax (under constant cost), and price, being determined on the basis of this amount plus some additional percentage which the firm feels it can realize, will be increased by at least the same amount.[34] If the old price were at the optimum level, the new one will be too high for maximum profit, but so long as all the firms keep to the same basis of pricing, the high level will be maintained.[35] Actually, the old price under such pricing methods was probably not at the optimum level; the new one may be nearer than the old, and there will be even less incentive to cut the new price.

Where several lines are carried, as far as a tax on a line yielding no profit is concerned, to raise price by the amount of the tax cannot make continued carrying of the line profitable, and it will almost inevitably be dropped,[36] unless further price increases are made in the manner indicated above. Apart from the latter possibility, average-cost pricing has no particular significance for incidence in this case. Where, however, average revenue exceeds average cost in the line taxed, such a price policy will lead to a greater price increase than would a marginal policy, the incidence being the same as under pure competition. The practice is of particular significance as to the effect on prices in the untaxed lines. If the monopolist is to maximize profits, the lower marginal cost for the other lines after one is taxed dictates lower prices. But at the same time marginal cost falls, average cost rises, because a larger amount of overhead must be allocated to the non-taxed lines. So a price increase is likely in these lines, even though such is directly opposite to a policy which would maximize profits if each firm acted independently. This policy is much more profitable, or less unprofitable, if all firms act in like manner. If one tries to raise the price of non-taxed lines while others fail to do so, his demand will be so elastic that he will be forced to reduce his price or lose a large part of his sales. If all act in the same manner, the demand is much less elastic, and the increase much more profitable. If the prices are increased by sufficiently great amounts, exodus of firms may be avoided even though there were no excess profits before the tax.

Thus, in general, average cost pricing will mean greater shifting, especially in the short run. When price is determined on the basis of average cost plus a certain desired percentage of profit, the tax will probably increase price by the amount of the levy, under constant cost, even though the optimum increase is less, since average cost is raised by this amount. Further, short run marginal cost is, for amounts below the old equilibrium, very much less likely to be of decreasing nature than average cost including overhead; this factor also involves greater price increase with average cost pricing. In the absence of excess profits, or in cases in which the firms adhere strictly to a policy of obtaining a certain rate of profit on capital, the price increase will be greater than the amount of the tax, as the overhead costs are spread over a smaller volume of output. In some cases, however, average-cost pricing will cause increases so great as actually to reduce profits to producers; not only do the latter suffer, but consumers bear a needless burden.

VARIATIONS IN CONSTANTS: The same formal considerations in regard to shifts in demand, alteration of production functions, and changes in factor prices apply as in the preceding cases. The reactions of changes in these factors will, of course, be different from the previous cases; for example, the effect on price of demand increases will be different with monopolistic competition and limited entry than with pure competition. The presence of oligopoly is of particular importance in introducing differences in reaction; for example, a fall in costs may not produce a weakening of oligopoly elements comparable to the strengthening of the latter caused by the imposition of the tax; accordingly there may be no reduction of burden for consumers of the taxed article despite a general decline in factor prices. The latter is, of course, unlikely to occur on any great scale so long as the industry taxed is relatively unimportant in relation to the economy as a whole.

CONCLUSION:

In concluding this chapter, it is desirable to emphasize the comparison of incidence under conditions of monopolistic competition with that under the conditions previously discussed.

There is at least one case in which incidence is similar to that under pure competition. Where monopoly elements are present, but excess profits are absent because of free entry, the price rise will be exactly the same as in the case of pure competition, apart from possible but not inevitable modifications mentioned below. With constant cost, price will rise by the entire amount of the tax in either case, since there are no other possible sources of payment; the entire direct burden of the tax rests upon the consumers, the owners of the factors forced out of use suffering additional indirect burden. In either case, complete increases come only with exodus of firms. When cost conditions for the industry are not constant, modifications will be the same with either type of competitive condition. The fact that the firm operates under conditions of decreasing cost is of no significance for incidence, as firms will operate at the same level of output after the tax as before.

However, there are numerous factors which produce differences in incidence in the two cases. In the first place, in the period prior to establishment of long-run equilibrium, the amount of price increase will be very different. In monopolistic competition, increase comes directly, from the action of the individual firms. Exodus serves primarily to allow restoration of profitable operation, though in addition it facilitates the increase. But with pure competition, no substantial increase is possible at all without exodus, since no firm can make any price change without losing all sales. It is true that, in theory, some immediate output reduction will occur with pure competition. At most, however, the rise would be slight,[37] because of the steep upward slope of the short run marginal cost curve for volumes of output within a certain range below the old equilibrium. With monopolistic competition, the marginal cost curve may be falling instead of rising in the section in which it cuts the marginal revenue curve, and a greater price increase will occur. Actually, with pure competition, no immediate output reduction at all is likely to occur in cases in which no close calculation of costs is made; price rise will come only with exodus. It is difficult to conceive of a wheat farmer cutting his output (assuming wheat to be his most profitable crop despite the tax) when the price he receives falls slightly.

Apart from theoretical considerations, there are other factors which lead to the same result. For reasons purely psychological, and inexplicable in economic terms, it seems that when in one case a certain price rise will lead to the same increase in profits as a certain output reduction would in the other case, there is more likelihood that the former would be made than that the latter would be made. Further, if comparison is made between a situation in which price increases at once, output reduction coming as a result of the increase, and another, in which price increase occurs only as a result of a reduction in output, cet. par., the average price at which the goods sold in the period will have been greater in the former case. Wherever retirement from business is necessary for price increase, the process is a very slow one in many cases, especially if no actual losses (in the business world use of the term) are being made. It is difficult to transfer capital from one line to another, even over time, without serious losses. In addition, there are numerous forces, personal and otherwise, which aid in keeping firms in a particular line even if normal profit is not being earned. Thus the greater the extent to which exodus is essential to full price rise, the longer will be the period in which the consumer escapes part of the burden to which he will eventually be subject.

Furthermore, the very conditions which give rise to monopolistic competition -- non-uniformity of product -- is responsible in many cases for the genesis of excess profits. When consumer-preference is established and made sufficiently strong, new firms can only with great difficulty take away sufficient business to restore profits to a normal level. In addition, the large initial investment necessary in many fields serves to check the development of new enterprises. Whenever such profits exist, there is a possibility that part of the tax may be absorbed therein; with complete absence of oligopoly, this must occur. As indicated graphically above, the absorption will be less than with pure monopoly.

However, certain elements of oligopoly are likely to be present whenever monopolistic competition exists, especially because of the chain relationships in the field. The elements are commonly manifest in such practices as uniform cost accounting methods and pricing on average-cost-plus bases. With such conditions, several modifications of the analysis are necessary. In the first place, even when excess profits exist, prices are likely to be raised by the full amount of the tax, since the latter represents an addition in full to average cost; when each firm is aware that the others will treat the item as an element by which to raise prices fully, each will take similar action, and the entire tax will be passed on by means of what is essentially a strengthening of the oligopoly position. A similar increase would have yielded greater profits to all if it had been made in the absence of the tax; the degree of monopoly was not sufficiently strong to allow this until an increase in cost definite and known to all produced uniform action. Monopoly profits will, of course, fall in the process, the receivers suffering a secondary burden. The price increase is similar to that under pure competition, despite the presence of excess profits.

However, it is entirely possible that prices will be raised, with constant cost for the <u>industry</u>, by an amount greater than the tax. The reduction in output increases the cost per unit when costs for the firm are of decreasing nature, as is typically the case under the circumstances. The firms are very likely to raise prices by an additional amount to compensate for this higher cost. This is especially likely to occur where no excess profits are made; the original number of firms will be enabled to continue operation. But even with excess profits, the firms may act in similar fashion if they consider the previous rate of return as the one which they are determined to get.[38] Thus consumers will be forced to bear not only the direct burden of the tax, but that part of the secondary burden which would otherwise rest upon monopoly profits.

It is not maintained that this result is inevitable with monopolistic competition; in many lines oligopoly elements are absent or are too weak to produce uniform action. But there is a definite possibility of a price rise of the nature indicated.

With strong oligopoly elements, the difference in incidence in the short run in contrast to the situation with pure competition is even more striking than in the longer period. With average cost pricing, the entire tax will be added to price at once; average cost at reduced volumes of output will almost necessarily be greater in the short run than that at the old equilibrium, provided that the capacity was properly adjusted, since the fixed cost will be spread over a reduced volume of output. Thus, the short run price increase will be greater than that in the long run if the firms follow strictly an average cost pricing basis, or will be of equal amount if merely the amount of the tax alone is added. This stands in sharp contrast to the situation with pure competition or pure monopoly. In both of the latter cases, the short run increase will be less than that which finally results when long run equilibrium is reëstablished.

There are other factors which act to produce further significant differences in incidence in the case under consideration in contrast to those previously discussed. The exact results of these factors depend upon the particular circumstances of the cases, and few generalizations can be made as to the effects beyond pointing out possible directions of modification introduced by them. In the first place, the possibility of shifts in elasticity of the demand curves of the individual firms must be mentioned. The curves may be made more elastic, for example, in the case of exodus of firms, if those formerly purchasing from the firms which cease operations have little preference as among the remaining. When any change of this type occurs, the level of output and the cost per unit for each firm will be altered, and the price rise modified accordingly. With pure competition, no such change is possible since the demand curves for the products of the firms are necessarily perfectly elastic; with pure monopoly, the elasticity can be affected only through the effect of the manner in which the tax revenue is spent.

Another source of modification is introduced by the existence with monopolistic competition of expenditures on selling activities. The reduction in the number of firms and the price changes made by competitors may alter the optimum amount of selling expenditures to be made at various price levels and cause greater or less price increase. When production is carried on by the firms at different levels of output than before the tax, as when oligopoly is strengthened, the likelihood that optimum selling expenditures are different at the new volume also modifies the price change. To the extent that advertising expenditures are influenced by profits made or cash available, part of the tax will be borne out of revenue formerly paid out for this purpose.

Likewise, product variation is of particular importance with monopolistic competition; reduction in quality provides an additional means of escape from the tax burden, one especially attractive in many cases because the consumers will be less aware of the quality change than the price increase. This is not the necessary result, however; in some cases, it may be profitable to offer a more costly product as a result of the other changes. When products are varied, discussion of incidence is made difficult by the inability to measure relative utilities to the consumers of different qualities of products.

A phenomenon of particular importance with the conditions under consideration is the production of multiple lines of commodities. Not only does this factor serve to increase greatly the use of average cost pricing methods, with the results previously discussed, but it is of significance for incidence in other regards. In the case of lines which make no contribution to overhead, for example, price will increase by the full amount of the tax, without exodus of firms, even though no excess profits exist in the field. Where some contribution to overhead is made and exodus occurs, part of the burden will pass on to consumers of goods other than those of the article subject to the tax. The purchasers of the latter escape part of the burden which they would otherwise pay.

Finally, the reactions to changes in factor prices and shifts in demand schedules resulting from the manner in which the tax funds are expended will differ in this case in contrast to the other situations. The exact difference depends on the particular circumstances of the individual cases. But, in general, when only one industry is subject to the levy, changes of this nature are not likely to be of practical significance in any case.

All that has been said in this chapter applies equally well to the effects of any change in cost as well as a tax, subject to a few modifications. In regard to the latter, in the first place, the increase in cost of any other item may facilitate readjustment in relative use of different factors; an increase in wages will in many cases make profitable the use of additional capital equipment. Secondly, the expenditures on other items -- for example, labor -- do not vary directly with total volume produced, as does the type of tax under consideration; the cost curves will be altered in a different manner than in the latter case, and the price increase will be affected accordingly. Finally, the reaction of oligopoly elements will not necessarily be the same as in the case of a tax. This is, of course, especially true when firms do not use the same amounts (relative to output) of the commodity the cost of which has increased; there will be less certainty that the competitors will act in uniform fashion, and accordingly common action resulting in full price increase is much less likely. Very few types of increase in cost are as definite and uniform for all firms as a tax per unit of output; the less definite the cost increase, the less likelihood is there of full price increase.

Thus, in summary:

1. With monopolistic competition, in the special case of absence of excess profits, incidence will be the same as with pure competition apart from the possible operation of certain modifying factors indicated in the analysis above.

2. The importance of monopoly profits provides possibility of absorption of greater amounts of the tax. Even without any feeling of mutual interest, however, price increase will be greater, cet. par., than with pure monopoly.

3. Despite excess profits, price increase will normally approach that of pure competition. The importance of oligopoly elements, with common cost accounting and average-pricing methods, allows the tax, which appears as a common and uniform increase in cost, to facilitate a price increase by the full amount of the levy. The increase is thus greater than with pure monopoly, the price level being adjusted nearer to the full monopoly level. This is, of course, not the necessary result; few fields are entirely free of price cutters, the activities of which interfere with the price increases. The increase will be checked also in the fields in which demand for the products of the firms is very elastic for price levels higher than the old for reasons other than the presence of price cutters.

4. In many cases, not only will price be raised by the full tax, but by an additional amount to compensate the firms for reduced volumes of output. Strong oligopoly and strict average cost pricing will bring this result, and allow retention of the original number of firms even when no excess profits existed. Not only is the consumer forced to bear the entire tax, but likewise the secondary burden normally resting upon owners of the factors forced to leave the field or suffer reduced returns.

5. In the short run period, the difference is particularly striking in contrast to incidence under pure competition. The price increase, in full or in part, comes at once without exodus of firms; the latter, when it occurs, serves for the most part simply to restore profitable operation. With strict average cost pricing, the immediate price increase will be greater than that after readjustment of capacity has taken place.

APPENDIX TO CHAPTER IV

THE PROCESSING TAXES OF THE AGRICULTURAL ADJUSTMENT ACT

Throughout this analysis, reference to actual taxes on particular commodities has been avoided. Determination of conditions of cost and competition in any line requires extensive investigation beyond the scope of this report, and generalizations as to incidence based on external indices of these conditions are likely to lead to serious errors. One group of taxes, however, has recently received extensive empirical treatment by the Bureau of Agricultural Economics, and a summary of their findings in relation to the conclusions reached in this study are of interest. The levies in question are the processing taxes imposed under the Agricultural Adjustment Act during 1933, 1934, and 1935.[1] Before presenting the summary, it is necessary to orient these levies in terms of the analysis of the preceding chapters. The taxes, levied upon the first processing of the commodities, were of specific nature, and represented fairly high percentages of the sale prices of the articles. The tax upon hogs ranged (at different times) from $.50 to $2.25 per 100 pounds,[2] which sold for from $4.00 to $11.00 in the period.[3] The wheat tax was $.30 a bushel, the latter selling from $.50 to $1.30 during the period.[4] The tax on rye was $.30 per bushel,[5] selling from $.50 to $.85.[6] Cotton was taxed 4 cents a pound, selling from 6 to 14 cents.[7] Tobacco was taxed on an average of 3.9 cents,[8] the price ranging from 7 to 23 cents.[9] The corn tax was 5 cents,[10] the price $.39 to $1.07 a bushel.[11] The rice tax was $1.62 per barrel[12] selling from $1.51 to $3.24 per barrel.[13] Peanuts were taxed 1 cent per pound,[14] selling from 1 to 4 cents.[15] Sugar will be omitted from this summary because of the complexity of the situation and the resulting obscurity of the results. The taxes are accordingly specific taxes levied upon manufacturers, in fields characterized by the existence of monopolistic competition. Accordingly, the expected result would be immediate price increases, by fully the amount of the tax, or, more likely, more than the tax. Where, however, the industry uses the entire supply of the basic product, the supply is likely to be extremely inelastic, if not entirely so in the short run. Accordingly, it is possible that this initial price rise would be followed by a fall in price of the basic product; this would not, however, be permanent, in the absence of excess profits in agriculture, but would remain over a long period of time because of the importance of irrational elements in the determination of the volume of investment in this field.[16] No exodus of firms in processing is likely unless the demand for the product is quite elastic and raw material prices do not fall; the processors can be expected to bear little of the burden except temporarily prior to exodus when the latter is required. The burden in the short run will fall upon consumers where demand is not too elastic and other uses exist for the product, upon producers where no alternative uses exist, and upon distributors, in part at least, where other outlets are available and demand is elastic.

The method used by the Bureau can be summarized briefly. The margins of the processors were determined, before, during, and after the tax, to ascertain whether or not this group had borne any of the burden; the margins of the wholesalers and retailers were similarly analyzed. The burden on the consumer was determined by an analysis of the elasticity of demand, to see whether producers could profitably raise prices, and by study of actual retail price variations. Changes in basic price levels were considered to discover if any of the tax passed back onto producers. This type of analysis is subject to the usual difficulties of empirical technique in economics, particularly the inability to exclude the effects on the prices and margins in question of factors other than those under consideration. Likewise the analysis is essentially of short run reaction. Nevertheless, the conclusions are of interest, and because of their clear-cut nature, in several cases at least, of significance.

The studies show that in only two cases, corn and tobacco, did the processors bear any burden at all, except perhaps incidentally through reduced volume.[17] The margin of hog-processors increased by almost exactly the amount of the tax, despite the fact that the latter amounted to four times the original margin.[18] After the tax was removed, the margin fell quickly to the old level.[19] In the case of wheat and rye flour millers, the margin between wheat and flour rose by approximately the amount of the tax, falling back when the tax ended.[20] With cotton, the margin rose more than the amount of the tax, although other costs were also increasing during the period of the tax.[21] With tobacco, because of the complexity of grades, uses, and time lag between purchase and sale, the conclusions are not clear. Cigarette margins increased by three times the tax; other products experienced much smaller increases, often by amounts less than the tax. Apparently most of the tax was passed off onto cigarette buyers alone.[22] In the case of corn for human consumption, the margins rose more than the tax, but because of changes in cost and competitive conditions, it is not clear that processors escaped all burden.[23] Peanut processors apparently escaped burden.[24]

As far as wholesalers and retailers were concerned, studies of margins indicate that there was no absorption of the tax by these agencies.[25] In the case of hog products,[26] cigars and cigarettes,[27] and peanuts,[28] the margins actually increased during the period, as would be expected in the light of markup practices to be discussed in Chapter VII. In the other lines, the margins remained virtually unchanged.[29]

In the case of wheat, rye, and cotton, study of the demand situations, of the impossibility of a substantial fall in raw material prices because of the world market, and of actual retail price changes shows that the tax was passed forward to the consumer. Inelastic demand conditions, especially with the first two products, coupled with a world demand of such nature that the decreased home consumption could be absorbed without price decline (except in cotton, in which apparently a slight decline resulted), allowed processors to increase prices without serious demand loss or fall in raw material prices.[30] With tobacco, the evidence indicates that, so far as cigarettes are concerned, price increased by an amount greater than the tax, this being made possible by the very inelastic demand for this product.[31] For other tobacco products, apparently the entire tax was not shifted, the remainder of the burden being borne by cigarette consumers.[32] In the case of peanuts, the conclusion is reached that the consumer likewise was burdened with the levy.[33]

Analysis of conditions in the producer markets indicate that in the cases just mentioned, no significant price decline to agricultural producers occurred. This situation is possible because only one use of the products was taxed; the relatively inelastic demand in the taxed line, coupled with the ability of the other markets to absorb the additional supply without serious price decline, prevented any secondary price decrease of the finished product arising from a fall in purchase price of raw materials to the processor.[34] Only in the case of cotton did the decreased consumption lower world prices sufficiently to allow a small portion of the tax to pass back onto the producer.[35]

In one case, however, namely, that of hogs, the processors were unable profitably to raise prices because of the recognized high elasticity of demand. If this commodity had been one with a world market, processors would have had to absorb the tax, or, in time, except with excess profits, quit business in sufficient numbers that hog product prices would have risen to cover the tax, regardless of demand elasticity. However, the market for this product is not world wide, and few alternate uses exist. Accordingly, the price of the raw material fell. Rather than increase prices initially, which they would have done with a more inelastic demand, the meat packers were enabled by their monopolistic position to force down hog prices directly. This would have been only a short run phenomenon, however, in the absence of excess profits in hog production, were it not for the benefit payments being made. Studies of the retail prices of hog products showed that apparently no change in these prices occurred as a result of the tax or its removal;[36] studies of income received by hog producers indicates a decline in prices as a result of the tax.[37]

Thus, in general, the relevant conclusions of the preceding chapters are borne out in the main by the statistical analysis of the processing taxes. Since the processors operate under conditions of monopolistic competition, with considerable degree of oligopoly, immediate increase in prices by the full amount of the tax, which was to be expected except with very elastic demand, was found in all cases except hog products, for which demand was shown to be elastic. The tax, a definite known cost to which all were subject, produced essentially a strengthening of oligopoly, and an increase in price by the full tax, apparently without the exodus of firms necessary in the absence of oligopoly. There was no definite evidence of an increase above the tax necessary to maintain the old number of firms or the old level of excess profits. This amount may have been of such little significance with the inelastic demands as to be unnoticeable in the statistical work, or may have simply not occurred. No evidence is presented as to excess profits or exodus of firms; because of other dynamic factors involved, it is extremely difficult to measure the effect of a tax on the latter.

V

SPECIAL AD VALOREM AND GROSS RECEIPTS TAXES

The analysis up to this point has been made solely in terms of specific taxes, levies made at a constant figure per unit of physical output. However, commodity taxes are commonly levied on an ad valorem basis, as a percentage of sale price, or, what is the same, as a percentage of gross revenue of the firms selling the product. General levies are universally on this basis, since from a practical standpoint it is much easier to impose a reasonably similar burden on different articles by means of an ad valorem than by a specific levy. In a world in which prices of different goods are constantly varying in diverse patterns, to attempt to tax a wide variety of goods with specific levies would require constant readjustment of tax rates if relative burdens on different lines were not to vary greatly. Thus the analysis of incidence must next be extended to ad valorem levies, on the firms in a single industry; not only is this question of importance in itself, but the discussion provides a basis for study of incidence of general sales levies.

PURE COMPETITION:

In general, under pure competition, ad valorem levies, just as specific, represent additions to cost affecting all firms, and must force price increases. However, as price changes, the tax per unit changes in the case of the ad valorem whereas it does not in the case of the specific, and accordingly the final price change is modified. It is necessary to analyze the case in detail to determine exact difference in incidence in the two cases.[1]

A change in technique of graphical presentation is desirable for ad valorem levies.[2] Since the tax per unit at each volume of output depends upon the price at which that output can be sold, the tax will be treated as a deduction from net revenue rather than as an addition to cost. Further, such taxes are most commonly levied on the sale price net of the tax;[3] thus, for each volume of output, the tax cannot be determined by applying the rate to the demand price at that output, but rather on the basis of the formula $Y = x + Kx$, in which Y is the demand price for the given output, x is the price net of the tax, and K is the tax rate. Thus, for each level of output there are two average revenue figures, the average gross revenue (AR on Chart 17), and average net revenue (NAR), the previous figure minus the tax. Average net revenue is not only the net return to the firm,[4] but likewise the base to which the tax rate is applied. The net revenue curve bears a definite relationship to the gross revenue curve, the distance between the two being greater at lower output levels. The rate at which the two diverge depends upon the steepness of the average revenue curve and the rate of the tax.[5] The two curves converge at zero price, as the tax is nil at this point.[6] The marginal of the NAR curve is less steep than that of AR, since it starts at a lower point on the Y axis and terminates at the same level on the X axis.

CONSTANT COST: On Chart 17, the incidence of an ad valorem tax of 50% is indicated, in an industry of pure competition and constant cost. Output is reduced from Z to S, and the price rises from P to P', as a result of the exodus of firms. The price rises by exactly the amount of the tax at the new equilibrium, since both are measured by the distance between AC and AR at the new output level.[7] In terms of the individual firms (Chart 17A), NAR falls from H to K as a result of the tax, causing losses for the firm. Some firms will withdraw; NAR moves up from K until it reaches H, at which point exodus stops. In order that NAR rise from K to H, AR must have risen from H to L; the tax at the new output is HL, the amount of the price rise.

Thus, under constant cost conditions, price rises by an amount equal to the rate times the original price, since it is to the latter level that net average revenue -- the base of the tax -- must come when equilibrium is reëstablished.[8] The same percentage of the tax -- one hundred -- is added to the price as in the case of a specific levy, and the incidence is the same in the two cases.

The problem of comparison between relative price increases in the case of the two types of levies can be pursued further. If the comparison is between two levies which impose the same burden at the old level of output, the increase will be greater in the case of the ad valorem. For equivalent burden, the ad valorem rate must be greater than the ratio of the specific levy to the old price, since, at the old output, after the tax is imposed, net revenue is less than the old price, and the rate on this smaller base must be greater to give the same burden as the ratio of this burden to the price.[9] Then when output falls and price rises as firms go out, the tax per unit rises, and when equilibrium is reached, the price rise will be greater than with the specific, which does not increase per unit. In terms of Chart 17, to give the same burden at the output, the NAR curve with a specific levy (SNAR') would pass through D; since the curve is parallel to AR, it would intersect AC farther to the right than S (at Q). But in each case, the full amount of the tax at the new equilibrium is added to price.

On the other hand, if comparison is made between a specific tax ($SNAR_2$ on Chart 17) and an ad valorem tax the rate of which is the ratio of the specific tax to the old price (that is, between a 50-cent tax on an article selling for $1, and a 50% tax), the price increase will be exactly the same in both cases.[10] Temporarily, the price net of the tax with the ad valorem levy will fall, and the tax burden will be less than if the old prices remained, and thus less than with the specific tax. When adjustment has been made by exodus of firms, the net price in each case will again be that of the old level (thus the NAR curves intersect at S), and the price rise will be the same. The fact that price rises from $1.00 to $1.50 does not cause a greater rise with the ad valorem, as the tax is levied net of the tax, and the net price rise from $.667 to $1.00 simply restores the tax burden to the same level as the specific, which is not affected by the temporary net price fall prior to final equilibrium. On Chart 17, the NAR curve with a specific levy representing a burden of 50% of the original price would, at the old output, pass through S, and cause the same price rise as the ad valorem levy in question.

DECREASING COST: With decreasing cost conditions the price increase will be greater than under constant cost, cet. par., since with the sloping

AC, output reduction must be carried farther before NAR intersects AC than if the latter were horizontal. Further, the price rises by more than the amount of the tax after readjustments have been made; on Chart 18, the price rise, the distance between P and P', is necessarily greater than the tax, SP'. The increase in price is measured between AR (at P') and a horizontal line through the old price, the tax between AR and NAR at the point at which the latter crosses AC (at S); since with decreasing cost, AC will be higher than it was at the old equilibrium, the amount of the tax will be less than the price rise.[11] A given output reduction will cause a greater rise in price than in tax, since the latter is a percentage of the former;[12] under constant cost, reduction for equilibrium is such that price rises by just the amount of the tax; when reduction is carried farther, as it must be with decreasing cost, the price rise will be greater than the tax. But, nevertheless, the same percentage of an ad valorem tax will be added to price as of a specific levy. Since the NAR curve of a specific levy imposing the same burden at the new equilibrium (SNAR) must pass through S, the price increase from this tax will obviously be the same as in the case of the ad valorem, and the price will have risen by the same percentage of the tax.[13] Since, so long as demand and cost curves are straight lines, the same per cent of this tax will be shifted regardless of the size of the tax,[14] the general statement can be made that under the conditions assumed, the same percentage of an ad valorem tax will be added to price as of a specific tax. However, if either curve is not straight, it becomes possible for a larger percentage price increase to occur in the case of one kind of levy than in the case of the other.

If comparison is made between an ad valorem levy and a specific levy imposing the same burden at the old level of output, (SNAR' on Chart 18), the price rise will be greater with the ad valorem, for the same reason as under constant cost, but, so long as the curves are straight lines, the same percentage of the tax will be added to price.[15] However, if, for example, the slope of the AC curve steepens above its point of intersection with the NAR curve of the specific levy, the percentage increase with the ad valorem levy will be greater, since at the point of intersection of AC and NAR (on Chart 19), the tax will be less than the distance between AR and an extension of the slope of AC before the change in slope in the latter (EP"), and thus represents a smaller percentage of the price increase than does the specific. If the cost curve had turned the opposite way, the percentage increase would have been less than with the specific. It is impossible, however, for the actual price rise to be less with ad valorem, since, under the assumptions, ad valorem NAR must be below specific NAR at all price levels above the old equilibrium.

As to relative price increase of a specific and an ad valorem levy at a rate representing the ratio of the specific tax to the old price, the increase will no longer be the same, as is the case under constant cost. The NAR curves of the two levies ($SNAR_2$ and NAR on Chart 18) will cross at the old price level, because the latter point is that at which they are assumed to be equal.[16] Thus, for all higher price levels, the specific curve is to the right of the ad valorem curve, and so cuts AC at a point of greater output and lower price.

INCREASING COST: Under increasing cost conditions, the price rise will be less than the amount of the tax because of the decline in production costs at lower outputs. On Chart 20 the upward sloping AC curve will intersect NAR farther to the right than would be the case if it were horizontal. Along the same line of reasoning as in the latter case, the percentage of price increase will be the same as with a specific levy so long as the curves are straight; under such circumstances, the distance between AR and a line horizontal through the old price is a constant percentage of the distance between AR and AC for the respective levels of output.

An ad valorem tax will, as in the other cases, cause a greater price rise than a specific tax imposing the same burden at the original level of output, for the same reason as before.[17] However, as to the case in which a specific tax is compared with an ad valorem at the rate of the ratio of the specific levy and the old price, the increase is now greater with the specific, since the NAR curves of the two (NAR and $SNAR_2$) cross at a point (H) above their intersection with AC, which is below the old price level for all lower levels of output; below this point (H) the specific NAR curve stands to the left of that of the ad valorem, and causes a greater price rise.[18]

Thus in general, under pure competition the theory of incidence is very similar for ad valorem taxes and specific levies. With constant cost, the price will rise by the full amount of the tax actually paid; the rise likewise is equal to an amount determined by applying the tax rate to the price prevailing before the tax. Under decreasing cost conditions, price will rise by somewhat more than the amount of the tax at the new equilibrium, and by an even greater amount more than the product of the rate times the old price. Whether a larger or smaller percentage will be added than with a specific levy depends on the nature of change in slope in the demand and cost curves. If both are straight lines, the percentage rise will be the same. Under increasing cost conditions, price will rise by less than the amount of the tax, and by an even smaller amount less than that determined by applying the tax rate to the old price, since price net of the tax falls as output is cut.[19]

MONOPOLY:

Attention must next be given to monopoly conditions.[20] In this case, for relative incidence to be shown, the net average revenue curves with the two levies (SNAR and NAR on Chart 21) must intersect at the level of output of the new equilibrium with the ad valorem levy (ON). When demand curves are straight lines, the marginal revenue curves must cross at the same horizontal level as the crossing of the average curves, the curve with the specific levy passing to the left at lower price levels. Thus, at the level at which the latter cuts the marginal cost curve, it is to the left of the ad valorem equilibrium, and the price rise is greater (to P''' instead of P_2). This conclusion is independent of cost conditions. When the demand curve is not a straight line, it is impossible to generalize definitely as to the relative incidence, since the net marginal curves may cross above or below the point at which either intersects the marginal cost curve. It seems likely, however, that the marginals will cross in the neighborhood of the intersection of the average curves, and thus the specific will be to the left of the ad valorem net marginal when the marginal cost curve intersects.

When comparison as to price rise is made between an ad valorem tax and a specific tax yielding the same burden per unit at the old output (SNAR' and NAR), so long as, after the tax, at the old output level, profit could still be made, the price rise will be less with the ad valorem levy. Since in this case the specific and ad valorem net average revenue curves cross above the cost line, their marginal curves must also;[21] since the specific curve goes to the left of the ad valorem curve below their intersection, and thus is to the left when each crosses the cost line, price will be raised more with the specific levy. Thus on Chart 21, SNAR' and NAR intersect at the old equilibrium output (E); at price levels below this intersection, SNMR' is to the left of NMR and thus the price rise with the specific is greater (to P" instead of to P_2). On the other hand, if the intersection of the NAR curves is below their intersection with MC, the intersection of AC and the NMR curves will come above the intersection of the latter, and there will be more rise with the ad valorem levy.[22] This is most likely with decreasing (marginal) cost conditions, and least likely with increasing cost.[23] In all cases, the percentage of the ad valorem tax added to price will be less than that of the specific.

As in the case of pure competition, comparison can also be made between a specific tax and the ad valorem levy at the rate of the ratio of the amount of the specific tax to the old price.[24] Again, the price rise will be less with ad valorem so long as the intersection of the NAR curves with the cost curve is below the intersection of the specific and ad valorem NMR curves. Such would be the case on Chart 21; the NAR curve with the specific levy ($SNAR_2$) would intersect NAR at S; below this point $SNMR_2$ is to the left of NMR, and thus the price rise will be greater. The reverse would be true if the intersection of NMR and $SNMR_2$ were below the cost line. With increasing marginal cost, there is greatest likelihood of greater rise with specific; there is least likelihood under decreasing cost conditions. Since the specific NAR curve is lower in this case than that discussed in the preceding paragraph, the intersection with the ad valorem NAR is, cet. par., higher up, and is less likely to be below the cost curve.[25] In different terms, a monopolist will usually find it profitable to raise price less with an ad valorem levy than with a specific levy of similar burden, since the marginal cost curve, including the tax, will be lower, for ranges of output near the old equilibrium, in the case of the former than in the case of the latter. Thus marginal revenue does not need to be raised as far to again equal marginal cost. The monopolist will suffer greater losses of profits than if the tax were specific and imposed the same original burden, but further output reduction will make profits less, not greater.[26]

PRICE DISCRIMINATION: When different prices are charged in different markets, it appears that there will be no difference in price rise in the various markets from an ad valorem tax, since the smaller output reduction with the less elastic curve will offset the fact that a given reduction causes a larger rise in this case. Unfortunately, this is somewhat difficult to explain. Where the NMR curves on Chart 22 cross the cost line, AC, the two are the same distance below their respective MR curves, since each represents the same percentage of its marginal revenue curve. Thus, the relative output reduction in the two markets is the same as it would be if the tax were specific and of the height of the distance between NMR and MR at the point at which the former crosses AC. If the tax were specific, as previously shown, the output reduction would be just sufficient to offset the difference in price rise from a given reduction. Thus, in this case also the same will hold true. The only exceptions would be cases in which the demand curve changes slope, or in which the tax is so great as to carry NAR and NMR in one market below AC at all levels of output. In the latter situation, sales would cease in this market; in the former, the price rise would be modified along the lines indicated previously. Nevertheless, despite the fact that price rises by the same amount in each market, the incidence of the tax is not the same in each. In the market of the more inelastic demand, the old and new prices are higher than in the other (P' and P'^{t}, in contrast to P'' and P''^{t}); thus the tax per unit is larger in the former, and the price rise is accordingly a smaller percentage of the amount of the tax. With the inelastic demand, a smaller percentage of the tax will be passed on to the consumer than with the more elastic demand.

MONOPOLISTIC COMPETITION:

ABSENCE OF MONOPOLY PROFITS: There remains for consideration the case of monopolistic competition. Where monopoly profits are non-existent, prior to the tax, for each firm the average total revenue and average net revenue curves, which are identical, are tangent to average cost. When the tax is imposed, average revenue remains tangent to average cost, but average revenue net of the tax is below cost, and losses are being incurred. A new equilibrium can be attained only when NAR on Chart 23 has been restored to tangency with AC, the price being net average revenue at the equilibrium output plus the tax at this figure. A further requirement for equilibrium is that DD must pass through the point of the price thus determined; otherwise expected price will not be realized and NAR will not actually be at tangency. Considerable price increase will come about as firms readjust output to restore the reduced marginal revenue to equality with marginal cost. But DD can move to the right only through exodus of firms; the latter takes place as costs are not covered, since, as previously explained, as long as the original number of firms remains, the attempt of each to reach an optimum position will cause all to suffer loss. The process will continue until the point is reached where each firm, when adjusting output to an expected price, realizes this price and in so doing covers all costs and nothing more.

Since NAR, with an ad valorem levy, is of less slope than AR, the former comes to tangency with AC to the right of, and therefore at a lower production cost than the old equilibrium. Since the amount of the tax is the distance between the new equilibrium NAR and the new price, and the former is below the old equilibrium and the old price, the price rise is less than the amount of the tax. Thus on Chart 23 price rises from P to P'; while the tax is the distance between F and P'. Thus, not only is the percentage of the tax shifted less than with pure competition, but is also less than with a specific levy, under similar conditions.[27] The full amount of the tax is added with the latter either under pure competition or monopolistic competition without excess profits, so long as the industry is one of constant cost. In the case of a specific levy imposing the same burden at the new equilibrium, the NAR curve would be parallel to the AR curve, and thus reach tangency at the same output as before the tax. With the ad valorem levy, exodus of firms is greater, cet. par., than under pure competition; excess capacity is reduced, and production is brought nearer the optimum for those remaining. Thus, in the case of ad valorem levies, the necessary existence of decreasing cost on the part of firms in monopolistic competition with absence of monopoly profits becomes of significance for incidence. The price increase is less than if all firms had been operating at the optimum, part of the tax burden being absorbed in the reduction of production cost per unit.[28] If the industry as a whole is one of increasing or decreasing cost, the price rise will be modified accordingly, but in any case the rise will be less than under a comparable situation of pure competition.

When comparison is made with a specific levy of an amount equal to the product of the tax rate and the old price, the rise will be greater with the specific. The old net price is greater than the new one; the specific tax, thus determined, would be greater than a specific tax levying the same burden as the ad valorem at the new equilibrium. Since the latter specific tax causes a greater price rise than the ad valorem, the former must also. It is not clear, however, that a specific levy imposing the same burden at the old output will cause a greater rise, since the tax is smaller per unit than the ad valorem at the new equilibrium of the latter; this may offset the fact that tangency is at a higher point with the specific.

LIMITED ENTRY AND EXCESS PROFITS: Consideration must be given next to the situation characterized by the existence of excess profits and limited entry. It will be assumed at first that the firm is operating in a range of constant marginal cost, and that the industry is one of constant cost. The initial effect of the ad valorem tax will be that each firm contracts output until marginal cost equals the new lower net marginal revenue. On Chart 24 each firm would seek to reduce output from X to Y, to the point at which NMR crosses AC; price would rise from P to P'. As each firm does the same thing, NAR and NMR move upward, lessening the need for so great an output reduction as otherwise. Eventually a new equilibrium will be reached, at which each firm, in equating NMR and AC (MC), adjusts output to such a level that the AR curve appropriate to this level of output on the part of the other firms crosses DD at the same output level at which NMR equals MC. On Chart 24, the final price would be P"; NMR' intersects AC (MC) at the same level of output at which NAR' crosses DD', and AR' crosses DD.

A smaller percentage will be added to price than in the case of a specific levy, always as long as the curves are straight lines, and in any case than with a specific levy imposing the same burden at the new price. The NAR with a specific levy of equal burden would pass through H. Since its marginal curve would then pass to the left of the ad valorem net marginal at the same level, and thus intersect AC farther to the left, greater price increase would be produced, as well as a price rise of a larger percentage of the tax than with the specific levy.[29]

When comparison is made with a specific tax of the same burden as the ad valorem at the old output, it is found that the relative price increase varies with conditions. The NAR curves cross at the same level of output as the original;[30] the marginal curves cross at the same price level as the intersection of the net average curves. If this latter point is above the cost curve (that is, if K were above AC on Chart 24), there will be greater increase with the specific tax because the net marginal curve with the specific levy will be to the left of that of the ad valorem when they cross the cost curve. The reverse is true if the tax is so great as to exceed profit per unit at the old equilibrium.[31]

The same line of reasoning applies to a comparison between the ad valorem tax and a specific tax of the amount of the ad valorem rate times the old price. In this case, since the specific is greater relatively to the ad valorem than in the preceding case, the marginals cross farther to the left; the specific marginal may even start below the ad valorem marginal. Accordingly it is more likely that the price will be greater with the specific levy than it was in the other case. But such is not necessarily the case if the tax at equilibrium is sufficiently greater than the old tax per unit of output.

In order to compare the price increase with that under pure competition and under monopoly, it is necessary to consider the nature of the shift in the line of equilibrium output. The left origin of this line is the same as of NAR and NMR, since at and above the level of price at which demand is zero, obviously there can be no output at all; below this point, as long as the cost curve is a straight line, or, if not, does not rise above the demand curve at the latter's origin, some output will be made. The right or lower origin is the same as before the tax, since at a price level of zero, the tax is zero, and the output the same as if there were no tax.[32] Thus the movement in EO is similar to that of DD and DDM. Since the slope is steeper than DD (NAR under competition) and less steep than DDM (NMR under monopoly), the price increase will be less than under pure competition, and more than under monopoly. The more firms in the field, cet. par., the nearer will the equilibrium line be to AR and the greater will be the price increase.

MODIFYING FACTORS: With two exceptions, it seems unnecessary to reintroduce the various modifying factors presented in the previous chapters. The significance of these factors appears to be the same in relation to ad valorem levies as to specific; what has been said about them before need not be repeated at this point.

Selling Costs: One factor which does require attention is that of selling costs. With ad valorem levies, where selling costs exist, there is a new possibility of modification of incidence. As was previously pointed out, with a specific levy, incidence is formally the same with selling costs as without, where tangency of AC and AR exists, only if the total revenue curve and the curve of revenue net of selling costs (TR and ANR on Chart 14) remain in the same relation to each other as firms leave the field. With an ad valorem levy, not only must this condition hold, but the two curves must be parallel, as is the case on Chart 14.[33] Otherwise, since with an ad valorem levy, tangency of NAR and AC is at a different level of output than the old AR-AC tangency, incidence will be different with selling costs than without. The nature of the difference will depend upon the direction in which ANR and TR converge. Furthermore, where ANR and TR are not parallel, the relative price rise from specific and ad valorem levies is altered.

Where firms operate with excess profits, the existence of selling costs may likewise influence incidence with ad valorem levies in a different manner than with specific. The possibility of readjustment in selling outlays as a result of the tax may cause the price increase to be different than would otherwise be the case.

Average Cost Pricing: The other factor deserving consideration is average cost pricing. The initial effect of this practice will be to lead firms to add to the price an amount equal to the original price times the tax rate. As output falls as a result, further readjustments may be made. In the short run, average costs are almost certain to be falling at larger volumes of output; thus the output reduction will lead to increases in cost per unit and further price increases. Thus, this practice, just as with a specific levy, leads to a price increase far greater than that indicated in the theoretical analysis. The firms, attempting to spread overhead over a smaller number of units, raise prices far more than would be profitable were the oligopoly elements to remain unstrengthened.[34]

Over a longer period, the net effect depends to a considerable degree on the location of prices prior to the tax in relation to the optimum point. If prices were too low[35] because of the pricing practice followed, the increase from the tax may well be permanent. Where such is the case, the previous analysis of the difference in effect of ad valorem and specific levies breaks down, since the two types affect average cost in such sufficiently similar way that there will be little difference in percentage of the tax added to price. The ad valorem levy thus loses its superiority as a means of reaching monopoly revenue.

However, if the original price were at the optimum or above, the practice may have little effect on final incidence, even though it causes greater price increase in the period of adjustment. If tangency of AC and AR prevailed before the tax, the pricing practice cannot prevent the exodus of firms. Temporarily it may do so, if all firms act in the same way; each can profit, however, by price cutting, and once some firms start the rest will be pulled down. Likewise, where excess profits are present, the result will be similar so long as oligopoly prevails. Where, however, strong oligopoly elements are to be found, or, with multiple lines and agreements on bases of pricing, the excessive increase may be maintained more or less permanently. With a small number of firms, and with the cross-trade raiding danger well known, each may raise by the full tax and not take advantage of temporary gains from price cutting. Each is foregoing possible profits because his price is too high; none will lower, if all have raised thus, for fear of starting a price war. Here again the increase from ad valorem will be similar to that with specific.

In general, in the common situation characterized by the existence of semi-oligopoly, and excess profits on the part of some firms, the significance of average cost pricing for tax incidence is that a tax will stimulate a shift nearer a complete monopoly price. If each firm prices on an average cost-plus basis, the full tax, apart from production cost changes, will be added to price. Each firm could gain by cutting under this, but none does for fear of starting a price war. The increase, which would be excessive for maximum profit if monopoly price were realized in the first place, is not too great because the latter condition does not hold. Since firms in such conditions are almost certain to be operating with decreasing average cost, the reduced output will raise average cost by lessening the volume over which overhead must be spread, and lead to a price increase by more than the tax. Under such conditions an ad valorem levy will affect price in substantially the same manner as a specific levy. The typical difference will be that the price rise with ad valorem will be greater than with a specific levy of the rate of the ad valorem rate times the old price, since, with higher production cost per unit at lower outputs, the tax per unit will rise and cause a greater price increase.[36] The fundamental factor which causes a smaller price increase with an ad valorem than a specific levy in most cases involving any monopoly elements is the fact that the net marginal revenue curve with the specific levy passes to the left of that with ad valorem at a level of output low in relation to the old optimum. When output determination is made on an average cost rather than a marginal cost basis, this fact is no longer of significance.

SUMMARY:

In summary, as to the incidence of ad valorem levies with monopolistic competition, with absence of excess profits the incidence is not the same as with pure competition (thus differing from the situation with specific levies) since net average revenue and average cost come to tangency after the tax at a point of lower production cost than the original equilibrium level. Firms are brought nearer to the level of optimum production, and price rises by a smaller percentage of the tax, cet. par., than with pure competition. As in the case of the latter, equilibrium can be reëstablished only through exodus of firms.

When excess profits exist, the percentage of tax passed on is less than in the case of a specific levy, so long as the curves are straight lines, or when two levies of the same burden at the new output level are compared. The rise is less than with competition, cet. par., and more than with monopoly. As far as comparison of specific and ad valorem taxes imposing the same burden at the old output, and of a specific levy and an ad valorem at the rate of the ratio of the specific to the old price are concerned, the relative price increases depend on the relation of the height of the tax to the profit per unit at the old equilibrium. Ordinarily, the rise will be greater with specific, especially in the second of the comparisons mentioned.

The analysis must take into consideration the significance of the various possible modifying factors previously mentioned, especially selling costs and average cost-plus pricing. The former may affect incidence if the output readjustment causes a change in selling expenditure and returns per unit thereof. Average cost pricing lessens the difference in incidence between ad valorem and specific levies, and, as in the case of the latter, will lead to very much greater temporary price increase. With both it will in some cases lead to permanently greater increase, especially where possibility of excess profits because of limited entry exists but where there is sufficient competition of the semi-monopolists to prevent realization of a full monopoly price.

VI

GENERAL PRODUCERS SALES TAXES

Ad valorem or gross receipts taxes may be levied not only upon single industries, but upon all producers, or upon certain broad classes thereof, such as manufacturers.[1] This type of tax involves combination into a single levy of special sales taxes upon each particular line of industry, and, in general, the problem of incidence involves merely the summation of the allocation of burden in each line affected by the tax. The general nature of the levy, however, introduces certain modifications into the incidence of each part of the levy, and affects the manner in which the total burden is divided among the classes in the economic society.[2]

INITIAL PRICE INCREASES - VARIATIONS AMONG LINES:

It must be emphasized at once that the price increases in the various lines will not represent uniform percentages of the sale prices despite the fact that the levy takes a uniform percentage of gross returns. The factors which are responsible for the differences have been treated at length in previous chapters, and can be summarized briefly:

1. Cost conditions. Price increase will be greater, cet. par., in lines of decreasing cost than in those of increasing cost.
2. Conditions of competition. Price increase will be greatest with monopolistic competition and strengthening of oligopoly, comparatively great with pure competition and monopolistic competition without oligopoly or excess profits, least with pure monopoly and optimum pricing policies.
3. Conditions of demand. With increasing cost conditions, the price increase will be greater, the greater the steepness of the demand curve; the reverse is true with decreasing cost.
4. Degree of rationality of investment. The greater the extent to which entry and exodus of firms is not entirely economically rational, the smaller the price increase.

Furthermore, the period necessary for final reëstablishment of equilibrium and the nature of incidence during the period of adjustment is not uniform among the various lines. Price increases can be expected at once when any monopoly elements are present, except under peculiar cost and demand conditions; the short run increases will be less than those in the long run because of differences in cost in the two periods. The only exception is to be found when strong oligopoly and average cost pricing allows continued covering of fixed costs despite the lower volume. With pure competition, no price increase will occur until firms leave the field; this process often requires considerable time. The nature of fixed investment, both as to importance in relation to total capital, and extent of depreciation, influences the period required for final readjustment in various lines.

After a period of time, however, in the absence of the factors considered below, price increases would be almost universal.[3] In most cases the largest part of the tax is passed on to the consumer groups, with some remaining on receivers of monopoly profits and owners of specialized factors of production. However, the fact that the tax under consideration is of general nature results in considerable modification in each industry of the price increase which would have occurred had the industry in question alone been subject to the levy.

MODIFYING FACTORS:[4]

REDUCTIONS IN THE RATE OF INTEREST: One result of the general price increase is a reduction in total capital investment, since the total level of output has fallen. In terms of the classical explanation of capital and interest,[5] this leads inevitably to a reduction in the rate of interest, as the supply of savings exceeds the demand for use in investment purposes. The reduction in interest facilitates an expansion in output, the reduction in cost allowing sale at a reduced price. The consumers are thus freed of a portion of the tax burden, at the expense of money-capital owners in general. The cost reduction allows also an increase in monopoly profits, receivers of the latter likewise being freed of a part of the tax burden. If the reduction in the return to capital owners does not produce a decrease in the volume of savings, interest must fall until the total volume of investment reaches the same level as before the tax. In this case the total output will be the same as before; consumers and monopoly owners will be freed of all tax burden at the expense of the capital-owning group. If the fall in interest does reduce the volume of savings, total investment in capital equipment will remain below the original level.[6] A redistribution of employment will occur in favor of the consumption goods industries, and a portion of the tax burden will remain upon the consumer because of the reduced use of capital equipment in production. Thus in terms of the classical explanation of the theory of interest, a substantial part of the tax, if not the entire burden, would necessarily pass onto capital owners. Thus consumers would be freed, in part at least, from the levy. It is strange that the various discussions of incidence which are based almost entirely on classical economics ignore this possibility.[7]

The classical theory of the rate of interest, as has been pointed out by J. M. Keynes, is based upon the assumption that the demand and supply schedules of capital are independent. Actually, as Keynes has indicated, the two schedules are interdependent, in that a change in either will alter the total level of income and accordingly affect the other schedule.[8] When this phenomenon is recognized, the incorrectness of this explanation of the theory of interest is apparent. In terms of the Keynesian analysis, interest cannot be considered as a reward for saving, but rather as a reward for the surrender of cash. The rate of interest is determined by the relation of the demand for money to hold, for purposes of liquidity, and the supply of money (broadly defined, to include commercial deposits), as determined by government and banking policy.[9] It is profitable for business men to expand investment (the process of creating new capital goods) up to the point at which marginal efficiency of capital -- the expected return from new capital goods -- is equal to the rate of interest which must be paid for capital. Thus, given the marginal efficiency of capital and the interest rate, there will be a certain volume of investment. The total amount voluntarily saved (that is, not spent for consumers goods) out of any volume of income depends upon the <u>propensity to consume</u>. Since the total volume of investment must equal the total volume of saving, the total income must be such that the amount which people wish to save out of that income will equal the volume of investment, determined as indicated above. At the equilibrium point, for each firm and each industry, marginal efficiency of capital is equal to the rate of interest, and to the rate of profit where there is no bonded indebtedness. If at any time marginal efficiency of capital exceeds the rate of interest in any industry, capital will flow into this line until the two are again equal; the reverse is true if the opposite relation exists.[10] With conditions of monopolistic competition, the significance of the effect of additional output in lowering prices, and thus in reducing marginal efficiency of capital, must be taken into consideration in the determination of the latter at each output. The addition to net revenue from additional capital is less than the net revenue gained directly from the sale of the produce of the additional capital.

Thus the reduced volume of investment caused by the tax does not necessarily lead to a fall in interest. The apparent "excess savings" will not actually exist, as the fall in total income caused by the reduction in investment reduces the total volume of savings. However, some decline in interest rates is almost inevitable. There will be reduced demand for cash for commercial purposes as the volume of transactions falls; any fall in wage rates, to be discussed below, will reduce the general price level and cause a lessened need for money for business purposes. Furthermore, a reduction in liquidity-preference may occur. The latter is essentially a psychological phenomenon; a general temporary reduction in returns to capital owners who have loaned their funds for investment purposes may make them more willing to forego liquidity at given possible rates of return; the demand schedule for cash will be reduced accordingly. However, these forces cannot in themselves lower the interest rates to such an extent as to restore the original volume of investment, if the original equilibrium was a stable one. They will ordinarily, however, cause part of the burden to shift to the capital owning class.

There is a further possibility of interest reduction. With the reduced volume of output, unemployment will be increased; the government and the central banking system may take steps to increase employment by increasing the supply of money. In a rapidly developing economy, the original volume of employment may be restored easily, since the original interest rate will have been high in relation to the levels below which it cannot easily be reduced.[11] In this case, the entire burden will pass to capital owners, unless the reduced interest lowers the volume of savings and thus forces the government to cut short its increase in cash. The result is exactly the same as that advanced on the basis of classical economics; the point of difference is that the decrease in interest, in terms of the Keynesian analysis, does not come automatically because of the excess of savings in relation to investment as the latter is reduced, but only as a result of conscious effort on the part of those in control of the supply of money.

In an economy which has reached a relatively high rate of development, it may be very difficult for the government to reduce interest rates sufficiently to restore the original volume of output.[12] There may be a constant volume of unemployment at all times, if the marginal efficiency of capital has fallen to the level below which the interest rate cannot be driven. The effect of the tax is to increase the volume of unemployment. While the increase may stimulate the government to new effort to increase employment, it is likely that a part of the net decrease will remain.[13] Thus, the consumers of goods will continue to bear a portion of the tax burden, and a secondary burden will be suffered by those who lose employment permanently.

Wherever expansion of output takes place as a result of the reduced interest rates, there is likely to be some readjustment of relative prices of different lines of commodities. The firms in various industries will be affected differently by this particular type of cost reduction, and the differences will not always be comparable to the original variations in reaction to the cost increase produced by the tax. In some cases, the two variations will be comparable; for example, in general, monopoly prices will fall less from a given interest reduction than competitive prices, but the difference is exactly the same as that between the original increases. In others, however, this will not be true; industries making relatively great use of fixed capital will expand in comparison to other lines, and the prices of the former will be lower in comparison to other prices than before the tax. Likewise, variations in price changes will arise where oligopoly elements are present; the effect of a cost increase in strengthening oligopoly will not necessarily be offset by the effect of a cost reduction, and prices may remain relatively higher in these fields.

One special feature in relation to output expansion must be mentioned. With monopolistic competition and relatively free entry, a chronic tendency to excess capacity is to be found in many fields. That is, not only do firms fail to operate at the optimum over the long period, but because of fluctuations in demand, of the hopes of new firms to oust old from their positions, of the introduction of new processes, there is constant tendency for physical plant to be excessive at all periods except in times of peak demand.[14] When a tax is imposed and output is reduced temporarily the excess capacity will increase. Accordingly, when interest rates fall, firms will be exceedingly slow to increase investment, simply because their plant is already excessively large. In contrast to this, with pure monopoly conditions, there is no reason, except poor business foresight, for plant to be too large; with pure competition, reduction of output will take place only as plants cease operation, paving the way for the construction of new ones as interest rates fall. But with monopolistic competition, the effect of the fall in interest rates is very much slower to manifest itself. In the end, however, it will, if entry is at all rational, increase the number of new firms seeking a place in the sun, and lead to price reductions. Temporarily, however, the presence of the excessive capacity will require greater interest reduction than otherwise to restore the old volume of output.

REDUCTIONS IN WAGES: One further influence upon incidence that must be mentioned is the possibility of a decline in wages coming about from the existence of unemployment produced by the tax. Even in terms of the classical theory of interest, some fall in employment is possible[15] if the volume of savings is curtailed as a result of the decline in interest rates. When it is recognized that there is no assurance of any substantial decline in interest rates, it is obvious that the total volume of unemployment created by the tax may be of considerable size. In terms of the orthodox theory of wages, real wages must fall until all those that seek jobs at the new wage levels find employment; thus the consumer as such will be freed of any tax burden which remains despite interest rate reductions, except to the extent that a smaller supply of labor is available at the lower wage rates. Apart from the latter, the consumer can suffer only indirectly, as a result of the readjustment in the structure of production that will come about if the lower interest rates cause a reduction in the total volume of savings.

Thus in terms of the classical theory of distribution, the burden of the tax will pass for the most part onto workers and receivers of property income.[16] The entire theory of distribution is based upon an assumption of a given level of output and income, subject to modification, given the state of the arts, only as the supplies of the factors change. Since a burden can rest upon the consumer group only if total output is reduced, logically in light of the analysis under discussion only if the supplies of the factors are affected by reduced return can the sales tax pass onto consumers as such in the form of higher prices. As long as the same amounts of capital, labor, and land are available, total consumption must remain the same, since the entire supply of the factors must find use in production, and all goods produced must be consumed.[17]

There are several forces which interfere with this process of reëmployment through wage reduction, however. In the first place, the activities of labor unions and governmental bodies serve to check the decreases in wages and thus to prevent absorption of the tax in this manner.[18] Secondly, it is not by any means certain that a fall in money wages will produce a reduction in real wages and an increase in employment. The classical argument is based on the assumption of a given level of income; when the effect of wage changes upon purchasing power and total income is taken into consideration, the relation between money wages and unemployment becomes very complex. In general at least with relatively pure competition, a reduction in money wages is likely to be accompanied by comparable reductions in purchasing power and prices. In this case the volume of employment will not be affected significantly.[19] This problem has received extensive attention in recent years and cannot be analyzed in detail at this point.[20]

SHIFTS IN DEMAND CURVES: The general nature of the levy under consideration introduces a further modification into the analysis. The demand schedule for each firm, in particular equilibrium analysis, is built on the assumption that the volume of income and the prices of all other commodities remain constant. In the discussion of the incidence of a tax on a single line of goods, the existence of this assumption creates little difficulty, except in a very few special cases previously mentioned. But, in the case of a general levy, in which the prices of all goods are changed, the significance of the interrelationships among price changes in various lines must be taken into consideration.[21]

The change in price of each commodity will cause the demand curves of other goods to shift; the curve of each one will be affected by the price changes of other commodities. To the extent that no interest rate reduction occurs, all prices will be rising. There will be an increase in demand -- a shifting of the curve to the right -- for those commodities for which the demand is relatively inelastic. The price rises in the cases of the elastic demand commodities will cause less income to be spent on these lines, and thus leave more to be spent on other commodities. The demand schedules for the elastic demand goods shift downward because more income is spent on the goods of inelastic demand. These shifts in demand affect the price changes of the various goods, in a manner depending upon the cost conditions in the different lines.[22] The result is different in the short run than over longer periods. In the former, those lines experiencing demand decreases are very likely -- and necessarily with pure competition -- to have price decreases as a result; in the long run, change may be in either direction. One further factor must be mentioned: to the extent that output and income remain below the old level, total demand for commodities will be less; rather than a uniform reduction in demand for all lines, there will be a shifting of demand in favor of products of high income inelasticity. Demand inelasticity in relation to price and in relation to income are not necessarily closely correlated, but it would appear that in general "necessities" would have demand schedules inelastic for both price and income change, with the reverse true for luxuries. But it is likely that there are individual exceptions.[23]

To the extent that declines in interest rates or wages allow restoration of the old price levels, of course the demand schedules will tend to resume their original character. Some modifications will remain, however. As previously pointed out, the cost reductions will not affect the relative prices in exactly the same manner, in the reverse direction, as did the original cost increases. Furthermore, redistribution of incomes will occur as a result of the interest and wage changes. Accordingly, the original price relationships will not be exactly the same as prior to the tax, and thus will be subject to further modifications as a result of the influence of shifts in demand schedules.

It must be noted that goods pass through a different number of processing stages. Butter, for example, passes through only one stage; cotton is processed several times before it reaches the form for final consumption. Unless the tax laws are written in such a way as to tax each good only once in the process of manufacture, different goods will bear different tax burdens from this source also, and the necessary price increases and demand shifts will be modified. A tax on a second stage in processing will not only cause further boosting of prices to the consumer, but by checking sales will cut the output of the producer in the first stage of the process, and cause further changes in price at this level according to cost conditions. Also, goods at the point of manufacture bear different percentages of final sale value: transportation costs will be greater on some; retail margins differ as between goods; varying amounts of service will be performed in the sale of different goods. Thus, the increase in retail prices from a given tax at the manufacturing stage will differ as between commodities similar in all other respects but this, and the resulting reaction on amounts sold will be different. If comparison is made between the effect of tax levies on two commodities, of similar cost conditions and identical demand schedules, one of which has far more margin between manufacturer and consumer than the other, the tax will cause much less price rise in the case of the product of high intervening margin. Since the tax comprises a much smaller percentage of retail price, a given additional production cost will produce a rise in retail price which is a much smaller percentage of the latter. Under the assumptions, however, the absolute rise will be the same in the two cases. If any of the intervening charges are determined as a percentage of cost of the good to the distributor, the absolute rise in retail prices will be greater with the one of high distribution costs.

THE SIGNIFICANCE OF THE EXEMPTION OF CERTAIN LINES:

The analysis has to this point ignored the fact that some lines of activity (those other than physical production) are free from the tax. The untaxed lines will provide an outlet for capital forced to retire from other lines (assuming a fall in interest rates); because of the limited number of such lines, the rate of profit in these will quickly be brought down, and the analysis of further effects is the same as that presented in the preceding paragraphs. The fact that enterprises engaged in physical distribution, which comprise one of the chief groups exempt, depend for business upon the volume of goods passing from producer to consumer lessens the possibility of escape. Profits in these lines will fall as physical production falls, just as surely as if they were subject to the tax. The fall in interest rates will, however, eventually lower margins of distributors and check the price rise to consumers. If interest rates do not fall at all, there will be no increased investment in untaxed lines, and the existence of the latter will merely be of significance in relation to relative shifts in demand.

SUMMARY:

Thus, in general, a general gross receipts tax on producers is shared between capital owners, consumer groups, and receivers of monopoly profits, with possibility of burden on wage earners as such. The burden will fall entirely on the first group only if the same volume of output is maintained through interest rate reduction; it will remain entirely on consumers and monopoly owners only if interest and wage rates are unchanged. The reduction in demand for money for commercial purposes will inevitably bring some interest reduction; the difficulty in lowering interest rates substantially in a developed economy will likely prevent full restoration of the old output. To the extent that the latter condition prevails, in addition to the direct burden of the tax, there will be further indirect burden on those thrown out of work as a result of the tax.

Thus, the general nature of the levy under discussion is of significance, in relation to comparison with a levy on a single line, in four ways. In the first place, a general levy leads to some reduction in interest rates, a phenomenon which may be of considerable importance if the government takes conscious action to lessen unemployment caused by the tax, whereas a tax on a single line will not. Accordingly, there exists with the general tax a force which restrains price increase -- namely, a fall in the cost curves; this may be sufficiently great, and must be, if the old output is to be restored, to compensate for the higher cost. In the second place, similar considerations apply in relation to reduction of wages. There are, however, serious checks to substantial money wage declines, and it is not certain that a fall in money wages will affect real wages or the volume of employment. If it does not, no further burden will be shifted to the labor group. Some shifting to wage earners, particularly to higher salaried groups, is at least a possibility, however. Thirdly, with a general levy, the demand schedule and elasticity of demand for each commodity will be changed by the tax because of the changes in prices of goods other than the one in question. This provides an additional factor in determination of the new price equilibria which is absent in the case of a tax on a single line. Finally, the tax will, in many cases, especially in a developed economy in which full employment can be obtained only with difficulty, cause permanent reduction in volume of output and income. Such a reduction in income will produce both a reduction in demand for almost all commodities, and a reallocation of demand as between lines. Thus, taxes on commodities in general fall in the main partly on consumers, to the extent that total output falls, and partly on capital owners, to the degree that interest rates are reduced.[24] The workers as such, especially certain groups thereof, and monopoly profit receivers, may likewise share the burden. Because of the shifts which occur in demand, the relative burdens on consumers of individual products will be different than that which would be indicated in the analysis of a tax on such commodities considered individually.

VII

RETAIL SALES TAXES[1]

Of great practical importance at the present time is the problem of incidence of the general retail sales tax, a levy imposed upon all or nearly all sales at retail, to final consumers.[2] The tax has been widely adopted in the United States during the depression, and has come to provide a substantial source of state revenue in many cases. The determination of the incidence of this levy is again a question of pricing, of the alteration of the price for retail service, the retail margin, as produced by changes in conditions of supply and demand as a result of the tax. Unfortunately, however, the theory of the determination of the price for retail service, which must serve as the basis for the present analysis, has received very little attention from economists in the past. The traditional value analysis, even as modified by the writers in the field of monopolistic competition, oversimplifies the problem, assuming implicitly that goods are sold directly from physical producer to consumer, or that the retailer serves merely as a conduit through which demands of consumers are transmitted to the manufacturer, the price of retail service being determined in the same manner as that of any facilitating agency in production. Far removed from this type of analysis are the sections in texts on retailing and retail practices, or in government investigations of retail practices, describing the manner in which retailers actually set margins.[3] The latter concern short run phenomena entirely, and fail to take sufficient account of the economic forces operating over longer periods which influence the levels at which prices are set. Nevertheless, some statement of the nature of the determination of retail prices is essential before consideration is given to retail sales levies.

TAXES ON SALES OF SINGLE LINE RETAILERS:

RETAIL PRICE DETERMINATION:[4] As a first step, the situation will be considered in which each retail unit is confined to the sale of a single product. For each firm producing retail service -- each retailer -- at each margin there is a certain number of units of the commodity which the retailer can sell -- or, in other words, a certain number of units of retail service. The series of these amounts for different margins is the demand schedule for the service of the retailer, and likewise shows the average revenue receivable for sales of the various possible amounts. This series can be represented by a demand or average revenue curve. There is likewise, of course, a marginal revenue schedule and curve based upon the average revenue schedule. The demand curve for the services of the group of firms as a whole is almost certain to be quite inelastic. A lower retail margin would lessen direct consumer purchasing from producer or wholesaler in some cases, but for the most part it would increase sales only to the extent that the lower total retail price allowed the sale of a greater volume of goods upon which the retail service was performed. The retail margin represents in most lines from 20 to 35 per cent of the sale price;[5] a change in this margin could not, except under unusual circumstances, cause a proportionate or greater change in demand. Retail service is in general not considered by the consumer as a source of utility in itself; the utility gained therefrom is not balanced against that gained from other goods, but rather is considered as a part of the utility gained from the particular physical good. Thus a reduction in margins would cause relatively little reallocation of demand in favor of retail services, but, by lowering the sale price of physical product plus retail service, would aid the sale of the total product.

The demand curve which confronts the individual retailer, however, is usually elastic, since trade will shift rather easily as between firms if price changes are made, provided the others do not make these changes also. Particularly is the part of the curve for price increases elastic; for decreases, in many cases at least, the demand curve which the retailer considers as his is made inelastic by the realization that any price cut will be followed by similar action on the part of competitors.[6] Thus, the typical retail demand curve contains a sharp break in the region of the prevailing prices; the marginal curve accordingly contains a very steep or perhaps even vertical section.[7] (See Chart 25, curve AR.)

This would not be true in all cases; with high quality luxury shops, the individual demand curve is quite inelastic throughout. For some types of products, such as staple groceries, the demand curves would be almost perfectly elastic, since goods are bought primarily on a price basis. But because of the importance of location, of personal attractions, of quality reputation, of different services provided, completely perfect elasticity could not prevail except in extremely rare cases The inelasticity of the sub-price portion of the curve arises out of the fact that the importance of "chain relations" in retailing produces a very large element of oligopoly at all times.[8] In almost all cases stores have near-by competitors who in turn have other close competitors; the same is true of the latter. Each firm realizes that a price cut on its part will spread quickly, and so fail to gain the expected demand increase. Such a situation is absent only with high quality luxury lines, with isolated neighborhood stores, or with others highly differentiated by location or other means from competitors.

Likewise, there is a cost curve for each retailer. The nature of the curve is in general that indicated in Chapter I as typical of all firms. For certain increases in output, cost per unit declines as indivisible factors are more adequately utilized; beyond this point cost per unit of retail service[9] increases as a result of the greater difficulty of coördination. (Chart 25, curve AC.) There is good reason to believe that the curve is comparatively flat, falling slowly, and rising slowly beyond the optimum, since the size of a store, and thus the capital investment and the labor force, can, at least over a period of time, be adjusted to different levels of output without such significant changes in cost as occur in physical production from the use and more complete utilization of capital equipment.

Each retailer will seek to adjust his margin to the level at which he can sell such an amount of service (that is, perform the services of retailing on such a number of goods) that the marginal revenue from sale of the last unit of service equals the marginal cost. Beyond this point, additional units could ordinarily be sold only at lower margins, and, because of the inelasticity of the lower part of the demand curve, great price reductions would bring only a small increase in sales. Under the extreme case in which nearly pure competition exists in retailing, increase beyond this optimum point will be checked by rising marginal cost. In certain cases both rising cost and falling revenue will act together in determining the location of the equilibrium. The deterring factor to a reduction in units of service to raise the margin is particularly strong in most cases because of the sharp increase in elasticity above the old price; a slight increase in margin would bring severe loss of trade, except in the case of the instances previously mentioned. Where free entry exists, average revenue will be equal to average cost, the average cost curve being tangent to the average revenue curve at or near the point of change in slope of the latter (M on Chart 25). Where excess profits exist, the average revenue curve cuts through the average cost curve. Because cost and demand conditions will differ as between firms in the industry, the price levels for the different retailers in each line will, of course, differ.

THE EFFECT OF THE IMPOSITION OF A TAX: Before completing the discussion of retail price determination, the effect of a tax on the situation portrayed above will be indicated. If perfectly free entry and absence of excess profits exist, any initial increase in price to re-equate marginal revenue and marginal cost will be inadequate without exodus of firms, or strengthening of oligopoly just as in the case of a similar situation in manufacturing. Actually, because of the change in elasticity of demand above the old price, the marginal revenue curve will be vertical or almost so within the range of output concerned, and there will be little or no price increase at all in the absence of strengthening of oligopoly. Exodus of retailers will occur until the margin has risen by the full amount of the tax, apart from changes in cost in the industry as a whole. (On Chart 25, the price will rise to M'.)[10]

This increase in retail margin and thus in retail price will be followed by certain reactions which will modify the final increase. The rise in margin will lessen the demand for goods from the producer; this will produce curtailment of output, and exodus of firms where no excess profits exist, and modification in production cost according to cost conditions in the industry. The latter, of course, will be different in the short run than in the long run. The effect of the decreased demand on production cost will be the same, cet. par., as that which would be produced[11] by a reduced output resulting from imposition of the tax directly upon the manufacturer. The change in purchase price may in turn modify the retail margin. If production cost falls as demand falls, the retail margin may expand by increase in oligopoly elements. Firms which would otherwise have gone out are able to take advantage of the falling purchase price of goods to remain in business, as the other firms fail to reduce prices. The situation is, of course, unstable. Or temporarily, the margin might fall under the common retail practice of determining markup as a relatively constant percentage of purchase price. This would, however, not be permanent, as losses would increase. If production cost rises, exodus of retailers will be greater than otherwise as the volume of sales falls; the retail margin will rise if a constant markup figure is used. This will be only temporary if MR-MC pricing is used; if not, the flow of new firms into the field (or the reduced exodus) may serve to bring the margin down, or may only have the effect of increasing the amount of excess capacity, and leave the price unchanged.

Where goods are purchased through wholesalers, new possibilities of modification of incidence arise. Wholesale costs may change as a result of the reduced volume. An increase in average cost is most likely in the short run because of the smaller number of units over which total cost is to be spread. But, in general, since wholesale margins represent only a small part of the retail price, chances are not great of significant modification from this source.[12] Thus, only when physical production, retailing, and wholesaling are all performed under constant cost conditions will the retail margin, and the price of the commodity to the consumer, rise by exactly the amount of the tax.

Where limited entry and excess profits are to be found in retailing, price will be increased as a result of the levy, though, except in the case of average cost pricing and strengthening of oligopoly, by less than the amount of the tax. The reduction in sales of the product will be less than in the previous case, and the resulting changes in cost of manufacturing will differ accordingly. It should be noted further that the change in costs of producers and wholesalers will produce different changes in retail price than those which would occur in the absence of excess profits in retailing.

New complicating factors are introduced where elements of monopoly exist both in manufacturing or wholesaling and in retailing. Under such circumstances the retailer's purchase price is determined by relative bargaining power of the groups concerned. The levying of the tax provides an excuse to renew pressure on the manufacturer to lower his purchase price, and the psychological effect of the tax may weaken the resistance of the manufacturer. The lowering of the purchase price will bring a restoration of the old retail margin (net of the tax) without any price increase; there will be no reduction in sales or loss in employment. Such action is possible only if excess profits exist in manufacturing. However, if only normal profits are earned in retailing, this may occur, either through pressure of organized retail groups, or by the realization on the part of manufacturers that price reduction will mean less loss in profits than would occur from a fall in output. In this case there would be no need for exodus of retailers.

Thus, in general, when a tax is levied on the sale of an article carried by retail units selling no other commodities, the margin will rise, through exodus of firms, by the full tax, subject to modifications produced by changes in cost of doing business, and in purchase price of goods handled as the volume of business changes. When excess profits exist in retailing, some of the burden must remain on retailers unless average cost pricing practices (to be discussed in detail later) result in boosting of prices by all firms by the full amount, or more, of the tax. With monopoly profits in production, part of the burden will ordinarily fall on this share. When monopoly elements exist on both sides, the modification of relative bargaining strength by introduction of the tax will influence the final incidence.

TAXES ON SALES OF MULTIPLE LINE RETAIL ENTERPRISES:

THE THEORY OF RETAIL PRICING WITH MULTIPLE LINES: There are, however, two essential characteristics of retail trade which have been ignored in the preceding analysis, and which, as it will be seen, play important roles in determining the incidence of retail sales taxes. In the first place, there is the large number of goods produced -- in the form of various lines carried -- by the typical retail store; the second is the great possibility and importance of quality and service variation in the field of retail trading. Attention will be given first to the former. Of all industries, none is characterized to the extent of retail trade by the number of "goods" produced; that is, by the number of articles handled. It is true, of course, that the products are very similar in most cases; the service performed in the retailing of a loaf of bread does not ordinarily differ significantly from that in the case of a pound of sugar. But obviously they are not the same, and must be differentiated for purposes of analysis. There are a number of factors responsible for this situation. One is the strict limit to the market for retail service on any one product because of the importance of the time element from the point of view of the consumers. Retailers cannot ordinarily supply customers over a wide area. Thus, total profits can be increased and indivisible factors utilized more fully only by taking on additional lines. These indivisible factors are of great importance in certain cases; there is a minimum possible floor space; managerial functions can be performed more economically on a larger scale (within limits); city-wide advertising and established reputation can be best utilized only with a variety of lines. Once a plant is established, additional lines can, again within certain limits, be carried at extremely low additional cost. Finally, the convenience of customers, and thus demand, is greatly increased when a wide variety of lines is carried under a single roof.

Furthermore, not only is a wide variety of services produced, but a very large part of the total cost is "overhead,"[13] for which no one product is definitely responsible, and which can be allocated among products only on some more or less arbitrary basis.

Just as in the previous case, at any one time, for each firm there are revenue and cost curves for each line carried. For each commodity, these curves are of the same general nature as those for the product of a single line store, and it would seem that the setting of price would be exactly the same as in the previous case. For any one good, the actual price might be different if the good were carried by multiple-line stores from what it would be if the good were carried by single-line stores, because the location of the cost curves would likely be different in one case than in the other. However, the method of price setting would seem to be the same. But, if the realm of theoretical analysis is left for the moment, and actual retail pricing methods considered, it becomes very obvious that the analysis is inadequate. The usual pricing method of retailers -- that of adding a certain percentage markup to the purchase price of the good -- does not involve the determination of marginal revenue and marginal cost schedules, and the setting of price at such a level as to equate the two. Rather, the method is essentially an "average cost" method of simply arbitrarily dividing the total cost, including the overhead, among the various products carried.[14] Thus it would appear that either retailers are not following methods of pricing which yield them maximum returns, or in some way, the theoretical analysis is inadequate.

The solution to the difficulty is, I believe, to be found by extending the analysis to consider the question of long-run or normal price, and the significance of the conclusions reached in regard to normal price as to the setting of price at any one time. With many lines of goods carried, and most of the cost overhead, there is simply no true average cost for any one commodity. For each line carried, there is a small amount of special cost for which the line is responsible, but most of the firm's cost is overhead; no one article carried is responsible for any certain part of this cost, inasmuch as the dropping of a line or the taking on of an additional one will not affect the total. The overhead must be incurred if the store is operated at all; the total amount of course can be adjusted to some extent according to changes in total volume, or total number of lines carried, but the variations produced by changes in any one line would ordinarily be so slight as to be of no consequence.

Firms must cover special costs on a line, or will not carry it; also total revenue minus special costs must cover total overhead. But there is no necessary way in which the overhead must be divided as between different goods, and thus no true average cost for each line. As a result of this situation, the use of marginal pricing methods would create a constant tendency toward an excessive number of firms in each line, more than could operate profitably. Temporarily, each firm would come to depend on certain lines for the covering of overhead. Further expansion in sales of these lines, beyond a certain point, would be unprofitable, since although marginal cost might be low, marginal revenue would be also, for in order to sell additional units, price would have to be lowered on all units. However, if a firm takes on new lines -- ones sold previously by other stores -- marginal revenue (per dollar of sales) would appear high, since prices of goods already sold would not be affected. It would likely be profitable to cut prices on these new lines below those charged by the stores already carrying them; whether this were done or not, the other stores would become unable to cover costs, because of loss in volume, lower prices, or both. But, just as it was profitable for the first group to enter the fields of the second, the second would find it equally profitable to enter the fields of the former. Throughout the retail industry this process would go on. Thus drug stores would take on candy at a very low average margin simply because some additional net revenue can be gained; grocery stores would start carrying drugs for just the same reason. As margins and/or volumes fall, some stores would go out of business; price increases due to this exodus would take place not only in the case of the lines which were being carried by an excessive number of firms, but also in the case of the other lines in the general field. But the new equilibrium will not remain; it will become temporarily profitable for stores to act in such a way as to start the whole process over again. The net result will be extreme variation as between margins in various lines which are unrelated to cost differences and which will not tend to disappear. Further, there will be constant shifting of margins neither produced by cost changes nor representing movement toward an equilibrium, and constant store mortality unrelated to changes in efficiency or demand. Since the entrance of excess firms into each line is just as inevitable as their subsequent exodus, variation away from normal profits is just as much to be expected as changes toward them. The variations must be considered a normal result of the use of marginal pricing methods in the field; there would be no normal price for any line, and constant price cutting and entrance of firms into fields unwarranted by demand would result. The existence of extreme variations and fluctuations in margins becomes the only normal element in the situation.

Because of the inherent instability and constant disaster to existing firms if strict marginal revenue-marginal cost pricing methods were used, a system of pricing which developed in the earlier days of retailing when conditions were much simpler and knowledge of costs and methods of pricing much less than today has remained, despite the fact that at any one time marginal revenue and marginal cost are not necessarily equated by the method. The usual method of pricing in retailing is the use of a percentage markup figure, the determining of the margin on each good by the application of a more or less uniform percentage figure to the purchase price of each commodity. The determination of the markup involves the allocation of the overhead uniformly -- subject to certain modifications mentioned below -- over the goods carried. The result is that each dollar volume of the goods carried bears an average share of the overhead. The price is thus set on the basis of the average cost of the product, the latter determined simply by assigning an arbitrary average amount of the overhead to each unit of service performed, a unit of service being measured by a unit of revenue received for the products on which service is rendered.[15] The markup figure is established sufficiently high to cover, at the estimated volume of business, the direct operating expenses, "overhead" or fixed expenses, and a rate of profit which is desired, or which is believed to be obtainable. The markup figure of course depends not only upon the total cost, but also upon the expected total volume of business. The latter varies inversely with the number of competing firms in the field.

Since direct cost of handling various goods differs according to risk, wastage, rate of turnover, floor space required, etc., the general figure is modified for individual lines according to the variations in direct costs. Of course, in certain cases it is obvious that lines are taken on at less than average markup simply because firms realize that the cost of handling them is low due to excess capacity. But ordinarily this type of policy is not followed.

There are several other factors which affect margins. One of the most important is the use of class prices -- the selling of goods only at certain definite price intervals, as the sale of neckties only at $1.00, $1.50 and $2.00 levels.[16] Articles whose prices based on markup would come between these levels are moved into the nearest group. In some cases this practice is designed to insure even prices. Thus variety stores will normally sell articles which on a strict markup basis would sell for 9 cents at 10 cents, primarily for purposes of convenience. There has been, however, a definite trend away from this practice in some fields such as in the grocery trade. In other cases the chief purpose of class prices is to reduce the volume of stock on hand and thus increase stock turn.

Also of growing importance is the practice of resale price maintenance, which results in the removal of the determination of the margin from the hands of the retailer.[17] Usually, however, the manufacturer must take into consideration the desires of the retailers; failure to allow a margin of comparable height to that on other lines carried by the retailers will likely cause the latter to drop the line or fail to push it. Likewise ordinarily the manufacturer will not set the margin higher than that usual in the field since the sale of the product will be checked by increased margins without benefit to the producer. There will be some variations in each direction, however: a producer who has securely established a reputation for his product may set the margin below the usual level; in other cases the margin will be increased in order to encourage the retailers to push the product.

In addition, many modifications unrelated to cost differences are necessary because of demand factors. Style and seasonal conditions will dictate changes from the average figure. Furthermore, there will be varying degrees of price competition. Even with the method of pricing in common use, there will be price cutters, firms attempting to gain from increased volume at low cost per unit. These firms will be much less significant than they would be if marginal pricing methods were used, as to the general realization of the strength of oligopoly is added the powerful force of the desire for an average markup on each line in checking price competition. The prime factor leading to price cutting in retailing is the extremely low cost of handling a product when "cost" is calculated on the basis of marginal cost; when average cost, including an average share of "overhead," is used as the basis for policy, no longer will the expense of handling additional units appear so low. Nevertheless, the severity of price cutting will differ inevitably as among lines, and accordingly variations in margins will be produced.

Not only do firms attempt to price on an average cost basis, but also they will take on a certain line only if they expect that the desired average markup, as modified by peculiar cost conditions of the line, will be covered. The chief exceptions to this include the cases in which the product makes a considerable indirect contribution to revenue, as in the case of loss leaders, or is necessary for a complete general line.

In general, the average cost method of pricing brings about the establishment of a quasi-normal price for each line, in the sense of a standard which firms attempt to gain over a period of time. This is not a true normal in the usual sense of the term, since it is not automatically established by flow of firms into and out of the field. Also there are many exceptions, which do not necessarily tend to disappear. If price cutting in a particular field drives the margin below average, there is no necessary tendency for it to return to the average, since firms will not leave the field if they fail to recover an average share of overhead on one line, provided that they can make up the deficit on other lines, nor will they necessarily drop the line. If the deficit in one line does cause the failure of firms, margins will rise in all lines, and not only in the one in which an average margin was not earned. Nevertheless, the widespread use of and belief in the markup system does provide a norm which firms strive to get and which ordinarily will be realized. If free entry exists over a period of years, the standard price will include an average share of a normal rate of return, and of all other costs with operation at a level of output less than the optimum by an amount determined by the degree of slope in the demand curve. If free entry does not exist, the standard includes an average share of the excess profits the amount of which depends on the degree of entry limitation.

Thus the retention of a method of pricing which at first appears to be at great variance with that method of pricing which in terms of theoretical analysis would yield maximum returns is essential to reasonable stability in the retail field.[18] With lack of any true average cost for each commodity, use of the marginal cost method would bring continuous instability in the retail field. While the present method does not necessarily insure maximum profits at any one time, it does insure greater safety for the retailer over a period of time. Partial realization of this, coupled with the strong tradition of the markup method, the greater ease of determining average than marginal cost, and the fact that this method seems the most obvious way to insure covering of overhead, serve to insure continuation of the method.[19]

The markup method of pricing, of course, does not insure uniformity of price in different stores, since the markup percentage varies according to the average cost of the store.[20] Uniformity in the latter is in turn prevented by differences in services rendered, volume of business, and efficiency of operation. The higher cost stores, of course, will not always be able to use a higher markup figure; they may be forced, at least in some lines, to readjust the markup figure to meet competitors' prices.

Thus because some firms enjoy lower costs, and because occasionally a store will turn to marginal pricing principles, some stores find themselves unable to use as high a markup figure as they would like to use, or to gain sufficient business at a usual markup to allow satisfactory profits. Accordingly in recent years various retail groups have sought legislation to prevent price cutting, the laws being directed especially at loss leader and other marginal cost price policy.[21] Some of these laws (the Fair Trade Laws) simply legalized resale price maintenance; in a number of states, however, the laws actually prohibited sales below cost. The laws are not clear as to the meaning of cost, nor are judicial interpretations yet uniform or complete; in general, however, the cost is interpreted to mean at least an average share of overhead for each line. So far, in actual enforcement, simply a minimum markup figure typically below the average (often around ten per cent) is required. Thus, the average cost method of pricing — the concept that each line should bear a normal share of overhead -- has come to be accepted in law.

As to the extent the markup policy is used, the Federal Trade Commission concludes its chain store price analysis with the statement:

> Pricing at a set average markup over cost is the rule most frequently reported by the chains. Next in order is the policy of meeting competitors' prices, which in turn is followed by the policy of selling at fixed retail prices determined in advance of the purchase of the goods, as exemplified in five and ten cent store chains. . . . . When a set markup is employed, the cost of the goods is treated as the basic figure and retail prices are set so as to provide the desired profit.[22]

The number following the markup method was slightly over half the total number reporting.[23] Further, since chain stores typically have sought to sell at low prices, and have in general employed the most advanced merchandising methods, it seems likely that a far larger percentage of the independent stores follow an average markup policy. In the case of the group which claims to follow the "meeting competition" policy, to the extent that the competitors are following an average markup policy, the prices set by this group will be virtually the same as if they had also.

THE INCIDENCE OF A TAX ON RETAIL SALES - MULTIPLE LINE ENTERPRISES:

Special Sales Taxes:

On Lines Not Contributing to Overhead Cost:

Now, with this summary sketch of retail price determination completed, it is possible to turn attention to the effect of a tax levied on retail sales. First of all, a tax on a single line of products will be considered. The result will differ according to the relation of average special cost and average revenue.[24] Where the former just equals or only slightly exceeds the latter before the tax, three possible reactions are possible. The firms may simply drop the line, immediately if average special direct cost is not covered as a result of the tax, or after a somewhat longer period if average special direct but not also average special overhead cost is covered. If this occurs, as would be inevitable under pure competition, it will continue until price and the retail margin have risen sufficiently that the entire tax will have been shifted to consumers; the retailers still carrying the line will be able to continue to do so. The only variation will be produced by a change in cost of handling the good, or by a change in manufacturing cost as volume is reduced. The latter change will differ according to cost conditions, and according to the degree of competition. With pure competition, an immediate fall in producers' prices is inevitable because of the time necessary for supply reduction in such cases; the final adjustment will come slowly. With monopolistic competition the short run reactions of the firms will likely approach the final adjustment, as immediate output reduction is possible. Final adjustment will differ only to the degree that long run marginal cost, and, without excess profits, average cost, differ from short run marginal and average. When manufacturing price falls, fewer retail firms will find it necessary to drop the line. Either retail price will fall, and cause the volume of sales to increase, or the margin will widen as the purchase price falls. The final adjustment will involve reduced investment and employment in manufacturing, with no exodus of retail firms, but some reduced employment and perhaps investment in retailing.

However, the more likely reaction is a direct increase in the retail price, by the full amount of the tax under average cost pricing practice. No one firm could take this action if the others failed to act without losing money on the article, since under the circumstances the point at which operations were carried on was the only one at which firms could cover cost so long as the prices of other firms remained unchanged.[25] But with universal use of the markup system, each firm realizes that the others will raise prices also provided that it does. Accordingly the demand curve appears much more inelastic, for ranges above the old price up to the point to which it is expected that other firms will boost prices.[26] (Note MK on Chart 25.) Above this, the curve turns sharply toward greater elasticity. Further, usually, the curve is seen to be of this nature only if the firm in question raises also to the higher level. Thus, average special cost and average revenue are restored to equality. The price will rise at least by the full tax, and probably by more, since, if there is any loss in the total sales of the product from the higher price, and if cost per unit of handling increases as business falls,[27] the higher cost must be passed on also. (On Chart 25, the price increase is from M to K.) If such an increase had been made before the tax, all firms would have gained some contribution to overhead from this article; this did not occur because no one firm would act because it had no assurance that the others would follow. The tax, however, is a definitely known cost, to which all are subject; each, under the markup system, realizes that the other firms will treat it as an item by which to increase the markup and so considers it in this manner itself.

There are certain instances, however, in which no price increase will occur. Certain products contribute more revenue than is actually obtained from their sale, by increasing sales of other products, either by allowing provision of a more complete line, or by serving as leaders. Some firms may see fit to leave the markup unchanged on these articles in the effort to maintain or increase their significance as leaders. Each firm may feel that any price increase whatsoever, even if followed by other firms, will destroy the effectiveness of the article as a leader, so that the demand curve, even under the assumption that other firms will likewise raise prices, will appear very elastic above the old price. Where the goods are necessary as an element in a complete line (i.e., sugar in a grocery store), no firm will drop them, despite the actual direct loss. There are limits, of course, to the direct loss firms will stand; if they feel that it exceeds the indirect gain, the line will be dropped. Otherwise, an attempt will be made to pass off the loss onto other goods; if this fails, there will be an exodus of firms, and a general increase in price of retail service. The tax will accordingly pass in the main to consumers of goods other than those taxed. In the cases in which price increase does occur, there will be changes in purchase price from change in manufacturing cost, and retail prices will be influenced in the manner previously indicated.

On Lines Contributing to Overhead:

However, the majority of lines will provide some contribution to the support of overhead. Under strict marginal revenue—marginal cost pricing, the price would rise by somewhat less than the tax. If the item gave only an insignificant contribution to overhead, or excess profits existed for the firm as a whole, this would be the final increase. If there were no excess profits, exodus of firms would occur; this would lead to a general increase in margin, and cause only a slight readjustment in the price of the good taxed. Thus, the permanent increase would be less than in the case of the type of commodity previously discussed. However, under usual markup practices, the tax will represent an addition to cost of the service of providing the good in question, and the markup will be increased, not only by the full amount of the tax, but likely by an additional amount to compensate for loss in volume of business over which overhead must be spread.[28] This amount will be greater in the short run than in the long, as in the latter it will be possible to reduce capital investment and other items "fixed" in the short period but not over longer periods. This latter item will be much more important than in the case of goods making no contribution to overhead; in the latter case, since no part of the overhead is supported anyway, there will be no further increase in markup on this account. By this means, which involves strengthening of oligopoly, all firms may be able to escape the tax, even though none enjoyed excess profits before.[29] The situation is not entirely stable, since any firm by cutting its margin (along dd' on Chart 25) can, provided no other margins change, increase its profit. But, because of the realization that other stores would follow, such action will not ordinarily be taken. In terms of the marginal and average curves, the area in which the average revenue curve changes slope sharply has been permanently lifted, so as to touch the higher average cost curve. A similar shifting could take place by the formation of a strong retail trade group. In this latter case, however, the excess profits would draw additional firms into the field, and cause a shifting of the average revenue curve to the left. With limited entry the excess would remain.

There is one situation in which even average cost pricing cannot prevent losses being incurred. If the old price was that of the optimum monopoly level, any attempt to add the full amount of the tax or more will simply increase losses. No solution is possible without exodus, which will allow the remaining firms to operate nearer the optimum. There will be some price increase also, just as a sales tax on a monopolist will bring some readjustment, but, apart from rare exceptions, by an amount less than the full tax. Of course, where exodus occurs, some of the tax will shift to other products, thus lessening the price increase of the good in question. Exodus will likewise be necessary when the tax is sufficiently great that an increase to full monopoly price will not be sufficient to eliminate loss.

It has been assumed above that the tax would be considered as an element to be included, where possible, in the markup of the particular product in question. Obviously, this is not necessary; the tax, while directly attributable to the product on which it is imposed, could simply be treated as an item in overhead, to be covered in part by all the products carried. If all firms treat the tax in this manner, as they may possibly do under a system of using a single average markup on all products, the burden of the tax will be spread widely over many lines. This must be regarded, however, merely as a possibility of slight importance, since the tax will ordinarily be regarded as a direct cost attributable to the product in question. The trend toward the use of cost accounting in the retail field lessens the likelihood of the burden being spread over other lines.

In some cases the relative importance of specialty and multiple line stores in the sale of the taxed product may have considerable influence on incidence. Where both types use similar markup practices, each will increase by roughly the same amount, and ordinarily shift the tax without exodus. One variation, however, arises out of the probable difference in per unit cost change as sales fall. If the cost in the case of one rises less than in the case of the other, exodus of the latter type, especially if it is the specialty and thus particularly dependent on this article, is almost inevitable. If losses cannot be eliminated without exodus, the position of the specialty shops is particularly weak. As multiple line shops leave, the margin on all goods rises for the remaining, and lessens the need for further exodus, and price rise in the taxed line. There is no similar compensating factor for the specialty stores, and much greater exodus is likely. Furthermore, if the multiple stores enjoy excess profits produced by other than the taxed line, whereas the specialty do not, the former do not need to raise price at all to stay in business, whereas the latter do; the position of the latter is accordingly weak. But so long as usual markup practices are followed, there is no great danger to the specialty groups.

In conclusion to this section, the incidence of a retail sales tax levied upon a single product will be compared with a tax levied on the sale of the same product at the manufacturing level. In general, the price rise would be the same in the two cases. The retail tax would appear as an added cost to the retailer rather than to the manufacturer. The former would readjust the markup on the commodity to include the entire tax, plus, in many cases, any increase in cost per unit coming about from the smaller volume of business; if the purchase price changed because of the effect of the reduced volume on price at the production level, the retailer will change his sale price accordingly. In case the tax is levied on the producer, when no excess profits exist, the price would rise by the entire tax, apart from changes in production cost. The retailer will apply the old markup to the higher purchase price, and thus pass on the entire tax, plus a small additional amount comparable to the additional amount added in the case of a retail tax because of reduced number of units over which the overhead must be spread. However, if the producer's sale price does not rise by the full tax, as will be the case with pure monopoly, or, at times, with any condition of excess profits, the final price rise will be less than if the tax were levied on the retailer.[30] Of course, the reverse situation is possible, in which the retailer, because the good is used as a loss leader, or because of a complete monopoly position, does not readjust markup, whereas an increase in purchase price would be passed on. Any change in cost of producing will be the same regardless of the type of levy, except in the cases in which final price rise is different because of other factors, since a given retail price rise will cause the same fall in output whether it comes about from increased cost to manufacturer and thus higher retail purchase price, or from a charge levied on the retailer and the subsequent readjustment of markup. In the short run, with pure competition in production, however, there is likely to be considerable difference. Because of the inelasticity of supply, an increase in cost will not bring any price increase for some period. When the tax is levied on the retailers, the price increase will occur at once; however, the reduced demand at the production level will cause a sharp drop in price and tend to restore retail prices to the old level for some period at least. Likewise, with oligopoly in production, an increase in cost and falling sales may have different effects in strengthening or weakening the elements of oligopoly, and some permanent difference in price increase may result. In general, a demand decrease may be less likely to bring a price increase than a fall in output due to decreased sales at higher prices.

Further, with oligopoly in retailing, the reaction to an increase in purchase price is likely to differ in many cases from that to a change in cost of operation. The former requires no readjustment of the relatively constant markup figure, but merely reapplication of the old figure to a new purchase price, a process of constant recurrence. The process of readjustment of margin is less commonly performed, and thus the force of inertia against change is greater; there will be less assurance of simultaneous action on the part of competitors. This factor is likely to bring greater increase when the tax is levied on producer than retailer; the chief condition in which the opposite tendency prevails is the case in which oligopoly exists in retailing in contrast to relatively pure competition or pure monopoly in manufacturing. The usual statement that a greater increase will occur from a producers' sales tax than from a retail sales tax because the initial increase in the former will "pyramid" because of the markup system[31] fails to recognize that the addition to price in excess of the tax made by dealers in the case of the producers' levy to compensate for lost volume has an exact counterpart in the tendency of retailers to add more than the tax, under the markup system, with a retail sales tax, for exactly the same reason. There is, in general, no reason why this increase should take place in greater degree in one case than in the other, except in the special situations mentioned.

One other difference between incidence of the two levies is the greater possibility of passing the tax off onto other goods in the case of a retail sales tax. Since retailers ordinarily carry more lines than manufacturers, there are more opportunities of so doing. Also the less careful use of cost accounting in retailing, the greater use of loss leaders and commonly the greater variety in intensity of competition in different lines in retailing tend to promote greater shifting of burden as between lines. Likewise, where exodus of firms occurs, the wider variety of lines in retailing causes the burden to be spread over a greater number of products. The retailer may, of course, distribute increased purchase prices over a number of lines, but he is much less likely to do so than he is to treat an increase in expenses in this manner.

General Retail Sales Taxes: Attention comes finally to the most important type of retail levy -- the general retail sales tax, imposed upon the sale of all goods at retail. There are a number of complicating factors in the analysis; for purposes of simplification, the immediate response of retailers will be considered first, then the accompanying and modifying influences, and finally the secondary reactions produced which modify the final result.

The Initial Reaction of Individual Firms:

The first reaction of the retailers will be to consider the tax as an element affecting the cost of handling each good. Regardless of the pricing practice followed, some initial price increase will be made on every product, except in the cases in which the average or marginal revenue curve appears perfectly elastic above the old price. Under strict marginal revenue-marginal cost pricing, and failure to consider the reactions of competitors to the firm's own price change, price will be raised initially by one-half the tax, when marginal cost is constant. It will be noted that, apart from differences in demand and cost conditions, the increase will constitute varying percentages of the retail margins, since the latter constitute varying percentages of total price, upon which the tax is laid. A heavier burden is imposed on retail profits in the lines in which the tax is a high percentage of margin, since with marginal revenue-marginal cost pricing, part of the burden, until exodus occurs, rests on store owners.

Actually, under usual retail pricing methods, as previously indicated, the initial price increase will be greater in most cases. The markup will be raised sufficiently to cover the increase in the expenses of performing retail services caused by the tax.[32] Since the latter represents a varying per cent of markup, the latter will be increased by varying percentages; the increase will, however, represent a constant percentage (apart from modifications introduced below) of the sale price added to the markup. Since some fall in volume will be expected, and in the short run average cost almost inevitably is of decreasing nature, the markup will be increased by an amount greater than the tax, to insure continued covering of overhead and provision of the original return on capital. The amount will vary in different lines according to cost conditions (which, however, in general are similar), and according to elasticity of demand. Where no excess profits exist before the tax for the firm as a whole, the price must necessarily rise by more than the tax, if the demand curve for the industry has any elasticity at all, for the firm to break even, because average cost per unit inevitably will increase at lower outputs under the circumstances. This must occur in every line, or, if prices do not rise in some, this must be compensated for by greater rise in others.[33] The increase is greater than would occur if equilibrium were reached by marginal cost pricing and exodus of firms, since the latter would bring operation nearer the optimum point. When excess profits exist before the tax, the price rise is more likely to be exactly the amount of the tax, unless the firms have become accustomed to the excess profit rate as a normal one, and continue to raise markup until this is again attainable, if possible. Otherwise, the increase of the markup by the amount of the tax represents the final adjustment. There will be some reduction in profits, despite the price rise by the full tax, if average cost rises as output falls. If average cost falls, profits may actually increase as a result of the addition of the tax to price. As previously indicated, the process of adding the entire burden can be carried through only because all firms act in similar manner. The long-established markup practices, involving the addition to the purchase price of a certain percentage, relatively constant except as modified by definite cost changes such as taxes which will be treated in more or less uniform manner by all firms in readjusting the figure, allow the firms to pass off the entire tax, ordinarily without exodus of firms or serious loss in profits. The smaller the excess over normal profits before the tax, the greater is the likelihood of a price increase greater than the tax.[34]

Separate-Charge Provisions: In recent sales tax legislation in the United States, definite attempts have been made to insure shifting of the entire tax, particularly through provisions requiring the charging of the tax as a separate item, and providing schedules of the amounts to collect on small purchases. In this case, there is no readjustment of markup, except as cost of providing service varies as volume falls; an amount determined by applying the tax rate to the price will be collected along with the latter. With separate charging, there are essentially two markups, the one applied by the retailer to cover his own cost and profit, and the one which he applies in behalf of the state to collect revenue for the latter. Such provisions are more important for incidence than they might appear to be because of the importance of oligopoly elements in bringing complete shifting without exodus. Without such legal provisions, other firms are not certain that the firms following fixed price or "meeting competition" policies will increase prices by the amount of the tax, and so are less ready to raise their own prices. The various provisions to insure shifting ordinarily will increase the assurance each firm has that the other firms will raise, and thus make full increase more likely than would otherwise be the case. This is especially true in lines where the markup system is not universally followed.[35]

Modifying Phenomena:

Retail Pricing Practices: There are, however, certain factors which modify significantly the results indicated above. In the first place there are certain retail pricing phenomena which interfere. One of these is the existence of customary prices. Prices on certain articles maintained over long periods can be altered only with great difficulty. That is, retailers realize that average revenue will fall greatly if the price is disturbed, and no change will be made; the tax attributable to this article will be spread over other lines. The line will be dropped only if it previously contributed nothing whatsoever to common cost, and made no significant indirect contributions.[36] Likewise, the absence of sufficiently small coin denominations will prevent the tax from being collected on items of small unit value; the burden will serve to increase total expenses that other goods must carry, and the markup on the latter will be increased. Another feature is the existence of price lines.

Experience has shown that some goods sell best in certain definite price lines; it will commonly be felt desirable to avoid any price changes which involve readjustment of class lines. If quality cannot be reduced, the tax burden and markup on other lines is increased. In all of these cases, so long as firms treat the tax in a uniform manner, there will usually be little difficulty to shove the burden off onto other products. In all cases, particularly in the first and third, a separate charging provision in the law will greatly facilitate the passing on of the burden. The separate charge will make it easier, from the point of view of consumer resistance, to raise the price. Consumers, being conscious of the tax payment as such in the case of other articles, will be less likely to object strenuously to price increases on customary-price lines. Where the latter are articles usually purchased along with others, the consumer will scarcely realize the departure from the customary price, since the latter will be quoted, and the tax added to the bill for the entire purchase. Likewise, as to price lines, the old prices will still be quoted, the tax appearing as a separate item when the bill is made out.

A further group of factors rigidifying retail prices include the existence of "suggested" prices by manufacturers, actual resale price maintenance, and legal and semi-legal price control. In the first two cases, it seems likely that ordinarily the manufacturer would readjust the retail price to include the tax; when this is done, the assurance that the tax will be shifted is increased. But there is less likelihood that any additional charge to compensate the retailers for lost volume of business will be forthcoming. It may be, of course, especially where retail merchant groups are strong, but there is great likelihood that the manufacturer will simply increase the retail price by the amount of the tax alone. With separate charging, the addition of the tax to the price would probably not be considered to constitute a deviation from the established price. In this case, any increase to compensate for lost volume would be extremely difficult. Some firms would probably drop the line, and additional pressure would be brought to bear on the manufacturer to increase the margin. But in many cases, undoubtedly the old set price would remain; the increase is the exact amount of the tax. Particularly will this be true if the original price was an "even" price, or one long established. With control of retail prices of this nature, immediate and complete shifting is much more certain to occur than in other cases, since it is impossible for any firms to attempt to gain volume by failing to raise prices. With legal control of prices, the price ordinarily is set on a "cost" basis: the tax, as an element in cost, would in general be added in exact amount to the price. Since all firms are forced to act in unison, complete shifting is more certain than under any other condition. If the cost of service rises from the reduced volume, a further increase to cover this is likely, much more so than in the case of a manufacturer-determined price. The producer is not under the same obligation to allow the retailer to cover costs as is a state agency.[37] In this case, separate charging is of significance only in the very short period. The price increase would ordinarily occur at once with separate charging; otherwise some time will elapse before the state agency can readjust the retail price.

Failure of Certain Firms to Raise Prices: A second and more significant modifying phenomenon involves the possibility of the failure of certain firms in the field to raise prices by the full amount of the tax. As previously indicated, any firm can gain from price cutting in the new situation after all have increased, provided other firms fail to act.[38] In graphical terms, the old curve (see dd, Chart 25) -- the curve of average revenue with prices of other firms unchanged -- will not ordinarily be tangent to average cost, the actual price being at the point at which the AR-dd curve crosses the average cost curve and intersects the DD curve[39] -- the demand curve with the other prices changing in like manner to the firm in question. Thus, any firm can gain by cutting along dd; only if it is realized that DD, or something near it, is the real average revenue curve below the old price, can the position be maintained. As previously indicated, this will ordinarily be the case. In retailing, with a high percentage of common and fixed cost, especially great possibilities of gain from price cutting, provided others do not cut, exist, as well as great danger because of the distance to which the cutting can go. Because of the realization of the latter, there is a tendency to hold to average revenue-average cost pricing, to avoid price cuts which might well lead to eventual collapse. The danger always exists, however, that some of the firms, especially those emphasizing high turnover and low margin at all times, will attempt to escape from the tax by selling an increased volume of goods. If the firm does not raise prices initially, its demand curve will shift to the right; at the old price, more goods can be sold, and the original level of profits maintained or even increased. If only a small number of firms attempt to act in this manner, they may be able to do so without interference, as the rest of the firms, not experiencing serious demand losses, avoid following in order to prevent a general price collapse. But if a number of other firms follow the price cut because they experience a greater demand reduction than expected, a general loss in profits will result, leading to failure of some firms, exodus, and eventual price increase with a reduced number of enterprises. Firms may increase prices in most lines but leave others unchanged.[40] If the firms chose the same lines to leave unchanged, and pass the tax on these to other lines, there will be no necessary loss in profits. But if the firms chose different lines to leave unchanged, a general collapse is likely just as if all prices had been initially kept low.[41]

It is because of this extreme importance of uniform action for full increase to occur without exodus that the provisions of laws requiring shifting are of importance. Obviously such laws do not make absorption of the tax impossible, inasmuch as merchants can reduce prices by the amount of the tax. But a powerful psychological force is added to the elements facilitating shifting. No longer does the force of inertia -- of letting existing conditions remain -- which is of great importance in short run incidence, and of some importance in the long run period, favor absorption, but instead serve to aid shifting. Further, such laws may lessen consumer resistance to the tax, giving less advantage than expected to those who cut prices. This is not necessarily the case; with separate charging, the consumer is made aware of the tax much more so than he would be otherwise.[42] But nevertheless, if he is aware of the law, he realizes that the retailer is expected by law to pass on the tax, and may make less effort to find a seller who will absorb the tax. When pure competition prevails, such laws are entirely futile, since no firm can raise its prices at all until exodus; with pure monopoly, and optimum pricing, they would not accomplish their purpose since the monopolist would reduce his net price. But under monopolistic competition, where not only the amount of short run increase, but also the extent of exodus of firms, and the long run incidence, depend on the strengthening of oligopoly elements, any factor which promotes common action will aid short run price increase, lessen the need for exodus, and cause greater long run price increase than would otherwise be the case.[43]

Differences in Elasticity of Demand: There are other factors which modify the relative desirability of price increases in particular lines. The very nature of certain articles makes the total demand for them more elastic than that for others. Thus when the firms realize that any price change, within the ranges important under the present considerations, will be followed by similar changes by other firms, and that accordingly the demand curve for the firm is of the same elasticity as that for the industry as a whole, the elasticity of demand for the product as a whole will be considered in changing prices as a consequence of the tax. It is not entirely clear as to whether greater elasticity will bring greater or less price increase. Because of the usual decreasing nature of the cost curves, it would appear that typically the more elastic the demand the greater would be the increase. With the elastic demand, the initial increase in price would produce a greater fall in output, so that the secondary increase would have to be greater to compensate for the greater volume loss.[44] With relatively slight differences in elasticity, this is likely to be true, if cost and revenue are carefully calculated. But the rule that with decreasing cost conditions price rise will be greater the more elastic the demand is valid only so long as the elasticity is not so great that the average revenue curve is steeper than the average cost curve.[45] When the latter curve is steeper than the average revenue curve above the old price, no price change at all is profitable; it is simply impossible to restore the original rate of contribution to overhead. In this case, the firm has the choice of dropping the line or accepting a smaller contribution to overhead; the latter involves a lowering of the cost curve of the product through shifting more of the overhead to other goods. Otherwise, as firms drop the line, the price will rise, and the demand curves of the firms still carrying it will shift to the right until losses are again avoided.

Secondly, where the curve is of relatively great elasticity, but the steepness is less than that of the average cost curve, it seems likely that in many cases firms will not realize the need for such a relatively great increase. The firms will be afraid to attempt an increase when it is obvious that a serious sales fall will occur, especially because the greater the price increase considered, the less certain will firms be that competitors will act in similar manner. Thus, while, in general, greater increases can be expected where demand is elastic than where it is inelastic because of the decreasing cost conditions, in many cases, the reverse is the case. This is true necessarily in those in which the demand increases in elasticity above the old price so greatly that the curve is of less slope than the average cost curve, and likewise in others where firms fear to take the chance of raising when a heavy sales loss is expected.

Secondary Readjustments:

Exodus of Firms: The picture of final incidence is not completed with the description of the price increases made by the firms as a result of the tax. In the first place, the attempts of firms to raise prices will not in all cases end the need for exodus. When strict marginal revenue-marginal cost pricing is followed on all lines, before and after the tax, with free entry and thus no excess profits, exodus cannot be avoided, as has been explained. The departure of firms will cause a price increase by exactly the amount of the tax, apart from possible changes in production cost caused by the reduction in number of firms. The entire tax will pass to the consumer as a result of exodus; the excess over this which is passed on with average cost pricing and lack of exodus will in this case not pass to the consumers; firms will operate at the same level of production as before the tax,[46] and thus at a level nearer the optimum than is the case with average cost pricing. As firms leave the field, the price reaction will be different for the various products carried, according to the degree of demand elasticity in the various lines. Thus, the final increase will be less in the case of the commodities of elastic demand, and more in the case of those of inelastic demand, than would occur if each type were carried by single line establishments. That is, the rise in contribution to common cost by the goods of inelastic demand will lessen the need for exodus which would be required if firms carried only those of elastic demand, since the latter need contribute a smaller amount to common cost than previously. The only force which could serve to prevent this would be a rise in the number of firms specializing in the production of goods of low elasticity, which would prevent an increased contribution to overhead of the original firm, and require a greater exodus of multiple line stores. This may be checked by the multiple stores if they cut margins on these products and gain additional income through greater volume.

There is one other situation in which exodus cannot be avoided, namely, when a sufficient degree of oligopoly prevailed before the tax that full monopoly price was realized. Under such circumstances, without excess profits, no possible price changes can enable firms to avoid losses, since the maximum monopoly price was being realized anyway. If oligopoly elements do not weaken in the process, exodus will continue until price has risen by the full tax. The continuing losses may, however, weaken these elements; price cutting is likely to start as firms strive desperately to avoid losses; the final result will be still greater exodus, and failure of price to rise by the full amount of the tax. Even a price decline is possible. There are likewise other situations in which exodus may occur and check the need for as great price increase as otherwise, by bringing production nearer to the optimum level. One is the case previously mentioned, in which average cost pricing fails to function properly, when some firms do not increase any prices, and eventually failures occur. Another is the case in which excess profits exist before the tax but the latter is of such great magnitude as to take all the excess and such an amount in addition that no price change possible will allow avoidance of loss.

Shifts in Cost: The problem of cost variation produced by the price increase and subsequent decline in sales must receive further attention. As previously indicated, the exact nature of cost conditions in retailing is not clear.[47] In the short run, except in rare cases with excess profits, average cost for levels of output below the original equilibrium is necessarily of decreasing nature as plant and personnel cannot be reduced substantially as volume decreases. Marginal cost may also be of decreasing nature, although not necessarily so at levels of output immediately below the old equilibrium output. In longer periods, with absence of excess profits, firms must also be operating in decreasing cost conditions, though of less severity than in the short run. Likewise, those firms enjoying excess profits may be operating under similar conditions. For the industry as a whole, it would seem that cost per unit will not change greatly as firms enter or leave. One factor of importance in some cases is the tendency for rent to increase as the number of firms increases; accordingly, when exodus occurs as a result of the tax, the reduced competition for suitable store locations will reduce cost of the remaining firms and check the price increase.[48] Apart from this factor, it would appear that neither external economies or diseconomies are likely to be of great significance. The decreasing cost nature of the firms would be of little significance for incidence under strict marginal cost-marginal revenue pricing;[49] as previously indicated, with average cost pricing, however, price rises greater than the amount of the tax are almost inevitable, especially where excess profits are absent. With the smaller volume of business, cost per unit is higher; accordingly, a price increase by the amount of the tax will not allow avoidance of loss, and a somewhat greater rise is necessary.

Likewise, the nature of the cost conditions in wholesaling and manufacturing will affect final price rise, as has been indicated in the analysis of a retail levy on a single line of goods. The reduction in purchases by the retailer as he experiences loss in volume will affect the volume of business in the case of all previous links in the marketing system handling the good, and in the case of firms in physical production. The cost conditions and the nature of competition are, of course, the significant factors in determining the price changes made by these firms as a result of reduced volume. In general, in the short run, in pure competition a fall in prices is inevitable, because of the inelastic supply; with monopoly elements there is likely to be an initial price rise. With the latter situation, in the long run, the price change depends on the cost conditions of the individual firm as well as those of the industry, as well as pricing practices followed and change in elements of oligopoly; under pure competition, the cost conditions of the industries are alone of concern, apart from demand elasticity.

One result of this variation in cost of physical production is the change in cost of goods purchased by the retailers. This will in turn lead to readjustments in retail prices. With pure competition in retailing, the entire price change would immediately reflect itself exactly in retail prices. Actually, however, with monopolistic competition, with the tendency to use a constant percentage of markup, an increase will at least temporarily be magnified and a decrease diminished in strength, as the markup figure is applied to rising or falling purchase price. This pyramiding is likely to remain permanently, since, in the case of a price increase, the additional increase will be necessary to compensate for lost volume; the reverse will be true with price declines. In the latter case, however, when other factors are requiring exodus to take place, the fall in purchase price may be a factor allowing a larger number of firms to remain in the industry. The firms may take advantage of the falling purchase price to readjust their rates of markup, whereas so long as the purchase price remained the same each would fear to increase his prices because of fear that the others would not do so. But this will not occur so long as usual markup methods are used.

Fall in Employment and Changes in the Rate of Interest: The second effect of the fall in demand at the wholesale level will be to reduce employment in wholesaling and production. This will supplement the decline in employment in retailing occurring as a result of the increase in retail margins and exodus of retail firms. According to traditional analysis, the fall in investment will bring down interest rates until the old volume of saving, except as modified by changes in returns to capital owners, will again find outlet in investment. The reduction in interest rates leads to a general decline in price of commodities, restores the old level of employment and removes the tax burden from consumers. The burden would rest on capital owners, except to the extent that decreased savings caused it to pass to consumers, or eventually to labor groups through wage declines. It is interesting to note that no discussion of retail sales tax incidence has considered this aspect at all; the usual brief analysis merely indicates that the tax will pass onto consumers, and ignores entirely the reactions on investment, unemployment and interest rates, which are inevitable under the orthodox theory of distribution on which the analyses are based.[50] Under the traditional explanation of the interest rate, a retail sales tax would not remain on the consumer at all, apart from consequences of the reduction in savings occurring at lower interest levels, but on the receivers of interest.

When the classical theory of the determination of the interest rate is questioned, the same considerations apply as indicated in the previous chapter. In general, some decline in interest is likely, but full restoration of the old volume of investment and employment is unlikely except in a rapidly developing economy. The fall in the interest rate, which depends to a considerable degree on government policy designed to lessen the volume of unemployment, will allow expansion of production, and sale of goods to retailers at lower cost; it will also allow retailers to operate on lower margins. Both factors will serve to reduce the price to consumers and offset, in part at least, the original price increase. In general, the possibilities and consequences of the interest rate reduction are the same as in the case of a general manufacturers' sales tax, and no detailed analysis is necessary at this point.

Variations in Quality of Service: A second important characteristic of retailing is the extreme importance of quality variation, of the variation in the nature and amount of service provided in transmitting a good from wholesaler or manufacturer to consumer. Goods can simply be placed on shelves or in barrels, in poorly lighted and furnished stores, in inconvenient out of the way locations, with little variety offered and no assistance in purchasing and no credit and delivery service. On the other hand, articles can be widely advertised, and sold with the aid of expensive display in elaborately furnished and well located stores offering wide variety of choice and numerous auxiliary services. Usually the quality[51] will be that of neither extreme; there is great possibility of variation if changes appear profitable.

The analysis of quality variation is difficult because of the lack of definite units in which to measure different degrees of quality. The only possible means is to indicate units of quality by dollars spent, over some basic level, on quality-service improvement. The analysis will become subject to further complications as it proceeds because of the need for consideration of two variables, quality and price, in relation to each other. At first, however, it will be assumed that the retail price cannot be varied, either because it is set by the action of someone beyond the control of the retailer, or because the latter has a definite policy of selling at certain fixed prices determined independently of the cost of the product. At a given price for the product, there exists, for each firm, a quality demand curve,[52] (QD on Chart 26), indicating the amounts that will be purchased if different dollar expenditures on quality and service are made. With dollar expenditures on quality measured on the Y axis, and units sold on the X axis, the curve slopes upward from left to right, indicating that larger quantities can be sold only if increasingly greater expenditures on quality are made. Since the most productive of the latter will be made first, the curve turns upward (increases in slope) as diminishing returns from quality expenditures set in. The marginal curve of this line indicates the additional expenditure in dollars necessary to sell additional quantities of the article.[53] There is likewise a curve for the industry as a whole; the total demand will vary according to quality offered very much less than in the case of the individual firm, as additional purchasers in the latter case can be drawn from other firms as well as from those formerly buying other goods. When an increase in demand for the product of any firm occurs, as from the departure of one firm in the field, more will be taken, at each quality, from each remaining firm; the curve shifts to the right.

The quality-supply curve indicates the amounts which the firms can afford to offer at each quality, or, in reverse, the maximum quality which can be offered at each level of output, with a given price (QS on Chart 26). The nature of the curve depends on the cost conditions of the firm. With increasing average cost, involving greater cost per unit of turning out larger amounts, additional amounts will be supplied only at lower quality, as only in this manner, at the given price, can the firm continue to cover cost. In this case, the quality-supply curve slopes downward from left to right. The marginal curve indicates, for each additional amount supplied, the addition to the total quality which the supplier is willing to provide. With increasing cost, the curve is, of course, declining, as with increasing quantities, successive additions which will be made to quality will decline because of the increasing cost per unit of supplying them. With decreasing cost, the reverse situation applies; successively better quality can be supplied as larger amounts are sold because of the declining cost of production. The marginal curve also rises. With constant cost, the average and marginal curves are horizontal and identical. Likewise, it must be recognized that as the number of firms in the industry varies, the quality supply and demand curves for the firms shift, the former according to the cost conditions in the industry. The normal situation for each firm, regardless of the conditions of the industry, involves a curve concave to the base line, with decreasing cost conditions at first, allowing the offering of better quality with increased amounts, replaced eventually by increasing cost. The marginal curve intersects at the highest point.

Each firm will expand output by raising quality to the point at which the product[54] of the amount sold and the excess of the quality which the firm could have offered at this output over the quality actually necessary to sell this amount is greatest. To increase output farther would increase the amount of additional quality per unit the firm would be willing to give to sell the greater amount sufficiently less than it would increase the amount the firm would have to give to dispose of the additional units as to offset the greater number of units on which an excess over costs is obtained. That is, additional units could be sold only if improvements in quality were made; beyond the optimum point, this additional quality would be so much greater than that which the firms would be willing to give to sell the additional amounts as to more than offset the greater number of units on which profit is being made. The optimum is thus reached at the point at which the marginals of the two curves cross, (with an output of OH on Chart 26), where additions to total quality that must be made to sell additional units is equal to the additional quality which the seller can afford to give to sell more units. Where several goods are produced, as in retailing, the difficulty of varying some types of quality -- for example, convenience of location -- on one good and not on others prevents any exact attainment of optimum quality for all goods. Variations among products will be made so far as is possible; when this does not allow attainment of an optimum position for each, an attempt will be made to strike a balance between quality requirements in different lines to gain maximum profits from the enterprise as a whole.

Where firms are free to move prices, for each price level there will be quality supply and demand curves of the nature indicated above. At successively lower prices, less quality need be given to sell a given quantity. The curves when plotted are below the old. On the other hand, the firms will be willing to give less quality at each point of output; the supply curves are also below the old. With each possible price, and location of curves, a certain total profit will be made. When the firm is free to choose both price and quality, that price will be chosen at which, with optimum quality adjustment made as described above, profit will be the greatest.

When free entry exists, the quality-demand curve for each firm will come to tangency with the quality-supply curve, either by price reduction or quality increase. Where the former cannot occur, entry of new firms will force down (that is, up, on the chart) the quality-demand curve since with a greater number of firms, a given amount of goods can be disposed of only at higher quality. This process continues until tangency of the curves is reached; at this point, there is no further excess gain to attract in additional firms. When price reduction can accompany inflow of firms, both quality supply and demand curves tend to fall (on the chart) as a result of the lower price; the decline in the demand curve will be checked by the increase in number of firms, and will eventually come to tangency with the quality-supply curve. If quality is unalterable, the curves are similar, but the actual quality is fixed independently of the action of the firms; the amount sold is determined by the intersection of a horizontal line at the level of the fixed quality and the quality demand curve. With free entry, price will continue to fall until the quality-supply and demand curves cross at the point at which the quality line cuts the demand curve. Thus, in general, when price is set, as by resale price maintenance, entry of new firms will exhaust excess profits by quality increase just as would be done otherwise by price decline. Where both can be changed, there may be some degree of each, although quality reduction may in some cases be profitable as new firms enter.

Now attention will be given to the problem of the significance of quality variation for tax incidence. First of all, the situation in which price is independently set will be considered. The immediate effect of the tax will be to lower the supply curve; that is, the firm will be willing to supply each quantity only at lower quality. Thus, at the old equilibrium quantity, the firm is no longer willing to supply the same quality as formerly, and therefore not enough to enable that amount to be sold. (See curve QS' on Chart 26). There are two possible reactions. In theory, with output determined on a strict marginal basis, despite temporary attempts to reduce quality, exodus of firms will take place until, for those remaining, the quality-demand will have risen (fallen on Chart 26 to QD') to tangency with the reduced quality-supply curve. Equilibrium for each firm will be reached, with constant cost for the industry, at almost the same output as before, but at reduced quality. The total amount sold by the industry will be less; thus, absence of constant cost in the industry will produce modifications in the location of the cost curve and thus of the quality-supply curve, and will modify the final quality change. In general, the entire tax is passed onto consumers by quality reduction -- with reduced convenience of location, variety of goods,[55] store furnishings, credit and delivery -- but with accompanying exodus of firms.

The actual reaction may in many cases differ considerably from that described above. As long as each firm ignores the possibility of quality change by competitors, no one can consider reduction of quality without fearing heavy losses in volume of business. If, however, each realizes that the competitors will cut quality also, provided that the firm in question does, a general quality reduction may take place very quickly, and in sufficient amount to cover the entire added expense of the tax plus the higher cost of operation per unit.[56] The position is not entirely stable, since any firm can gain by increasing quality provided that the others do not. But the close relations between dealers may serve to check this sort of activity. This process of quality reduction is comparable in effect to that of average cost pricing on price increase where the latter is possible. The quality reduction will be greater than in the case in which exodus occurs, since firms will be operating farther from the optimum. There appears to be less likelihood of this reaction than in the case of price change, because of the lack of the same sort of definite relation between tax and selling expenditure that exists between tax and price change. With average cost pricing, a 2% tax will suggest to all the firms the need for roughly a 2% price increase. But there is less assurance that such a tax will lead to a quality reduction of an amount such that the reduction in cost of production is equal to the amount of the tax. Accordingly, each firm will not feel as certain that the others will decrease service expenditures as would be the case in regard to price changes and will be less likely to act itself.

Where excess profits are maintained by limited entry, and at the point of operation the quality-supply curve is above the quality-demand curve, in theory at least, with marginal analysis, less quality reduction will occur than if there is no excess. Quality readjustment will be determined on the basis of the relation of marginal rather than average curves. But in this case, as well as in the preceding, if the firms expect the others to act in similar manner, each may act just as in the case in which there are no excess profits, decreasing quality to such an extent as to pass on all of the burden in this fashion.[57] There is also, however, a further possibility which cannot occur with absence of excess profits. There may be little or no quality reduction at all, if each feels that his quality-demand curve becomes extremely elastic below the old, so that any reduction would greatly reduce the volume of sales.

Under ordinary situations, of course, both quality and price can be varied. Without excess profits, and with exodus of firms, the latter leads, of course, to higher prices. But will the stores provide more or less service at these higher levels? The firms will be willing to supply higher quality goods than they would have if prices had not risen after the tax. If the price moves up so as to remove all tax burden from the firm, as it will in time, the firms will be willing to supply as high quality as before at each quantity level. But the movement of the demand curve cannot be judged so easily. There are two offsetting forces operating as the price moves up: the higher price results in a smaller quantity demanded at each quality, but the reduction in number of firms causes a shift in the demand curve to the right. If these two forces are mutually offsetting, the final adjustment, if full price increase occurred before quality change, would involve no alteration in quality at all. If either is stronger, the final quality will be greater or less than before the tax. Any change in quality will produce a further change in price, until a new equilibrium is reached. However, quality may be readjusted simultaneously. If quality is cut, as is likely to be the case, the price increase need not be as great as otherwise. Obviously, whether quality and price are readjusted simultaneously, or first one and then the other, the final equilibrium position will, under completely free working of the marginal price determining factors, be the same. But, actually, where friction is important, the order of change may be of considerable significance for incidence over long periods of time. While it is difficult to generalize as to the result, it would appear that, typically, an initial quality reduction, by lessening the need for exodus, will check the price increase. Part of the tax will be shifted to the consumer through price rise, part through quality reduction. This situation may remain over a long period, even though an optimum adjustment might require even higher quality than the old and still greater price rise, simply because the firms are not aware of their true optima. In some cases, if the initial action of all firms is to increase quality and service in a desperate attempt to get business, the exodus and price rise may be greater than if no quality change could be made. If some firms raise quality while others lower, it is impossible to say just what the results would be; neither group would realize the sales expected, and a restoration of quality toward the original level may occur.

When the price increase occurs without exodus, the quality supply curve must move up; the firms will be willing to supply more quality at each quantity level than previously because price will have risen by more than the tax, to compensate for loss in volume. But, without exodus of firms, the demand will be less as a result of the higher price; the quality-demand curve accordingly rises. Thus, inevitably, the optimum quality is greater than before the tax; the quantity sold is, of course, reduced, but is provided at higher quality. It is, however, questionable as to whether this is significant in practice or not; the excess of price rise over tax will probably not be great, and it is difficult at any time to calculate exactly the optimum quality. It is interesting to note that if the price increase is limited to the amount of the tax, by law or otherwise, the quality that producers can continue to supply at the temporary optimum is less than that necessary to sell the product. Losses can be avoided only by exodus or by a quality reduction by all firms sufficiently great as to decrease the quality demanded at each amount to such levels that an equilibrium can be reached between quality supply and demand.

When excess profits exist, price increase will occur. The amount of the increase will be less than the tax under marginal cost pricing, and equal to, or greater than the amount of the tax if average cost pricing is followed. Under the former, the quality-supply curve will be lower than before the levying of the tax. If the quality-demand curve remained unchanged, the marginal curves would intersect farther to the left,[58] and a lower quality would be given. However, the price change will cause the quality demand curve to fall (move to the left on Chart 26), inasmuch as the price rise is not, in this case, compensated for by a reduction in number of firms. It is impossible to state whether or not this reduction in demand will reduce or increase optimum quality over what it would have been if demand had been unchanged. The shift will move the intersection of the marginal curves farther to the left, and cause a greater output reduction than otherwise, but a given output can be sold only at a higher quality than before. Thus, the effect on quality variation depends upon the particular circumstances of the case. When average cost pricing brings an initial increase greater than the tax, to the point that profit per unit is the same as before, the quality-supply curve is greater than before the tax; the quality-demand curve is lower. Because of the former factor, the marginal curves will intersect farther to the right than if the price increase had been less, and the equilibrium quality is thus higher. But the quality-demand will likewise be less than before (the curve will be higher on Chart 26); again the effect of this demand reaction depends on the relative elasticity of the curves. Thus, it is questionable whether the fact that firms can readjust quality as well as price will usually lead to increase or decrease in the former when a tax is imposed. If price cannot be changed, the result is obviously quality reduction; where both can shift, the nature of the quality change depends upon the manner in which a fall in the quality-demand curve affects optimum quality, which in turn depends on the elasticity of the quality-demand curve and the nature of the marginal quality-supply curve. When quality-demand falls, a reduced quantity will be placed on the market; this in itself would allow sale of the output at poorer quality. But, when the quality demand curve falls, in order to sell any given quantity, more quality must be given, because price is higher. Whether the actual quality at the new equilibrium level is better or poorer than before depends upon which of these offsetting forces is greater in strength. Producers place less on the market; this would allow poorer quality. But the quality-demand curve has fallen, and thus given amounts can be sold only with more quality. The net result depends in each case on which force is greater.

In general, out of this discussion of quality variation comes the conclusion that if price increases are restricted by resale price maintenance or other legal means or simply by the strength of customary price, a reduction of expenditure on quality and service will occur. Where no excess profits exist, the decline in the number of firms, under strict marginal pricing, will inevitably increase the demand for those remaining, so that each can reduce quality and stay in business. Or, if all act together immediately in reducing quality, a phenomenon somewhat less likely to occur than a simultaneous price increase where the latter is possible, all may be able to shift the tax, and the further loss in profits from reduced volume, without any exodus. It is impossible to say whether or not a certain quality reduction is less injurious to consumers than the price increase which would otherwise result from the tax. Because often the consumer has no choice of buying the good with varying degrees of quality, the latter may be providing relatively little utility, and the quality reduction may be the less undesirable of the two possibilities.

Where both price and quality can be varied, the possibility of the latter introduces new factors in the determination of the final equilibrium. An initial quality reduction will lessen the need for price increase, and will likely remain over a period of time; an initial quality increase designed to obtain new business may likewise be more or less permanent, in a situation exactly similar otherwise to the previous. This will lead to greater price rise than would otherwise occur. Actually, under strictly optimum price-quality determination, there will be only one new optimum, which may involve greater or less quality provision than before the tax; the actual direction of quality change depends on the particular nature of the quality-supply and demand curves in the situation.[59]

The fact that different stores selling the same product provide different amounts of quality introduces no significant modifications not previously mentioned. As indicated earlier, the low quality stores, hoping to gain by greater volume, are least likely to raise prices. The high-quality stores may not suffer greatly from the failure of the low-price stores to raise; the ones chiefly affected are those supplying only slightly better quality than the price-cutting group. This middle group will suffer serious losses in sales; unless extensive quality reduction is made, exodus of firms will occur. The price-cutting group will gain much of the output lost by the middle group. If all the higher groups lower quality instead of raising prices, the lowest-quality group may be in a serious position, if demand increase from quality reduction by the other firms is not sufficient to eliminate losses. This group is unable to reduce quality because only a minimum is being supplied, and exodus is necessary. There is one important difference in the effects of price change and quality reduction in shifting demand as between firms. Where the former occurs, the low-price stores will almost certainly experience demand increases, even if they increase their own prices, since those buyers who have become accustomed to a certain physical standard as to goods purchased will seek the same amount of the articles with less service attached. There is no similar phenomenon in the case of quality reduction, as the buyers will simply remain with their old firms. Thus, the low-quality firms will experience less demand increase in the latter case, and will have greater difficulty to avoid loss. Thus, in general, the very high quality group will be most likely to pass on the tax and the higher production cost from reduced volume by price increases. The middle group, subject to more severe competition by the cut-price firms, will have more difficulty in escaping if the latter are important; if quality reduction, which is likely if the low service firms do not increase their prices, proves ineffective, exodus or permanent loss of excess profits is inevitable. The low-service firms are the ones least likely to raise prices, although normally they can be expected to do so because of markup practices followed. These different reactions of the various groups are made possible by the difference in quality and service provided by them, and accordingly the sale to relatively distinct groups of purchasers.

To the extent that quality reduction occurs as a result of a sales tax in place of price increase, those thrown out of work initially will be ones engaged in the production of retail service: advertising men, suppliers of store furnishings, retail clerks and delivery men, etc. There will, however, be no reduction in production of physical consumption goods; an equal number of goods will be passing through retail channels as before, though accompanied by less quality and service.[60] But this does not mean that total reduction in employment will be any less, unless a dollar spent on a physical commodity gives employment to more men than a dollar spent on retail service. Actually, the opposite is much more likely to be the case. Quality reduction simply brings greater increase in the amount of unemployment in retailing and the provision of retail service and less in physical production of consumption goods. When interest rates fall, much of the reëmployment will be in manufacturing; the net result of the tax will involve a shift in production from retail services to physical goods, and of employment from retailing and subsidiary industries to manufacturing. This may in part be temporary; as the retailers experience declines in purchase prices, they may expand service instead of reducing sales prices and thus prevent as great an increase in the sale of manufactured goods as would otherwise take place. This increase in service may be just as effective as a price decrease in expanding sales in one line, but cannot affect total sales in the economy as a whole as long as the propensity to consume remains constant.

The analysis in the preceding paragraph is based upon the assumption that changes in price and in quality will affect propensity to consume in the same way. Actually there is likely to be some difference. In the case of the initial price rise, propensity to consume is almost certain to rise, since many individuals simply save what is left over after they purchase the goods to which they are accustomed. This will check the decline in employment, and modify price change. However, when interest falls and output expands with reduced prices, the propensity to consume is likely to fall again. When quality is reduced, there will be a decrease in propensity to consume, inasmuch as individuals will be getting less quality for their money, and will be less inclined to buy.[61] The price decrease following reduced interest rates will simply increase this tendency, requiring among other things further interest and price declines. Only if service increases as retail purchase prices fall will the decline in propensity to consume be eliminated.

Shifts in Demand: One final modification of the initial price increase is produced by the fact that the demand curves for many goods will shift as prices rise. This will be of considerable magnitude with a relatively high tax, and will bring changes in retail prices according to cost conditions in retailing in the lines taxed, and according to changes in the prices charged by manufacturers and wholesalers as a result of the changes in volume. In general, the same considerations apply as in the case of a general producers' sales levy. Demand shifting will occur as between general groups of stores, from high-quality to low-quality stores, from those carrying luxuries to those carrying necessities, and as between lines in individual stores, especially in the case of firms carrying lower quality goods. These changes in demand bring further readjustments of burden as between lines, and increase still more the tendency for the burden imposed on the sale of certain commodities to shift in part at least to the consumer of other goods. When demand shifts as between lines in individual stores, there is likely to be less readjustment of price than might be expected; instead of reducing price on the article gaining demand and raising on the one losing, assuming both to be provided at decreasing cost, the retailer simply allows the former to carry a greater part of the overhead than before.

The Exemption of Certain Lines from the Tax:

Many retail sales taxes provide for exemption of certain articles considered to be absolute necessities, such as food.[62] In these cases, certain lines, for example, grocery stores, are thus exempted from the tax almost entirely, while most other lines will be entirely unaffected. The taxed lines will react as previously indicated; the untaxed groups will be unaffected at first except as demand shifts between lines as some prices rise and others do not. A reduction in the number of stores in the taxed lines may reduce costs and price in the untaxed lines by reducing the prices of more or less specialized factors.[63] If interest rates fall, expansion will take place in the production and service of the untaxed lines as well as of the taxed. Permanent price reductions will occur in the former lines; the absorption of some of the unemployed in these lines will prevent restoration of prices in the taxed lines to their old levels.

In many cases, however, stores will be subject to tax on only a part of the lines carried. In general, prices on the taxed lines will be increased, along lines previously indicated. The prices of the untaxed lines may also be affected; consumers of these goods may be forced to bear part of the burden on the taxed lines, if the stores act together in spreading the burden onto other goods. If exodus of firms occurs, and specialty stores cannot operate profitably in selling the line in question, an increase in margin on the untaxed lines is almost inevitable. Where exodus does not occur, and the taxed lines have more elastic demand curves above the old price than the untaxed lines, there will be a tendency to shift the tax burden to the latter. The consideration of the tax as an element of cost for which the good on which it is levied is directly responsible serves, of course, to check, but not prevent this. Likewise, where the untaxed lines are also carried by specialty stores which are entirely tax exempt, any attempt by multiple line stores to shift part of the burden to these lines will be checked by the substantial reduction in sales.[64]

CONCLUSION:

The chief feature of incidence of general retail sales taxes can be summarized briefly. The initial reaction of retail firms, operating inevitably in conditions of monopolistic competition, although with widely varying strength of the monopoly elements, will be to raise prices at least by the full amount of the tax, either by adding the tax to the regular price as a separate charge, or by readjusting markup to include this additional cost item. In addition, since retail firms operate normally in decreasing cost conditions, a further increase, to compensate for the higher cost per unit of the reduced volume of business, will ordinarily occur, especially where firms earn no excess profits and thus can escape loss only by such an increase. The short run increase will be greater than that in the long run, since plant can be adjusted in the latter, but not in the former; with average cost pricing followed in retailing, fixed costs are included in cost for price-making purposes. This immediate and full increase is possible only because of the importance of oligopoly in retailing. Because of the nearly universal markup practices, each firm ordinarily realizes that other firms will treat this tax as an addition to cost and raise prices fully, provided the firm in question does also; as each acts in this manner, the price rise brings a relatively slight reduction in sales. If strict marginal pricing practices were followed, and each firm ignored the action of his competitors, the price rise would be small. With excess profits there would be no further change; without excess exodus would occur. In this case, price would rise sufficiently to shift the full tax to the consumer; there would be no further increase necessitated by the decreasing cost nature of the individual firms. Laws requiring separate charging are of considerable significance because they serve to strengthen the forces leading to uniform action which is essential to immediate full increase.

However, the initial tendency to add the entire tax to the retail prices is subject to modifications. The differences in conditions of cost and competition under which various commodities handled are manufactured will cause different types of change in retail purchase prices as volume falls, and cause readjustments in the prices which retailers charge. Retailing costs will not be the same in all fields, and will differ even for lines in the same store, especially because some lines customarily contribute nothing to overhead. Further, demand elasticity will vary widely as between lines. In some cases the demand will appear so elastic that average revenue will rise more slowly (at reduced levels of output) than average cost. The line may be dropped; however, ordinarily a reduced contribution to overhead will be accepted, and further increase made in other lines. This can be done profitably if all firms act in similar fashion. Among the conditions which will produce such great elasticity are the existence of customary prices and class lines, which can be varied only with great loss in volume, an exceedingly great elasticity of demand for the entire product on the part of the consumers, as when close substitutes are untaxed, and a high degree of price competition. There is no certainty that all firms will raise; there is always likelihood that some firms will attempt to avoid losses by gaining greater volume at the old price level; if this occurs in a few lines, the multiple line stores will try to pass the tax on these lines off onto other goods. When, however, this occurs in many lines, price increases will be accompanied by severe losses in volume of sales. Accordingly, exodus of firms must occur before the tax is shifted to consumers, unless excess profits are sufficiently great. In one case exodus is inevitable; namely, when the original price was the optimum monopoly price because of great strength of oligopoly elements.

Where retail prices are set by manufacturers, or by law, there is even more certainty that the entire tax plus, ordinarily, some additional amount for higher cost of operation per unit, will be shifted immediately. Legal regulation of prices provides ordinarily that prices must be sufficiently high to cover cost. They will be adjusted accordingly to include the tax and higher operating costs. The manufacturer usually will be forced to readjust margins allowed; if the bargaining power of the retailers is weak, only the tax, or even less, will be added.

Wherever the retail price is beyond the control of the retailer and the latter is not able to force change, the tax will often be shifted by quality reduction. Delivery and credit will be eliminated; variety of goods reduced, etc. Again, this is profitable only if all firms act in unison, or those lowering quality will lose volume so heavily as to suffer loss. The uniform action is, however, likely to occur, and if sufficiently great may prevent any exodus. Where both price and quality can be varied, some change in the latter is almost certain, but the nature of the change depends on the peculiar circumstances of each case.

All that has been said above applies equally well to special or general retail sales taxes. It must be emphasized that in the case of the former, just as in the case of the component parts of the latter, part or all of the burden may pass onto consumers of other commodities than the one taxed. This will be the case if price increases will cause less loss in sales in the untaxed lines and if all firms act more or less in unison, or if exodus of firms occurs. Ordinarily, however, the tax will rest on the consumers of the commodity on which it is imposed. The source of the essential differences between incidence of special and general levies is the secondary reaction which occurs when the tax is of general nature. The reduction in sales caused by the increased prices will lessen the total volume of output and employment, except as checked by the rise in the propensity to consume as people use part of the income formerly saved to meet the higher prices. This decreased investment, employment, and income is likely to cause some fall in interest rates. In terms of the orthodox theory of distribution, the fall in interest will continue until all workers have been reëmployed and the old level of output restored. The entire burden of the tax, apart from modifications introduced by changes in the volume of savings, would be shifted to capital owners. Even when the orthodox theory is questioned, it will be realized that some interest rate fall is likely, and, with proper governmental action, may be of considerable amount.[65] Accordingly, production will expand, and the volume of retail business will increase. Not only can retail firms operate on lower margins, but the volume of physical production becomes greater. Prices at retail will fall because of the reduced production and distribution cost, and the burden will in part pass from consumers to interest-receivers.[66]

Thus, in general, while the initial reaction of retailers will be to add the entire, or in most cases, more than the entire tax to prices charged, there will be considerable variation as between price changes on different commodities. Furthermore interest rate declines coming about to restore, in part at least, the old volume of investment and employment, may serve to restore prices toward the old levels and pass a part of the burden onto interest receivers.

APPENDIX I TO CHAPTER VII

EMPIRICAL STUDIES OF RETAIL SALES TAX INCIDENCE

In recent years several empirical studies of retail sales tax incidence have been made, and the conclusions are of some interest, although the inadequacy of the technique must be emphasized. As to the latter, in the first place the studies were made very shortly after the taxes were imposed; of greater importance is the fact that the method of determining whether shifting occurred was to inquire of various retailers as to whether or not they thought they shifted the levy. Obviously, in many cases, retailers are not entirely aware of the extent to which they are shifting a tax, and any attempt to determine incidence in this manner ignores entirely secondary effects of the tax. The University of Mississippi School of Commerce study of that state's 2% sales tax law in 1933 showed that of the retailers questioned, 55% felt that they shifted the tax in full, and 22% in part.[1] Most of those failing to shift said that absorption was necessary because of competition. A more complete study was that of Haig and Shoup in 1934, of experience under the New York, Illinois, and Michigan laws.[2] In New York, with a 1% levy, less than one-fourth of the retailers subject to the levy felt that they were shifting any of the tax.[3] However, in cases of firms most of whose lines were subject to the tax, the percentage reporting shifting was very much higher.[4] The chief reasons given for not shifting the tax were "consumer resentment" and "pressure of competition."[5] The sample was fairly large, including about 20% of the firms in the lines of business covered. Certain less populous areas of the state were excluded from the survey. In the case of Illinois, the tax rate was 2% (1933); the survey was confined to Chicago, and Moline-Rock Island, with a sample of 20% in those areas. In Chicago, somewhat less than one-half reported shifting all or part of the tax, in contrast to three-quarters under the previous (up to 1933) 3% levy; in Moline-Rock Island, only one-fifth reported shifting.[6] Small stores in particular found difficulty in passing on the burden. In Detroit and Monroe, Michigan, the sample was similar to those in the other states. The tax rate was 3%. More than nine-tenths of the retailers reported shifting the tax; nearly all of these reported shifting all of the levy.[7] None of these laws made shifting mandatory; in practice, most of the retailers added the tax item as a separate charge.[8] In all three cases, the large stores found less difficulty in shifting than did the smaller stores. All of the studies were made during the year following the imposition of the levy. On the whole, in the case of the high (3%) rate, part of the conclusions reached in this study are borne out by the results of the empirical analysis. Apparently a tax of a lower rate does not appear to retailers, at least at first, as a sufficiently heavy burden as to warrant price readjustment. Over a period of time, the results might be very different.

The final study is that of the New York City sales tax made by Carl Shoup in 1935.[9] The New York tax rate was 2%, with separate charge provisions. The sample ranged from 10 to 20% of all stores in the various lines. Only 4% made no separate charge to customers on all or most all sales; one-half of these tried to comply with the law and stopped.[10] But only 57% stated that they charged separately on every sale.[11] There was a noticeable tendency for stores failing to shift with the 1933 law to shift with the 1935 law which included a separate charge provision. It must be noted, of course, that the fact that the tax item was added separately does not show that absorption did not occur, as it shows nothing about possible price reductions at the same time as the tax is added. Shoup concludes:

> In general, it seems clear that the doubling of the tax rate, the elimination of exemptions for small charges, and the official requirement concerning separate charging made a marked change in the superficial aspects of the sales tax in New York City, and probably had an appreciable effect, as well, upon short-term economic consequences, notably the degree of shifting.[12]

APPENDIX II TO CHAPTER VII

CHAIN STORE TAXES

One special type of tax on retail stores has attained such great importance in recent years as to warrant special attention. This is the levy imposed upon chain stores, in 1940 by 19 states, in general consisting of license fees graduated according to the number of stores operated.[1] The problem of incidence has been the subject of considerable dispute but of little detailed consideration.[2] Complete analysis would require more space than is warranted in this study, and only brief discussion will be given.

INITIAL PRICE INCREASE:

When such a tax is imposed, the costs of the chain stores are increased. If the stores price on the policy of obtaining a definite rate of return, they will attempt to increase the rate of markup and retail prices sufficiently to pass on the tax and, in many cases, the higher cost of operation from reduced volume.[3]

If the field in question is dominated by the chains (all of whom are subject to the tax) because of the inherent advantages of chain organization in the field, a relatively large tax may be passed off in this manner, provided all the chains act in uniform manner. Of course, such action, if taken prior to the introduction of the tax, would have increased the profits of all the firms, but with the given strength of oligopoly, that is, the amount of attention each firm gives to the effect of its own action on the policies of its competitors, any increase was impossible. No one firm could act alone in raising, and unity of action among the firms was not sufficiently strong to allow increases. But the imposition of the tax raised the costs of all the firms; each firm realized that the other firms were similarly burdened and that, because of markup practices common in the field, would raise prices by at least the amount of the tax provided the firm in question raised also. Since each reacts in the same way, the prices charged by all rise, and the burden goes on to the consumer. If pure competition existed in the field, no firm could raise without great loss in volume, and the prices would remain at the old levels until some of the firms had gone out of business. If complete monopoly had existed, increase by the full amount of the levy would not have been profitable since price was already at a level offering maximum profits. But with conditions of monopolistic competition and oligopoly, the effect of the cost increase is to cause each firm to act in such a way as to bring the price nearer to the full monopoly level because each firm considers the cost increase as an amount by which to increase markup in full. Only because the conditions in retailing are typically those of monopolistic competition and oligopoly is complete and immediate shifting possible without the failure of any of the firms.

THE EFFECT OF COMPETITION OF THE INDEPENDENTS:

However, in many lines the chains do not occupy such a dominant position, and are pressed by severe competition of independents and voluntary chains, although the prices of the latter groups are almost universally higher than chain prices.[4] Under such circumstances, not only will each chain realize that the other chains will be in doubt as to whether or not to raise, but it will also realize that even if they do, the constant prices of the independent firms, though still above the chain prices, make the demand curve very elastic, and render any price increase at all of doubtful gain. In other words, the average revenue curve will appear to be so elastic above the old price as to be of less slope than average cost, the marginal revenue curve being vertical within the range of the old and new cost curves; accordingly any price increase at all will merely increase losses. If the stores are operating without excess profit, some attempt to increase prices is almost inevitable. If successive increases fail to eliminate losses, eventual exodus of some firms must occur. If the differential advantage of chains over independents is solely one of price, and of such nature that a small reduction in the difference in prices will cause loss of virtually all chain business, this method of operation will be eliminated completely. The business of the chains will be taken by independents, as any increase in chain margins from exodus will lead to an inflow of independents, which will prevent sufficient rise in margin to allow restoration of chain profits. If, on the other hand, chains possess other advantages, such as greater variety of goods offered, superior display methods, etc., for which there is a definite demand, chain margins will rise as exodus occurs, despite the inflow of independents, since the latter cannot in this case compete completely with the chains. The result will be of this nature, likewise, if the tax is not too great relative to the chain price differential, and if relatively large groups of buyers prefer any price differential at all to the higher quality offered by the independent.[5] In the first case, the consumer will be injured despite the fact that the government obtains no revenue; this will be true in part in the second also, to the extent that chains are replaced by independents not subject to the tax. Where both chain and independent possessed certain advantages prior to the tax, each type of organization was extended until the advantages, including price differences, balanced. The tax interferes with the operation of the chain by lessening its ability to sell more cheaply, reduces its advantages in relation to those of the independent, and forces a readjustment of the relative spheres in favor of the independent. If the tax is sufficiently great, it will destroy the chain system entirely.

In general, the greater the extent to which the size of the price differential between chain and independent is due to competition of chains among themselves, and is not necessary to maintain total chain volume, the more able will the chains be to pass on the burden to consumers. It must be noted that the relation of the tax to the size of the differential of chain prices under independent prices shows almost nothing about the ability of the chains to withstand the tax. The difference persists only because of differentiation and quality difference; any reduction might transfer all business to the independents.[6]

THE SIGNIFICANCE OF CHAIN STORE EXCESS PROFITS:

On the other hand, where the chains earn excess profit, they are much more capable of resisting the effect of the tax than otherwise. Here, likewise, where independents are weak, some price increase, perhaps by the full amount of the tax, or more, is likely, but not inevitable.[7] The extent of the increase, if any, depends upon the estimate by the chains of the elasticity of demand in relation to cost conditions. If the demand is so elastic because of the presence of untaxed independents that the average revenue curve rises more slowly than the average cost curve, or if demand increases in elasticity so greatly above the old price that there is a vertical section in the marginal revenue curve, there will be no increase at all. This will, of course, be the case when the independents are strong, and the chains lack definite quality advantages. The tax will then be borne by the chains with no injury whatsoever to the consumer. If the tax takes part of normal profits as well as of excess, some exodus of firms is likely, though less than in the case where only normal profits are earned. The figures on retail profits presented in Beckman and Nolen indicate that in many lines extremely high profits on capital are earned by chains;[8] apparently a fairly high tax can be borne by the owners without facing liquidation, even if no price increase is made. More typically, however, where some chains in a field are earning excess profits, others are not. If the independents are weak, shifting is not likely to be checked by this condition. When, however, they are strong, the high-profit chains will not raise prices, and those with normal profit will find it almost impossible to raise and avoid bankruptcy. As they go out, some consumers may be injured since they lose their preferred stores; to the extent that the service provided by the remaining chains is similar to that of those going out, there will be no substantial injury. The remaining chains will gain additional business which may to a large extent compensate them for the tax burden. The tax is thus borne in part out of monopoly profits, in part out of the lower costs of operation on the part of the remaining stores produced by increased volume.

DIFFERENCES IN NUMBER OF UNITS IN VARIOUS CHAINS:

The previous analysis is an oversimplified statement of incidence, since it is based on the assumptions that the number of stores in the chain systems and the average volume of business per store are approximately uniform for all the firms subject to the tax. Neither of those assumptions is truly representative of the actual situations except possibly in rare instances. In the first place, the number of units in the systems varies widely; since the tax rates are graduated according to the number of units, the tax burden expressed as a percentage of sale price will be greater in some cases than in others. Where one or a group of large[9] chains of approximately equal size control most of the total sales volume, reactions from the tax are not likely to differ substantially from those described above. The chains bearing lower taxes may raise prices to the same extent as the large chains, thus increasing their profit per unit. However, they may consider it more profitable, if not afraid of retaliation by the larger chains, to raise only sufficiently to cover the tax which they bear; they may even consider it undesirable to raise at all, as they will benefit from increased volume as the larger chains raise. If they raise as much as the large chains do, the consumers bear a burden greater than the amount of the tax. There is not likely to be any permanent gain to the smaller chains, as the excess profits created will draw new firms into the field. If both groups increase by the exact amount of the tax which they bear, the consumers will bear the entire tax burden. If the smaller chains do not raise, their tax burden is absorbed in the cost reduction.[10] In the cases in which the smaller chains fail to raise, the effect on the profitability of increases by the larger chains is similar to the effect of failure by the independents to raise, as described above. If the large chains have price[11] or quality-service advantages, they can shift most or all of the burden; if not, they must bear the tax out of excess profits, or in the absence of the latter, contract the size of their systems until their tax burden is no greater than that of the other stores.

If the larger chains control only a small percentage of the total business, the majority of the latter being done by smaller chains subject to the tax, the latter, provided that the position of the independents allows, will normally raise prices sufficiently to cover the tax in the manner previously described;[12] the larger stores will have even greater difficulty, cet. par., to raise prices sufficiently to pass on the full tax burden than in the case above, and will be able to do so only if they have great price or quality-service advantages. Otherwise, as in the case above, they must bear the burden out of excess profits, or contract in size; in the latter case, the tax burden is reduced, but the customers may suffer burden beyond the amount of the taxes paid by the chains if smaller size means higher cost and higher prices, or reduced quality of service.

In other situations, however, no one group of chains will dominate; in some lines there is a wide range (as to number of units) of chains, with no one group doing any substantial portion of the business. It is difficult to generalize as to price changes under such circumstances. Each store may at first attempt to pass on the full burden of the tax which is levied on it; all will suffer losses in sales, the losses in general (except for the existence of prior price differences, or quality-service advantages) being progressively greater according to the number of units in the chain. The larger chains may be forced to eliminate a portion of the increase; they must then bear a part of the tax out of excess profits, or contract in size. Even if a high rate of return was earned prior to the tax, some levelling out in size of the chains is to be expected. Since this process will likely bring cost increases, caused, for example, by loss in strength of buying power, price will rise in many cases by an amount greater than the amount of taxes actually paid by the stores after they have contracted in size. Complete uniformity of size is not likely to be attained, because the difference in quality-service appeals used by the various firms will cause optimum size of operation to differ, both before and after the tax.

Thus in general, the diversity in the size of the chains greatly impairs the ability of the group as a whole to pass on the burden of the tax initially imposed upon them. When the large chains dominate, most or all of the burden may be shifted, although the failure of smaller chains to raise by an amount equal to the amount of the tax on the larger chains interferes with the price increases by the latter; where the large chains are of less importance or there is a wide range of sizes it will be difficult for the larger units to pass off the entire original burden. In some cases the levies will be borne out of excess profits. Most frequently, however, where the taxes are substantial in size, the larger chains will find it profitable to reduce the number of units in their systems, and reduce the tax burden. Not only will consumers lose in convenience of location, but since the reduction in size will commonly entail cost increases, prices are likely ultimately to be raised by more than the amount of the taxes finally borne by these stores.[13] In almost all cases some reduction in number of units is to be expected. The chains prior to the levy would have extended the number of units to the point at which the last stores established just covered the marginal cost of their operation. The tax will inevitably render some units unprofitable by increasing the cost of operations; this is especially true because the existence of the marginal stores increases the tax burden per store on the more profitable stores. Thus only in cases in which the larger chains possess sufficient initial price or quality-service advantages as to be able to raise price without losing any substantial amount of business can all of the initial tax burden pass to the consumers. However, after the reductions in size have occurred, the incidence of the amount of tax still paid by the stores will not differ substantially from that in the situation in which all chains are of equal size; to the extent that the larger chains have earned excess profits, more of the burden will rest on the receivers of this share than if chains were of uniform size.

DIFFERENCES IN AVERAGE VOLUME OF SALES PER STORE:

Chains differ not only as to the number of stores in the system, but also as to the average volume of business per store; the latter also causes the tax expressed as a percentage of sale price to vary. The differences are greatest between chains in different lines; for example, in 1936, the average sales in grocery and grocery-meat chains were $69,000, in variety chains $177,295.[14] Thus, with the tax applied to all chains, the burden on the consumer, and the number of chains forced out of business, will be greater in some lines, for example, grocery, than in others.[15]

Likewise, even within a certain field, the average volume of business per store differs. Some chains have followed policies of establishing a large number of small neighborhood stores,[16] while others have concentrated efforts in a smaller number of large units.[17] The significance of these variations is similar to that of differences in the number of units in the system. The small unit chains may possess price advantages which will allow them to pass on their full initial burden;[18] what is more likely, they may be able to increase prices sufficiently to cover the tax because of service advantages, in the form of greater convenience of location, even if this involves raising above the level of the large-unit chains. The nature of competition from the independents, of course, is always a factor affecting the ability of all chains to shift. In many cases, complete shifting by the small unit chains will be difficult even if the larger ones can free themselves of their burden, and revision of the small unit policy will be necessary if only normal profits were earned previously, and profitable even if the rate of return exceeded the normal one. As the chains reduce the number of units in order to increase the size of those remaining, the consumer will be deprived of certain advantages of convenience, for which there is no compensation to the government. The attempts to increase average volume of business per store may prove very difficult. The chains which followed the large unit policy before the tax may have obtained the best locations for such stores and built sufficient reputation for the type of service which they have been rendering that all or part of the old small unit stores will be forced out of business because they are unable to establish themselves on the large-unit basis. Their customers go to the remaining chains and to old or new independents. Mere reduction in the number of units, though reducing the tax burden, cannot allow the small unit stores to survive unless they are able to increase the size of the remaining units. Even in the case of those which do survive, heavy losses will be suffered in that cost of expansion of the stores retained is likely far to exceed the salvage value of the units closed. This cost will, of course, not be incurred by the chains which followed the large-unit policy from the beginning.

Thus, the existence of variations in average volume of sales per store complicates the explanation of the extent of price increases following the levying of a chain store tax; however, after the necessary readjustments as to size of stores have been made, the same considerations as to incidence apply as in the absence of these differences. The tax may be borne in part or entirely, to an extent depending on the strength of the independents, out of excess profits; if the latter do not exist, the tax must pass to the consumer, either in the form of immediate increases by the chains if competitive conditions allow, or through gradual increases made possible by exodus of some chains. Otherwise the chains and the tax base will disappear; a burden will remain on certain consumers as they are forced to buy at higher prices at independents or forego preferred types of quality and services.

PRICE INCREASES BY INDEPENDENTS:

In some cases it seems likely that independent store prices will rise as chain prices increase. The increase in the chain prices will, if the chains control a large part of the total volume of business, facilitate price increases by the independents since losses in sales to the latter will not be as great as they would have been prior to the action of the chains in raising prices.[19] However, the chains may not increase prices initially, as they will commonly not be able to do profitably if the independents' volume of business is large. Likewise, even if the chains increase, if there are a number of independents, no one will be able to take the initiative in raising, or too much business will be lost to other independents, and unity of action may be difficult. The situation is entirely different from that in which all firms experience cost increases. Finally, even if prices of independents are raised, the additional profits earned will draw new firms into the field; in some cases the loss in business by the other firms will precipitate price cutting and restore prices to the original level. In others, however, in which the use of the markup method of pricing is strongly established, the firms will avoid price cutting, or even raise price as new firms enter,[20] and the higher cost per unit will absorb the temporary excess profit, the price increase becoming permanent. An additional factor checking increase in prices is the increase in elasticity of demand for the remaining stores produced by the loss of business by the chains. The customers of the latter consist especially of those groups which buy primarily upon a price basis, and thus are more willing to turn from one store to another to gain advantage of lower prices.

If the chains leave the field entirely, some price increase by independents is possible, since the demand curves for the individual firms may become less elastic to price increases, provided all independents increase together, as the low-price group of firms is removed. The chains in general have stressed low prices and minimum of service; as they are destroyed, an intensification of quality-service competition, with subsequent cost and price increases, is likely. Of course, chains are not the only price cutters, but they have provided one of the strongest checks to the tendency to increase services. Thus, to the extent that this occurs, if all chains are driven out of business, the state receives no revenue, yet not only are the former chain consumers burdened in that they must pay higher prices than previously but also those formerly patronizing the independents may pay higher prices. There are, however, serious checks to the ability of the independents to boost prices; united action is often hard to obtain and individual action impossible; the increase in demand elasticity indicated above and the greater volume of business for each independent at the old prices lessen the profitability of price increases.[21]

It is well to note that even if chains are driven out of business, there is little gain to existing independent retailers. Some will gain excess profits temporarily, and others about to quit business will be enabled to remain. But, in general, an increase in margin will either be offset by an increased expenditure of service necessary to hold customers, or will be eliminated by an increase in the number of firms.

CONCLUSION:

Thus, in conclusion, a chain store tax will remain on the chains only in cases characterized by excess profits high in relation to the tax, and great elasticity of demand above the old price level. Such a situation is likely to be found only in lines in which independents are still dominant, but in which newly-rising chains are making high profits. This situation is, of course, unstable, since the chains are expanding; the tax, by checking this process, will interfere with price reduction and ultimately cause the shifting of the burden to consumers. With excess profits and a demand curve of not too great elasticity, some price increase will occur. In cases in which only normal profits are earned by the chains, price increase will be necessary, either directly or by exodus of firms. Immediate increase will be possible in cases in which chains have substantial initial price advantages over the independents not offset by quality advantages of the latter, or in those in which the chains themselves have strong quality-service appeals to their customers. The latter situation is less likely than the former. However, complete and immediate shifting is checked by the differences in burdens on the various chains; those chains bearing heavier burdens because of larger number of units, or smaller average volumes per store, will have difficulty in shifting the differential burden, unless they have price or quality advantages over the lower-tax chains. The higher-tax chains ordinarily will find it necessary to reduce the number of units in the system, and increase, if possible, the volume of business per store; after this readjustment has taken place, incidence of the levy will be as indicated above, but the revenue gained by the government will be less than it would first appear. In almost all cases, even when the chains can shift completely, some reduction in number of units is likely, as the marginal units will be rendered unprofitable by the levy.

In other cases, immediate shifting will be impossible, but as some chains go out, the remaining ones will be able to raise prices to pass on the burden. Where a slight price increase will cause loss of most all business, regardless of the size of the original differential, the chains will disappear. The former customers are injured since they are forced to buy at stores which they did not previously prefer. Ordinarily, without excess profits, some exodus is inevitable; the independents will gain the business of those customers to whom the old price differential barely compensated for the service disadvantages of the chains. The customers whose preference for the chains was originally somewhat stronger will be retained by the chains; they will pay higher prices. In some cases, prices in independent stores may increase, the consumers paying an additional amount for which there is no contribution to the state, which either allows retailers to remain in business who would otherwise have been forced out, or allows retailers to cover higher costs per unit caused by an inflow of firms into the field. Usually, however, price increases by independents will be checked either by the desire to gain from increased volume, the failure of the chains to raise substantially, or the inflow of the new firms into the field as profits of the old firms increase.

In general, the burden of the tax will be borne by the consumers, who commonly will suffer far greater financial injury than the equivalent of the amount of the taxes received by the state, to the benefit of independent retailers who would either have been forced out of business or not have been able to start up. The owners of the chains, of course, in some cases bear part of the tax burden out of monopoly profits; the chief injury to this group is the loss of their source of income in the field of retailing. If other investment opportunities of comparable returns exist, they suffer no permanent injury, except to the extent that they cannot withdraw all of their capital from the field without some loss. Whether the chains are able to remain or not, the principal burden of the tax is on the consumer group. The exact reactions will vary somewhat from line to line and from section to section. An exact statement of the incidence of a chain store tax in any particular line requires knowledge of the exact degree of competition in the field, the rate of profits earned by the various chains, and the price, cost, and quality differences between chains and independents, and between firms within each group.[22]

VIII

GENERAL SALES TAXATION

THE CONCEPT OF A GENERAL SALES TAX:

As the final step in the development of the theory of incidence of sales taxation, attention will be turned to a levy upon sales or gross revenue of all sellers of commodities and services, at all stages in the production and distribution process. For lack of a more universally accepted term, this type of levy will be designated as a general sales tax. It must be noted that the latter term is commonly applied also to general producers' and retail sales taxes without the qualifying adjectives;[1] in this study it is limited strictly to a levy upon all steps in the process of production and distribution. This levy must be distinguished from two other still more "general" types, the gross income tax, and the transactions tax. The former includes the receipt of personal incomes in the tax base; the latter includes also the receipts from sale of real property and titles to property of all types. The former represents essentially the combination of a general sales tax with a personal income tax; the analysis of incidence requires merely the addition to the discussion in this chapter of the theory of incidence of personal income taxation, which has been developed at length elsewhere.[2] To attempt any consideration of the problem in this study would carry the latter beyond its designated scope. The same considerations apply to the problem of incidence of those parts of the transactions tax upon sales other than those of goods passing directly or indirectly to final consumers.[3]

THE THEORY OF INCIDENCE:

INITIAL REACTIONS: The general sales tax represents merely a coördination into a single levy of the general taxes on producers and retailers already discussed, plus the addition of taxes on the intermediate wholesale steps.[4] Accordingly, to elaborate in detail the price changes resulting from this levy would involve in the main repetition of that which has already been presented. It is necessary only to point out modifications in incidence produced when these separate levies are lumped together into a single tax.[5]

When a general sales tax is imposed, each enterprise -- producer of raw material or finished good, wholesaler, or retailer -- will experience an increase in cost. Retailers, operating in monopolistic competition, will normally boost prices, as in the case of a retail sales tax, by the entire tax, or, with strengthening of oligopoly, by something more, subject to the exceptions and variations as between lines of goods indicated in the preceding chapter. Only in relatively rare cases will some or all retail prices in a certain line fail to increase. Wholesalers will react in similar manner; in this case, with a uniform tax rate, the price increase represents a much larger per cent of the margin than in the case of the retailers, and may be made with somewhat greater difficulty. Where all wholesalers act together, and where direct selling is impossible,[6] the demand for wholesale service will be very inelastic because the wholesale margin represents a relatively small part of the final sale price, and the increase can be made without severe loss in volume.[7] Likewise, manufacturers and other basic producers will attempt to raise prices, except where conditions approaching pure competition exist. With the latter, as, for example, in wheat growing, no increase is possible until exodus occurs, which requires some period of time. Where any degree of monopoly prevails, some increase will be made immediately, except in rare instances. The increase will be greatest with decreasing cost conditions and strengthening of oligopoly; with pure monopoly and optimum pricing, only part of the tax will pass onto consumers. Where no excess profits exist, and oligopoly elements are not strengthened, exodus is necessary for final equilibrium. Regardless of the state of competition, the long run increase would be different from the immediate because of the difference in cost conditions in the two instances.

SECONDARY REACTIONS - The Production Stages: However, in this case, secondary reactions absent in the case of levies on individual steps in the production process arise out of the actions of various links in the process resulting from the changes in price and volume of business made by other links because of the tax. The position of the manufacturer will be considered first. He will, of course, experience sales loss as he raises his price, or loss in profits if he is unable to do so, until he either ceases operation or enjoys a price rise as other firms leave. But, in addition, a decline in demand will occur as wholesalers and retailers raise their margins because of their tax burden, and sales to consumers decline further. This demand decline, which appears to producers as an actual shifting downward of demand curves, may cause significant modifications in prices charged, of kind and degree determined by the nature of cost and demand schedules. With monopolistic competition, for example, with decreasing cost, prices may be increased, especially with average cost pricing practices. With pure competition, prices must fall temporarily; only with exodus of firms can an equilibrium be restored. The price level at the new equilibrium depends on cost conditions for the industry as a whole. When increasing cost exists in manufacturing, a part of the tax levied on the retailer will pass back onto specialized factors in manufacturing, since the price to the retailer, net of the taxes levied on steps prior to the retailer, will decline as a result of the reduction in demand caused by the retail margin increase. Thus, rent of land used in physical production may fall, or, with excess profits, the return to the entrepreneur in production will be reduced.[8] In the latter situation, of course, some burden will rest on the producer regardless of the cost conditions. With decreasing cost in production, the retail margin increase intensifies the operation of the cost condition in leading to still greater price increase.

Manufacturers will experience increased raw material prices as well as decreased demand. This type of cost increase will lead to a similar effect upon price as a tax. Differences will be produced only because of the fact that a cost increase of this nature is equivalent to a specific rather than an ad valorem levy, and because reaction of oligopoly elements may be different in the two cases. With pure competition in manufacturing, this cost rise will speed and increase exodus; in the long run the entire additional cost will pass forward, as modified by the effect of the additional output reduction caused by this further price increase. With monopoly, the cost increase will pass on only in part, and monopoly profits will fall still farther; the same may occur with monopolistic competition and excess profits. However, a strengthening of oligopoly may result in an amount even greater than the tax passing to the consumer, with little or no profit reduction. In the cases in which intermediate links exist between retailer and manufacturer, these units will, in general, pass back the effect of reduced retail sales occurring because their own margins as well as those of retailers increase. Moreover, changes in cost in these units will lessen or increase the demand reduction for manufacturers; the existence of monopoly elements in these links may allow absorption of part of the demand decline. That is, these units will in some cases reduce their prices when the demand for their services falls, and accordingly the fall in demand experienced by the manufacturer is less. However, in cases in which oligopoly prevails, the demand reduction may be intensified.

The Retail Level: Next must be considered the secondary reactions of the retailer. The latter is subject to the tax, and likewise, at least after a period of time if not at once, to an increased purchase price of goods handled as producers and wholesalers, by direct action or through exodus of firms, pass forward the taxes levied upon them. The latter will in some cases be supplemented as a result of cost increase, in other cases reduced by the gains of less costly operation at lower volumes. With pure competition, in the short run there may be an actual decline in purchase price due to the effect of reduced demand upon price at the earlier levels; with any degree of monopoly, such a decline is possible, but an immediate increase is far more likely. In the long run an actual decline in purchase price could result only from collapse of oligopoly somewhere along the line, or sharply increasing cost conditions coupled with a severe demand decline caused by the increase of wholesale and retail margins, or irrational determination of the volume of production.

The retailers will, in general, transmit this increase in purchase price, at least fully, and usually with a supplement, into sale price.[9]

By the application of a constant markup figure to the increased purchase price, the sale price is increased by an amount greater than the tax. The difference compensates the stores for volume reduction, and thus allows the original number of stores to remain in operation, or maintain their excess profits. An increase in purchase price is even more certain to be shifted to the consumer than a tax on the retailer, at least in the short run. The forces of inertia are much more strongly in the way of shifting the tax when the markup must be readjusted than simply when the old markup is applied to a new purchase price. With the former, there is much less certainty that competitors will be increasing by the full tax or more, and so each firm will be less ready to make the increase itself. With separate charging practices, the inertia against an increase by the amount of the tax is perhaps no greater in general than that against an increase in purchase price, but there is even greater check to the additional increase necessary to allow maintenance of the original number of firms or volume of profits. In the short run, this may be more than offset by the delay in full purchase price increase, especially when exodus of firms is necessary somewhere along the line for price increase, in contrast to the immediate burden felt under the retail levy. However, when the situation in earlier stages is of such nature as to check immediate increase, the imposition of a retail levy is likely to lead to a temporary decline in purchase price.

Thus, in the long run, a twofold increase takes place in retail prices, one produced by a cost increase in retailing itself, the other by an increase in purchase price caused by the imposition of the tax upon producers and wholesalers. The final increase to consumers, apart from the effect of interest rate changes, to be discussed below, depends in part upon the cost conditions of producers, wholesalers, and retailers, in part upon the degree of competition in the three stages. The nature of cost and of competition in stages prior to retailing determines the amount of change in retail purchase price. The sale prices of these groups change as a result of the taxes upon them, as a result of changes in operating cost and strength of oligopoly as volume of business falls because of the price increases which each makes, and as a result of falling demand caused by price increases in stages subsequent to the ones in question. In turn, the price changes made by retailers as a result of the taxes and the purchase price increases (or, temporarily in some cases, decreases) depend upon conditions of cost and of competition in this field. To the extent that monopolistic competition accompanied by sufficiently strong elements of oligopoly to allow retention of the old number of firms, along with average cost and markup pricing practices, prevails, it is almost inevitable that the consumers will bear a greater burden than the amount of the tax. Only to the extent that monopoly profits are cut into, or the shares to specialized immobile factors, under increasing cost conditions, reduced, can part of the tax remain on those engaged in production. With pure monopoly and optimum pricing anywhere along the line, some tax burden will remain; with monopolistic competition, however, it is always possible that prices will be boosted sufficiently to maintain the old profit rate.

Thus, under conditions which are likely to be rather common, the portion of the tax levied upon earlier stages in the production and distribution process will tend to "pyramid"; that is, because of ordinary markup practices followed by distribution agencies, at each successive step, the price will be increased by an amount greater than the increase in purchase price caused by the tax. This will, in general, serve to compensate for reduced volume of business, and allow the old number of firms to continue in operation, at a point further from the optimum level of output.[10]

INTEREST RATE REDUCTION: However, one further reaction has yet to be considered. The reduced volumes of physical output and of retail service will lead to a reduction in employment, at each stage in the production and distribution system. A fall in interest rates, partly automatic, partly brought by governmental action, will serve to restore investment, output, and employment, as in previous cases. This process serves in part at least, and perhaps fully, in a rapidly developing economy, to remove the burden from the consumer and place it on the receivers of capital income. However, consumers of certain products will be burdened more heavily than those of others; some may actually experience price declines if the interest fall is sufficiently great. A general sales tax places an unequal burden on different commodities, because of the non-uniform number of independent steps in the production of goods. This is, of course, supplemented by the effect of differences in cost conditions, in elasticity of demand, competitive conditions, in special treatment of the lines by dealers. A readjustment of total output will occur; more of those goods will be produced which bear relatively light burden.

The fall in prices at manufacturing levels will lead to declines in purchase prices for distributors; the markup practices of the latter will, in general, intensify the retail price declines, the increased volume of sales allowing a reduction in cost per unit of operation and in retail margin. The latter will fall also because reduction in interest rates lowers cost of operation in retailing. Investment in retailing will increase, not only because of the fall in the cost of doing business, but primarily because of the greater volume of goods passing through, at the lower prices brought about by cost declines in manufacturing. The relative decline in output of lines bearing high burdens in contrast to those of lower will not apply to any degree as between firms on different levels; that is, the high burden on wholesaling will not cause a permanent relative decline in this type of activity (assuming that the number of independent links cannot be reduced), since the investment in the wholesale business depends primarily upon the volume of goods passing from producer to consumer. That is, the demand for wholesale service will be extremely inelastic up to the old level of output, allowing the relatively high burden to pass on to consumers, without any decline in wholesale activity relative to that in other lines.[11]

COMPARISON WITH THE RETAIL SALES TAX:

Before considering the problems of the significance of a general sales tax upon methods of doing business, the incidence of this type of levy will be compared with that of a retail sales tax providing the same total revenue. Obviously the final burden on consumers will be distributed as among consumers of various products differently in the two cases because of the different number of steps in production and distribution of different goods. But the chief problem is that of the relative distribution of the total burden between consumers and the groups engaged in production.

In the case of the two levies, there is the same total increase in cost of getting the goods from initial producer to final consumer; in one case the burden is placed entirely on the final seller; in the other case, it is distributed over the entire series of firms which handle the products. In general, the final price increase will be similar in the two cases, since the additions to cost in the earlier stages will tend to pass forward, reaching the retailer in the form of increases in purchase price, and being passed on by the retailer in general in the same manner as increases in operating cost. In the case of the retail levy, the retailer will pass on, normally, all, or more than the tax burden, to compensate for reduced volume; the reduction in demand at the earlier levels will produce changes in production cost and in strength of oligopoly, which will modify retail purchase and sale price. In the case of the general levy, at each level, the sellers will experience both increased operating cost and, in almost all cases, purchase price. These burdens will be passed on, without excess profits, in full. With excess, they may pass only in part. In the case of monopolistic competition with oligopoly, the excess increase necessary to allow the old firms to remain in business has an exact counterpart under the retail sales tax in the increase made by firms in earlier stages, when demand falls, to allow maintenance of the old profit level. When pure monopoly, or monopolistic competition and limited entry, or pure competition and increasing cost exist in any of the earlier stages, with a general levy, less than the amount of the tax will pass forward; with the retail levy, the demand decline at the earlier stages will produce an actual decrease in prices asked. It is impossible to compare exactly the amount of price change at the earlier stages in the two cases. With pure monopoly, and decreasing cost, there is apparently more increase with the general than the retail levy, since any demand decrease will produce an actual price increase under the circumstances, whereas a cost increase will not lead to a price increase greater than the amount of the cost unless the cost curve is very steep. With other conditions, however, it appears that the changes would, in general, be of similar nature.

The effect of production cost changes on retail price increase will, for the most part, be the same in the two cases. That is, to the extent that the other factors influencing change cause the same retail price increase in the two cases, the total output reduction will be the same, and likewise the change in production cost per unit. At each level of output, given the volume reduction, the cost change will be the same regardless of whether the latter is caused by demand decrease or output increase. The only difference is introduced by the fact that the tax will be distributed over various commodities in a somewhat different manner in the two cases, and since cost conditions differ between lines, total cost change will not be the same with the two types of levy. Likewise, to the extent that other factors, especially those to be mentioned below, cause different amounts of price increase, the difference will be modified according to the cost conditions present.

However, while in general the incidence of the two types of tax will be similar, significant differences are introduced by the fact that the transmission of the effects of the tax from one stage in the system to another may differ in the two cases because of the oligopoly elements involved. The comparison must be made between the reaction of the units in the production and distribution system to, on the one hand, an increase in operating expenses, along with increased purchase price and sales decrease, to, on the other hand, a relatively severe demand decrease for firms in all stages prior to the retail level, and a much greater cost increase for the retailer. Because of usual markup practices, it appears that there will be greater final increase with the general sales levy, since a large part of the tax will pass from one step to another as an increase in purchase price. There is more assurance in this case of sufficiently excessive price increases to allow maintenance of the old firms than there is of sufficient price increase to allow this when demand falls. Likewise, as previously indicated, the retailer is much more likely to pass on an amount greater than the tax when purchase price increases than when operating cost rises. Thus, in general, a general sales tax will bring greater price increase because exodus of firms, which would allow operation nearer the optimum, is checked. But this difference must not be exaggerated; very commonly demand reduction will bring the same type of reaction. Likewise, especially in the short run, there is an offsetting factor which may be of considerable importance. The retailer, especially with separate charge provisions, is almost certain to take immediate steps to free himself of the levy so far as possible. But with the general levy, the rate on each step will be very much lower; the intermediate firms may be less sensitive to cost changes, because of more nearly pure competition or other factors, and inertia may check for a long period of time any reaction at all on the part of these firms.[12] In the long run, with rational calculation of investment outlays, some change is inevitable; in shorter periods of time, a tax may be absorbed entirely. The demand decrease, with the retail sales levy, will not cause any comparable price decline, except where the absorption is due to conditions of pure competition. In the latter case, the decline in retail demand will cause a price decline comparable to the tax absorption with the general levy. But, even here there will be a lag before the price fall is transmitted forward to the retailer.

Apart from these differences, further modification arises out of the fact that the tax imposed upon each commodity is different in the case of the two levies even though the total burden is the same. This is due in part to the fact that margins of distribution and the amounts of value added by manufacture are not uniform; accordingly the prices in the earlier stages represent a greater part of the retail sales price in some cases than in others, and the tax does likewise. The other factor is the different number of independent stages through which various commodities pass on the way from initial producer to final consumer. The price rise will, of course, be greater in the lines characterized by a large number of steps in the process.[13] Since the conditions of cost and competition will be different in the various lines, the difference in the manner in which the total burden is allocated as among individual goods modifies the division of burden between consumers and other groups. Likewise, the shifts in demand between lines will differ in the two cases; this is of particular importance in the case of commodities which are close substitutes, yet require a different number of independent steps in production and distribution. There will be a severe loss in demand for the commodity requiring a greater number of stages.

As far as price declines occurring as a result of decreased interest rates are concerned, again the relief to consumers will be similar in the two cases. Output will be expanded at all steps as a result of the reduced interest cost. In the case of the retail levy, the fact that the tax stands on retailers alone will not result in any significant reduction in that type of activity in relation to physical production, since the total volume of investment in retailing depends primarily on the volume of goods passing through to final consumers. An increase in the latter to the level at which the old volume of output is restored will bring a similar increase in units of retail service provided. The demand for retail service will be the same at the margin which includes the tax as it was before at the old margin, as the purchase price of goods will be sufficiently lower to allow the sale of the same volume of goods at a higher margin. The difference in incidence between the two levies can be modified through the effect of interest rate changes only in so far as the changes in price apart from interest reduction are different, and in cases in which, due to oligopoly elements, the cost reduction will be transmitted forward differently. But, in general, since basic production is the sphere in which increased output from lower costs is of chief significance, in either case variations along such lines seem of little importance. In one respect, an interest rate reduction to allow the old level of employment may be made more easily with the retail than the general levy. With the latter, the prices at the intermediate stages as well as at the retail level will be higher than before; in the former, only the latter will be raised to any significant amount. Accordingly, more money will be required for circulation purposes than with the retail levy, and interest reduction will be more difficult.[14]

TAXATION BY LIMITED JURISDICTIONS: However, when the levies are imposed by limited jurisdictions, new variations between the two types are introduced.[15] As pointed out in an earlier chapter, in the case of a state tax on manufacturing, in many cases such a levy will check production within the state, and although bringing in no revenue, place a burden on the consumer, of an amount up to the level of the tax, because of higher production cost outside the state. In the case of a retail levy, only to a relatively minor extent will the possibility of outside competition interfere with shifting. Only in the case of merchants in borderline towns, and of products of sufficient unit value to warrant the trouble of out of state purchase,[16] will the type of problem met with in manufacturing be encountered in retailing.[17] Where out of state competition is possible, greater exodus of firms is likely, until the remaining group can be supported at the higher price, or lower cost of operation. However, with strong oligopoly, the greater demand loss may simply mean even greater price increases to allow maintenance of old profit margins. This will, of course, not be possible if the demand becomes sufficiently elastic. But, in general, a retail sales tax can be shifted without such difficulties, the possibility of outside purchase merely making demand somewhat more elastic than would otherwise be the case. Just as manufacturing cannot leave the state if raw materials are located within its boundaries and transportation costs are prohibitive, retailing cannot usually be driven out because the buyers are located within the state and the retailers must be in close contact with them. In sharp contrast to this, with the general sales tax, that part of the levy resting upon producers and intermediate distributors is likely, to the extent that the burden represents a differential to which competitors in other states are not subject, to interfere seriously with the ability of these firms to continue operation. Especially is this true of wholesalers, whose location is not tied to raw material sources to the same extent as firms engaged in physical production. Thus, where pure competition exists in these fields, price will not rise sufficiently to allow normal profits until all or at least a much larger number of firms than with a universal levy have left the field. With monopolistic competition, no degree of price increases will allow normal profits without at least substantial exodus of firms. Accordingly the burden to the consumer will not be compensated for entirely by gain to the state. Part of the burden will be due to more expensive production cost; the additional sums paid by the consumers will go in part to pay for transportation services and higher cost of operation in out of state sections.

Thus, under such conditions, consumers will be burdened much more severely under a general than under a retail sales tax. The loss of business to outside firms will be much greater with the former than with the latter; with the general levy, not only will the tax pass onto the consumer, but the latter will bear an additional burden caused by the shifting of production to areas of higher cost of production. If all wholesalers and producers leave the area, the tax rate must be as high as the retail rate to yield the same revenue; the consumer will pay as much tax as with the retail levy, but will pay an additional amount to compensate for higher costs of production and distribution, from which the state gets no revenue. Furthermore, interest rate reduction will not alter this difference between the two levies.[18] The reduction will apply throughout the entire area; production and distribution costs will fall, but there will be no readjustment of production to more efficient locations. If the same volume of employment is restored, part of the men will be engaged in tasks which would be unnecessary with more suitable location of operations. Essentially there are two "taxes," one collected by the state, the other collected by those engaged in unnecessary activity.

THE EFFECT OF THE GENERAL SALES TAX ON INTEGRATION:

The preceding analysis has been based upon the assumption that the number of times each good changes hands on its way to the final consumer is determined independently of forces whose operation is affected by the tax. Actually, of course, the number of independent links in the distribution system depends upon the relative cost of different methods of performing the services. A decrease in the number of firms will occur when firms can reduce cost of production by uniting with others. When a general sales tax is imposed, the tax burden can be reduced by uniting formerly independent units under common management, and accordingly integration is promoted.[19] The latter will not necessarily take place, however. The less integrated process must have possessed certain economies over a more completely integrated system, or the union of steps would have occurred before the tax; the gain from tax reduction must be sufficiently great to offset these economies, or no change in the number of units will occur. Where further integration does take place, the reduction in the number of times the tax applies will lessen the burden of the tax on consumers; this reduction will, however, not offset entirely the loss in revenue to the government because of the less efficient method of operation. This difference represents a net loss to consumers not offset by gain to anyone, since the total volume of output is reduced simply because less satisfactory methods are used. Likewise, in some cases those formerly operating as merchants will remain as independent organizations but will operate on an agency basis.[20] The same considerations as to incidence apply as in the previous case.

One important aspect of the integration problem was ignored in the previous paragraph, namely, the fact that in many lines of goods, the various competing channels of distribution have different numbers of independent steps. Thus, the chain store, which usually eliminates the wholesaler, and in some cases even the independent manufacturer, competes with the independent producer-wholesaler-retailer system. As indicated in the discussion of chain store taxes,[21] each type of distribution system has certain advantages, and the relative extension of each depends on the relation of these advantages. The imposition of a general sales tax, which improves, relatively, the position of the integrated system, checks the independent system; the latter will disappear entirely, if previously it possessed little advantage over the former relative to the tax burden. The former consumers of the independent units will suffer not only the burden of the tax on the integrated system, but also additional loss, either through higher prices or inferior quality and service than that formerly obtained, from the necessity of purchasing at the type of store not previously preferred. The severity of this loss depends, of course, on the relative strength of the advantages of this type of store for the consumers in question prior to the tax. To the extent, however, that the independent system possesses sufficient advantages to remain despite the tax, customers of these stores will contribute more to the state than those of the integrated system. But they will suffer less injury than if the stores they preferred ceased business entirely, and the additional sums which they pay will accrue to the treasury.[22] The consumers suffering most will be those tied to independents because of debt or other factors; they are unable to shift to chains, and are forced to bear the higher tax. Where excess profits exist in the independent system, the consumer may escape the additional burden on this type of enterprise. These stores may find it profitable to raise only to the extent that the integrated systems do, because to increase more would involve severe sales losses. Accordingly, the differential part of the tax is absorbed in monopoly profits; the burden on the latter is greater than would be the case with a retail levy. But such situations are not likely of great frequency.[23] One further aspect of the integration problem should be mentioned; the method by which the process takes place is commonly the introduction of direct selling by the producer, the latter bringing the intermediate links in distribution under his control. The weak financial position of some producers will place them at a disadvantage in this regard, and check the sale of the products of some firms to the gain of others. In summary, a general sales tax will serve very definitely to foster integration, thus increasing the burden of some or all consumers in certain lines by lessening efficiency of operation, without any offsetting gain to the government.

SUMMARY:

In summary, a general sales tax will be borne for the most part by consumers, apart from the effect of possible interest rate and wage reductions. The taxes on the firms in the various stages of physical production and distribution involve cost increases, and will result in increases in sale prices at each step. The latter culminate in increased purchase prices as well as higher operating costs for the retailer. The prices of the latter will, in general, be raised so as to pass on these two burdens to the consumers. The final increase depends, of course, in part upon the cost conditions in the various stages, and in part on the nature of competition. In the short run, there will be some delay before the taxes on firms in the earlier stages come forward to retailers; where exodus is necessary for increase, the delay will be intensified. Where economically irrational factors influence entry, there will be more or less permanent failure to shift. With monopolistic competition and usual markup practices in retailing, there will be a tendency to pyramid increases once they are made; not only are firms in such circumstances more likely to shift an increase in purchase price than an increase in operating cost, but an additional increase beyond the tax is almost inevitable with the application of a constant markup percentage to an increased purchase price. This excess increase serves to compensate firms for reduced volume and to allow maintenance of old profit levels and the original number of firms. Only in case of increasing cost conditions, and in some cases of excess profits, will part of the tax remain on groups engaged in production. An interest rate reduction, arising out of decreased need for cash for business purposes, and out of government action to reduce unemployment, will serve to relieve the burden on consumers and pass it to capital owners. Some labor groups may suffer from substantial wage reduction; these will, however, suffer from less unemployment than other groups. Regardless of interest reductions, however, consumers of goods which pass through a relatively large number of independent stages in the distribution process will suffer particularly severe burden.

A general sales tax, by offering possibility of escape of the levy by reducing the number of independent links in the production and marketing process, furthers the tendency to integration, and injures relatively the position of those channels of distribution with numerous separate links. In some cases, this may reduce production costs by forcing a change dictated by economic conditions, but delayed by mere inertia. More likely, however, integration will be forced beyond the limits to which it would be carried on the basis of efficiency of operation. Accordingly, prices to consumers will be raised by an amount more than that of the tax, to compensate for less efficient methods of operation.

The incidence of a general sales tax differs from that of a retail sales tax only to the extent that, in some cases, a reduction in demand at the earlier stages will affect price somewhat differently than the increase in cost which would occur with the general sales levy, and in others the shifting forward through the distribution system of the taxes on the earlier stages in the case of a general levy will result in a greater final increase. The latter comes about because firms will normally pass forward an increase in purchase price more completely than an increase in operating expenses, which requires definite readjustment of the markup figures. This will, in the short run at least, be more or less offset by the slow reaction of some of the firms along the line to the increase in operating costs. But, in general, the incidence in the two cases will be the same, since there is the same increase in total cost of getting goods to the consumer, which will bring roughly the same reduction in total output, and modify production cost in similar manner. As an example of the similarity, if pure competition prevails in physical production, the temporary absorption of the tax under the general levy, which may be more or less permanent with economically irrational determination of investment, has its counterpart with the retail levy in the form of a corresponding fall in purchase price for retailers caused by the action of falling demand on inelastic supply in production. The burden, of course, differs among various commodities because of the nonuniform number of stages in the production and distribution process. Otherwise, significant differences in incidence exist only when the levies are applied by limited jurisdictions. In the latter case, the retail tax will cause comparatively little loss of business to outside merchants. The part of the general levy resting upon earlier stages in the distribution process will, to the extent that it represents a differential burden to which these types of firms in other states are not subject through any type of levy, tend to drive this type of business out of the state. The result will be increased cost of production because of less economical location, and increased prices to consumers, on account of which no revenue accrues to the state.

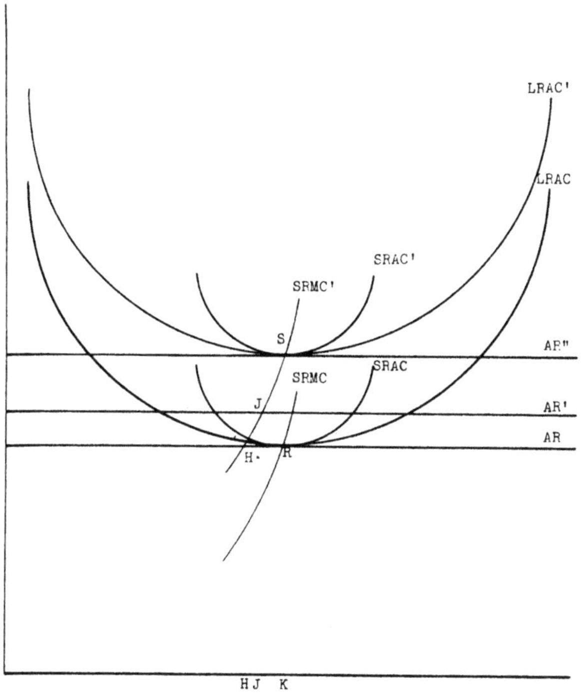

CHART NO. 1

Curves of the individual firms:

LRAC : Long run average cost, before tax.
LRAC' : Long run average cost, after tax.
SRAC : Short run average cost, before tax.
SRAC' : Short run average cost, after tax.
SRMC' : Short run marginal cost, after tax.
SRMC : Short run marginal cost, before tax.
AR : Average revenue, before tax.
AR' : Average revenue, after short run adjustment to tax.
AR" : Average revenue, after long run adjustment to tax.

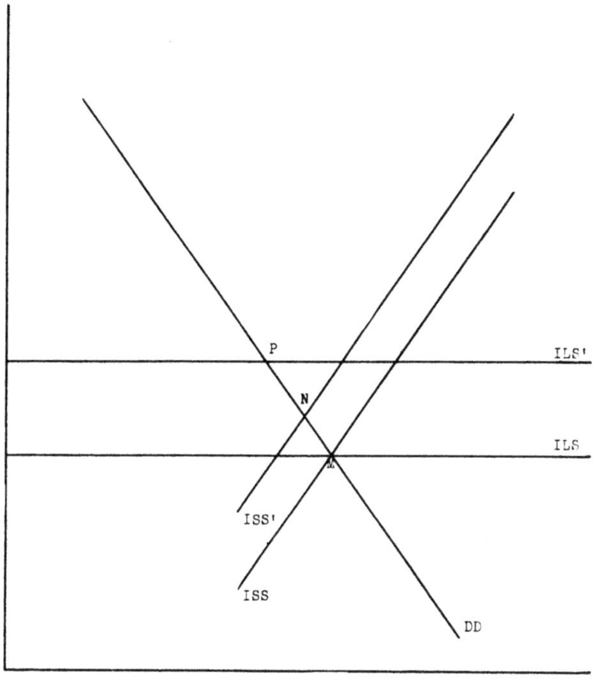

CHART NO. 2

Curves of the Industry as a Whole:

ILS : Long run supply and cost curve of the industry, before tax.
ILS' : Long run supply and cost curve of the industry, after tax.
ISS : Short run supply curve of the industry, before tax. (The summation of the portions of the marginal cost curves of all the firms above the average variable cost curves.)
ISS' : Short run supply curve of the industry, after tax, before readjustment of number of firms.
DD : Demand curve for products of the industry.

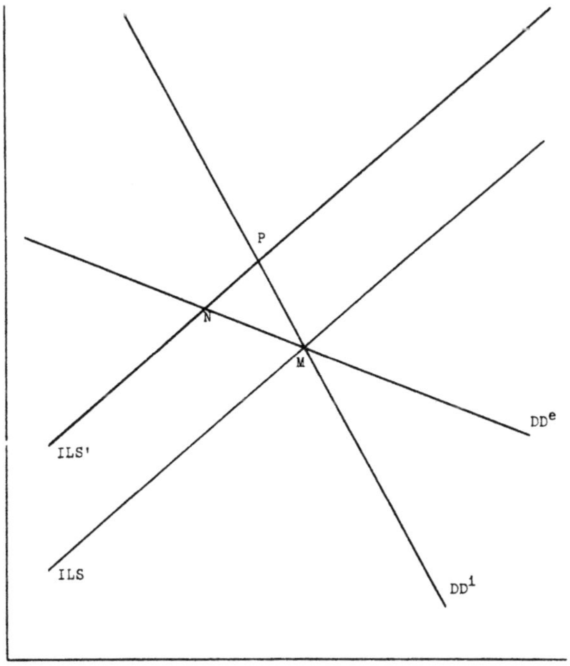

CHART NO. 3

Curves of the Industry as a Whole:

ILS : Long run supply curve, increasing cost, before tax.
ILS' : Long run supply curve, increasing cost, after tax.
DDe : Demand curve, relatively great elasticity.
DDi : Demand curve, relatively inelastic.

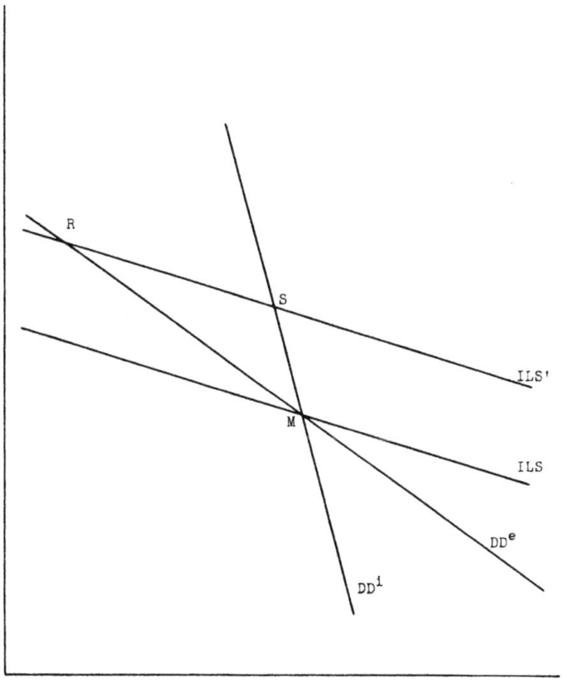

CHART NO. 4

Curves of the Industry as a Whole:

ILS : Long run supply curve, decreasing cost, before tax.
ILS' : Long run supply curve, decreasing cost, after tax.
DDe : Demand curve, relatively great elasticity.
DDi : Demand curve, relatively inelastic.

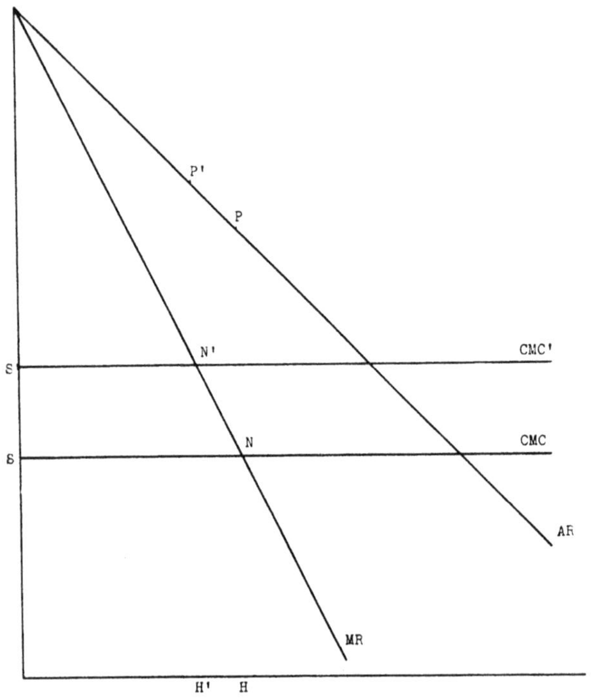

CHART NO. 5

AR : Average revenue. MR : Marginal revenue.

CMC: Cost, average and marginal, constant cost conditions, before tax.

CMC': Cost, average and marginal, after tax.

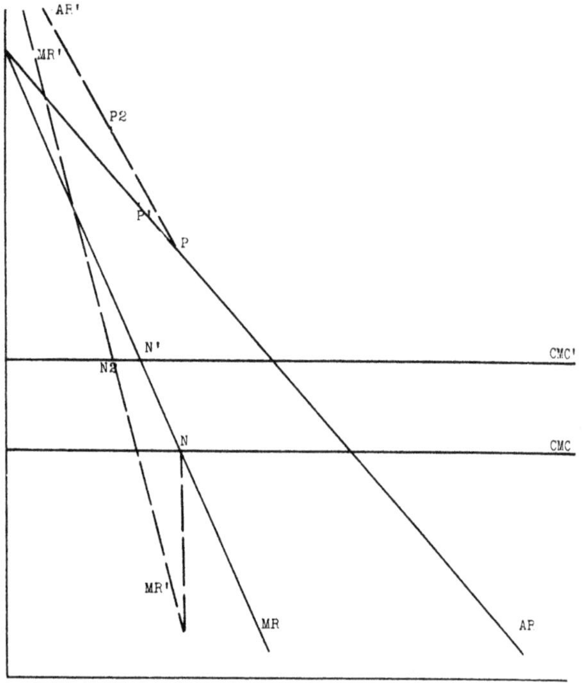

CHART NO. 6

AR : Average revenue, straight line demand curve.

AR': Average revenue, demand curve increasing in steepness.

MR : Marginal curve of AR. MR': Marginal curve of AR'.

CMC: Cost, average and marginal, constant cost, before tax.

CMC': Cost, average and marginal, after tax.

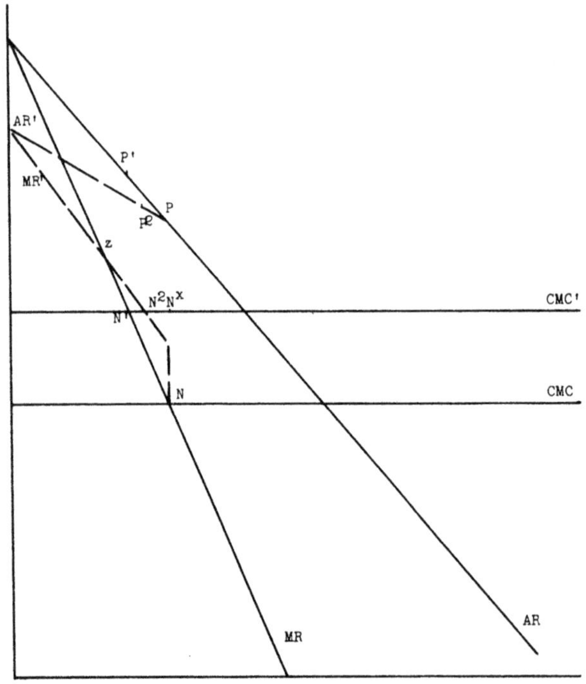

CHART NO. 7

AR : Average revenue, straight line demand curve.

AR': Average revenue, demand curve decreasing in steepness.

MR : Marginal curve of AR. MR': Marginal curve of AR'.

CMC: Cost, average and marginal, constant cost, before tax.

CMC': Cost, average and marginal, after tax.

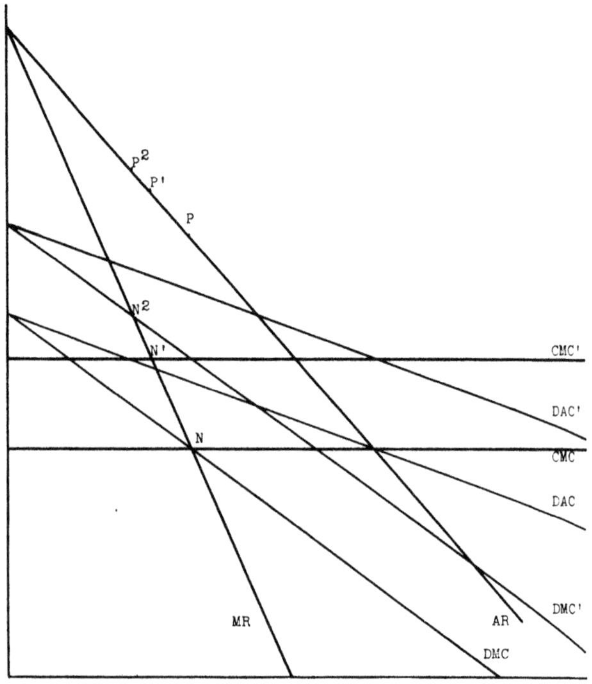

CHART NO. 8

AR : Average revenue. MR : Marginal revenue.

CMC and CMC': Cost, average and marginal, before and after tax respectively, constant cost conditions.

DAC and DAC': Average cost, before and after tax respectively, decreasing cost conditions.

DMC and DMC': Marginal cost curves of DAC and DAC' respectively.

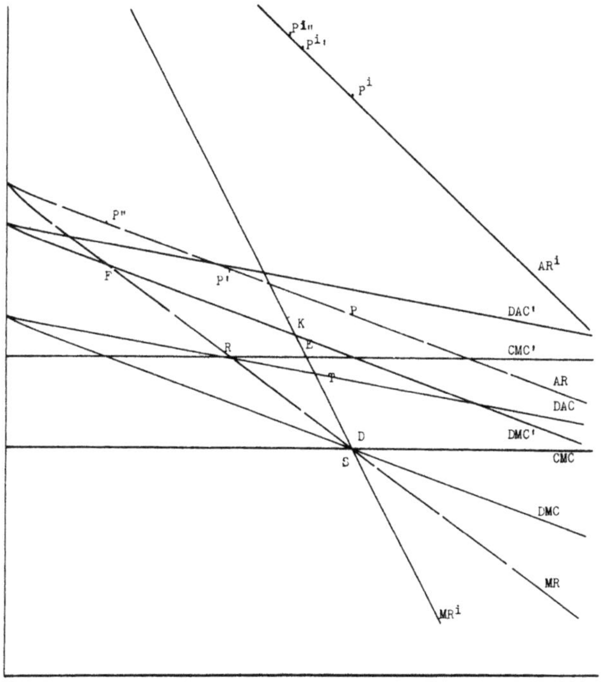

CHART NO. 9

AR : Average revenue, less steep demand curve. AR^i: Average revenue, steep demand curve.

MR : Marginal revenue curve of AR. MR^i: Marginal revenue curve of AR^i.

CMC and CMC': Cost, average and marginal, before and after tax respectively, constant cost conditions.

DAC and DAC': Average cost, before and after tax respectively, decreasing cost conditions.

DMC and DMC': Marginal cost curves of DAC and DAC' respectively.

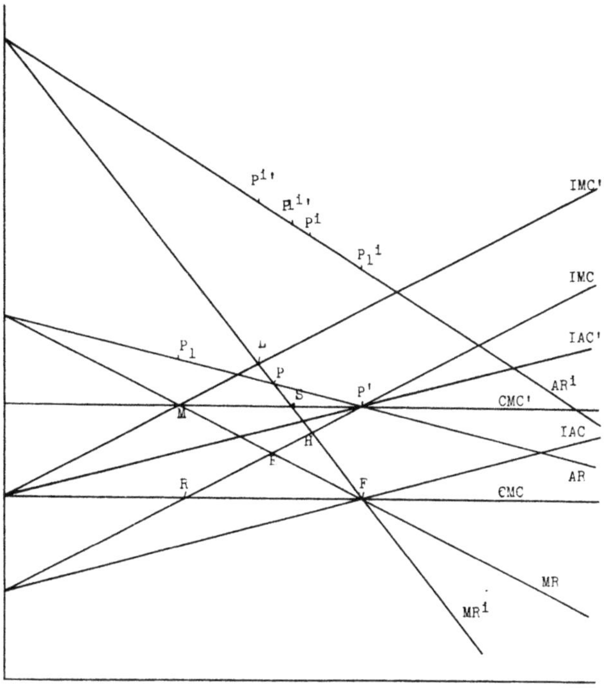

CHART NO. 10

AR : Average Revenue, less steep demand curve. AR^i: Average Revenue, steep demand curve.

MR : Marginal Revenue curve of AR; MR^i, Marginal Revenue of AR^i.

CMC and CMC': Cost, average and marginal, before and after tax respectively, constant cost conditions.

IAC and IAC': Average cost, before and after tax respectively, increasing cost conditions.

IMC and IMC': Marginal cost curves of IAC and IAC'.

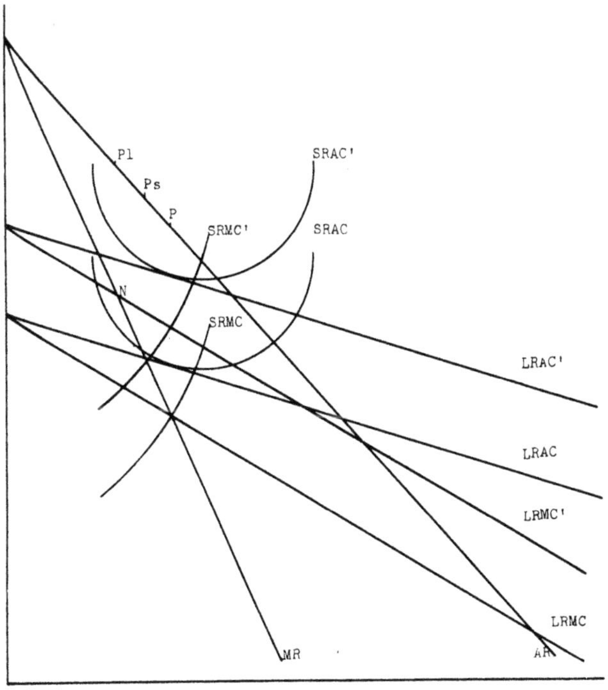

CHART NO. 11

AR : Average revenue. MR : Marginal revenue.

LRAC and LRAC': Long run average cost before and after tax respectively.

LRMC and LRMC': Marginal cost curves of LRAC and LRAC'.

SRAC and SRAC': Short run average cost before and after tax respectively.

SRMC and SRMC': Marginal cost curves of SRAC and SRAC'.

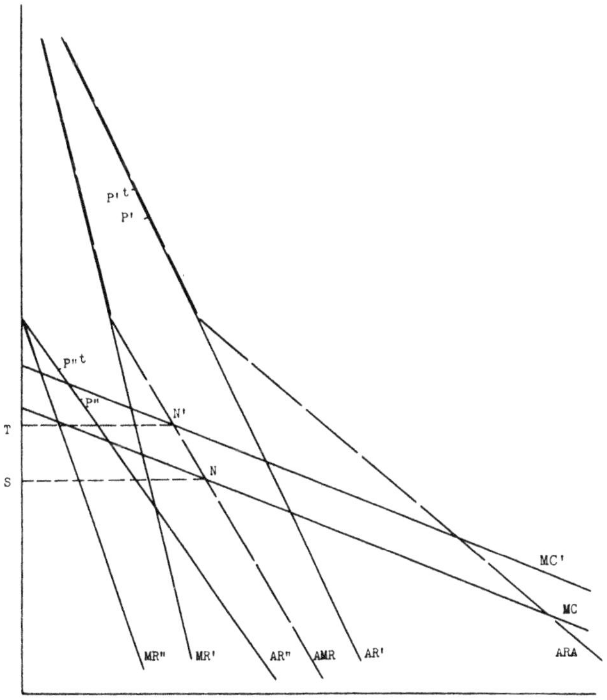

CHART NO. 12

AMR: Total Marginal revenue. ARA: Total Average revenue.

AR': Average revenue, market 1. AR": Average revenue, market 2.

MR': Marginal revenue curve of AR'.

MR": Marginal revenue curve of AR".

MC: Marginal cost, before tax. MC': Marginal cost, after tax.

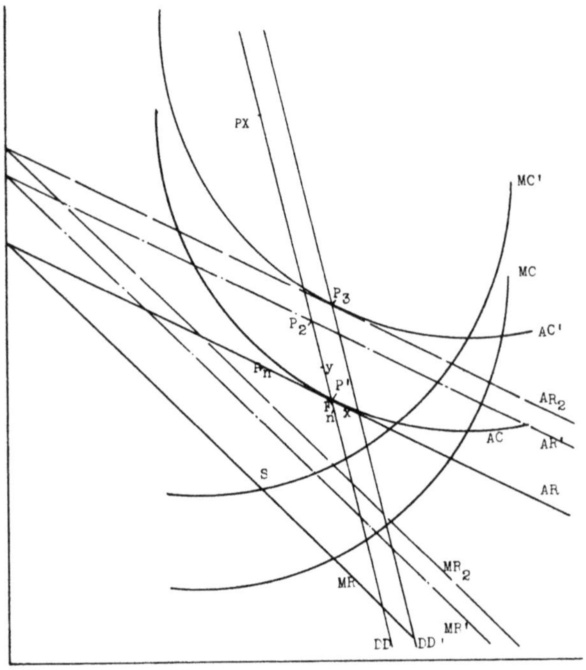

CHART NO. 13

AC and AC': Average Cost, before and after tax, respectively.
MC and MC': Marginal curves of AC and AC'.
AR and MR: Average Revenue and Marginal Revenue, before tax.
AR': Temporary equilibrium Average Revenue, after tax.
AR_2: Permanent equilibrium Average Revenue, after tax.
MR' and MR_2: Marginal curves of AR' and AR_2 respectively.
DD and DD': Average Revenue curves, assuming prices of other firms to be identical to prices of this firm, before and after tax respectively.

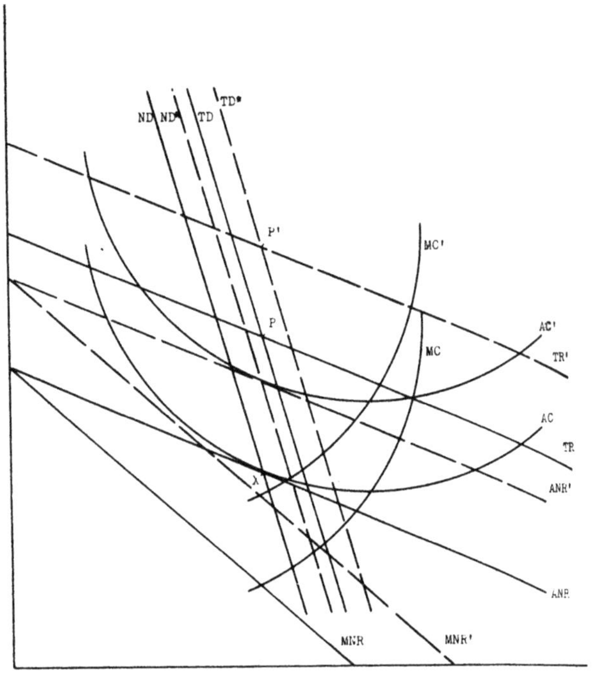

CHART NO. 14

AC : Average cost, before tax. AC: Average cost, after tax.
MC and MC': Marginal curves of AC and AC' respectively.

TR : Average gross revenue before tax.
TR': Average gross revenue after tax.

ANR and ANR' : Average net revenue (TR minus selling cost) before and after tax.
MNR and MNR' : Marginal curves of ANR and ANR'.

TD : Average gross revenue, assuming prices of other firms to be identical with prices of this firm, and given selling activities on part of other firms, before tax.
TD": TD, after tax.
ND and ND": Average net revenue, before and after tax, assumptions as of TD.

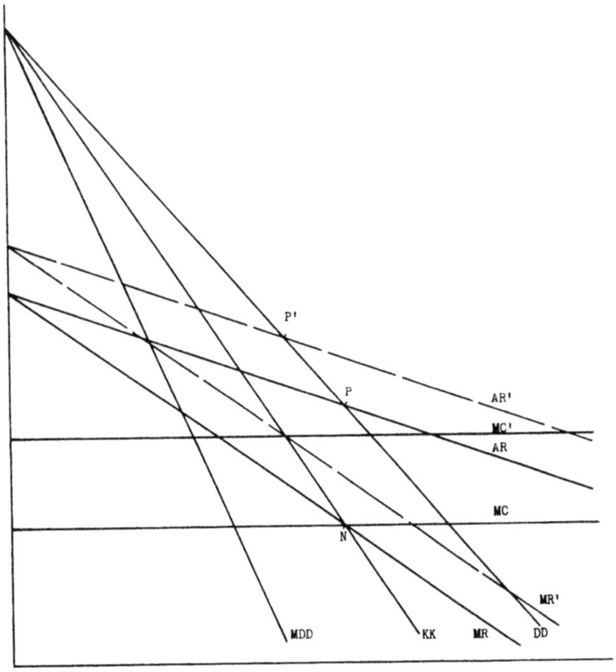

CHART NO. 15

MC: Marginal cost, before tax. MC': Marginal cost, after tax.

AR and AR': Equilibrium average revenue, with cost curves MC and MC' respectively.
MR and MR': Marginal revenue curves of AR and AR'.

DD: Average revenue, assuming prices of other firms to be identical with prices of this firm.
MDD: Marginal curve of DD.

KK: Line of equilibrium levels of output, with various possible cost curves.

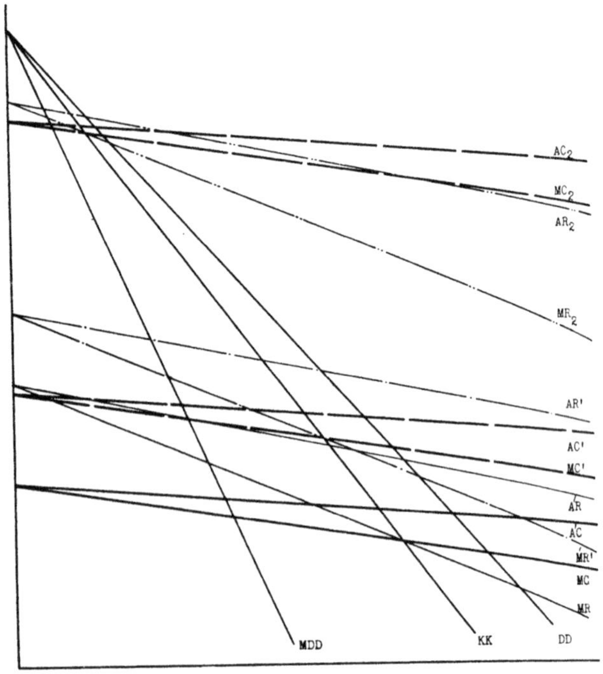

CHART NO. 16

AC: Average cost, before tax. MC: Marginal cost, before tax.
AC' and AC_2: Average cost curves after relatively small and relatively large tax.
MC' and MC_2: Marginal cost curves of AC' and AC_2.
AR and MR: Equilibrium average and marginal revenue, before tax.
AR' and AR_2: Equilibrium average revenue curves after imposition of the taxes of AC' and AC_2.
MR' and MR_2: Marginal revenue curves of AR' and AR_2.
DD: Average revenue curve, assuming prices of other firms to be identical to prices of this firm.
MDD: Marginal curve of DD.
KK: Line of equilibrium levels of output, with different possible cost curves.

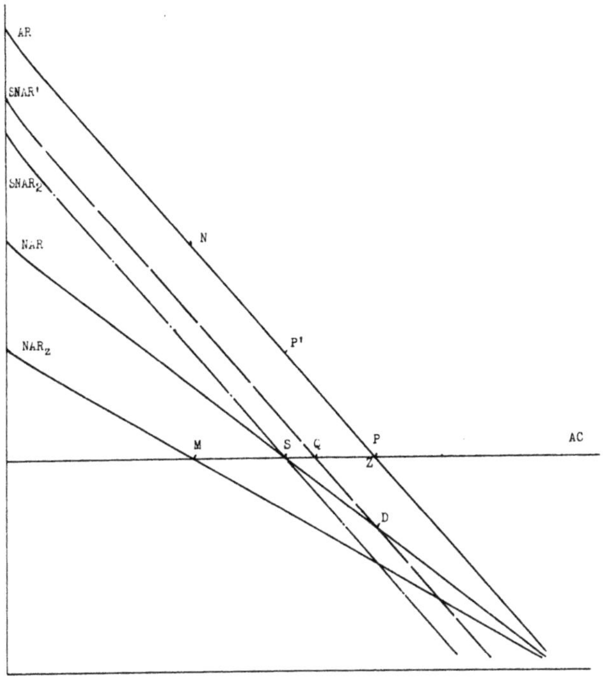

CHART NO. 17

AR : Average revenue, before tax. AC : Average cost.

NAR : Net average revenue, after tax, ad valorem, levied net of tax.
NAR_z: Net average revenue, after tax, ad valorem, levied on price including tax.

SNAR' : Net average revenue, after specific tax imposing same burden at old output level as ad valorem yielding NAR.
$SNAR_2$: Net average revenue, after specific tax yielding same revenue at new equilibrium as ad valorem of NAR, or after a specific levy at the rate of the ad valorem times the old price.

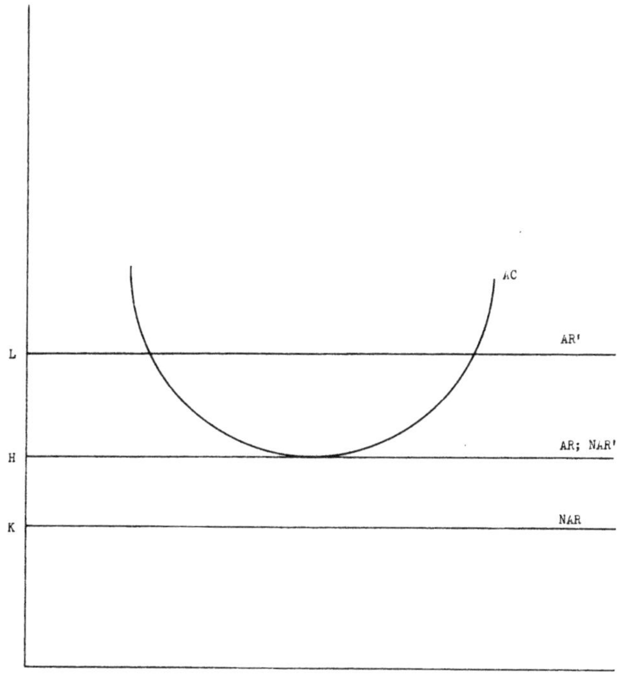

CHART NO. 17A

AC : Average cost.

AR : Average revenue, before tax.

NAR: Net Average revenue, after tax, before exodus of firms.

NAR' : Net Average revenue, after exodus of firms.

AR' : Average revenue, after exodus of firms.

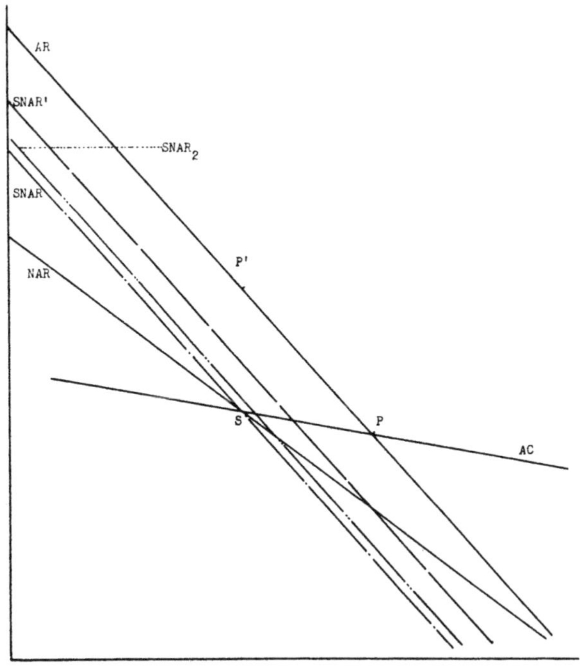

CHART NO. 18

AR : Average revenue, before tax. AC : Average cost.

NAR: Net average revenue, after tax, ad valorem levy.

SNAR: Net average revenue, specific tax imposing same burden as ad valorem of NAR, at new equilibrium of latter.
SNAR' : Net average revenue, specific tax imposing same burden at original level of output as the ad valorem.
$SNAR_2$: Net average revenue, specific tax at rate of ad valorem tax times original price.

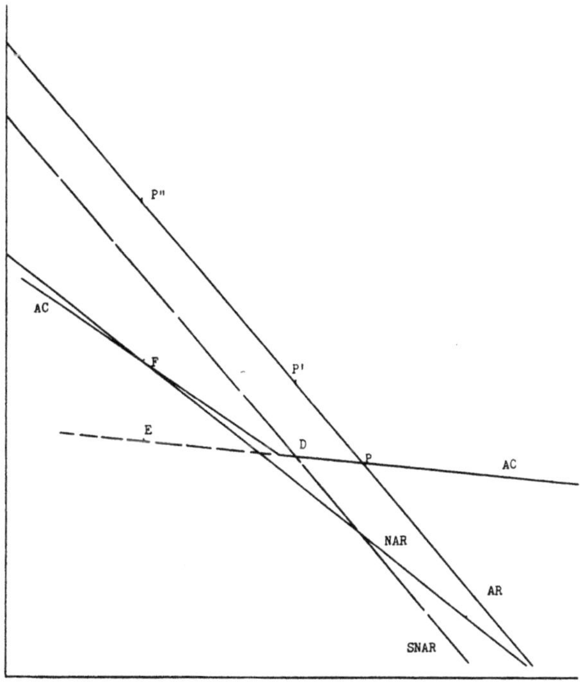

CHART NO. 19

AR : Average Revenue, before tax. AC : Average Cost.

NAR: Net Average Revenue, after ad valorem levy.

SNAR: Net Average Revenue, after specific levy imposing same burden at original level of output, as ad valorem of NAR.

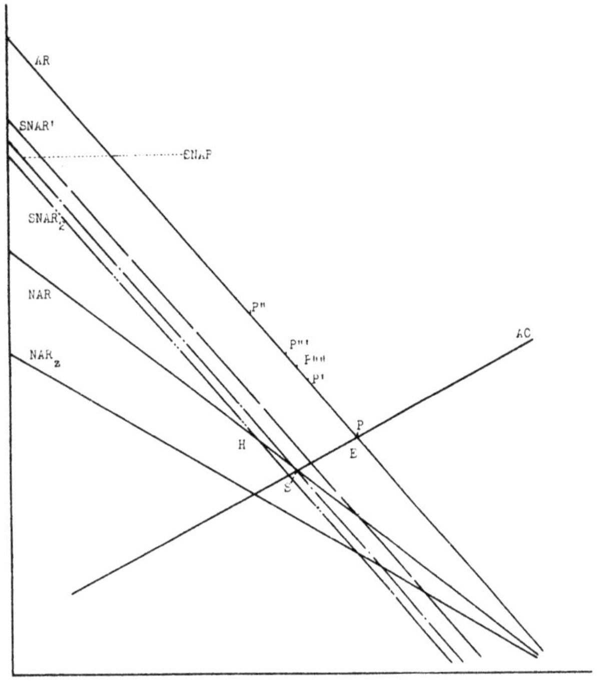

CHART NO. 20

AR : Average revenue, before tax. AC : Average cost.

NAR: Net average revenue, after tax, ad valorem levy, levied net of tax.
SNAR: Net average revenue, specific tax imposing same burden as ad valorem of NAR, at new equilibrium of latter.
SNAR': Net average revenue, specific tax imposing same burden at original level of output as the ad valorem.
$SNAR_2$: Net average revenue, specific tax at rate of ad valorem tax times original price.
NAR_2: Net average revenue, after tax, ad valorem. levied on price including tax.

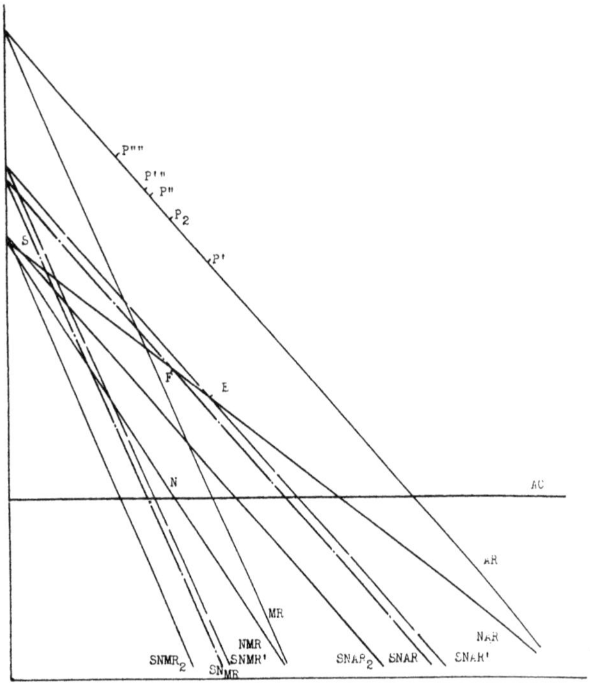

CHART NO. 21

AC : Average cost, and marginal cost.

AR : Average revenue, before tax. MR: Marginal revenue, before tax.
NAR and NMR : Net average revenue and net marginal revenue, after ad valorem tax.
SNAR: Net average revenue, specific tax imposing same burden as ad valorem of NAR, at new equilibrium of latter.
SNAR': Net average revenue, specific tax imposing same burden at original level of output as the ad valorem.
$SNAR_2$: Net average revenue, specific tax at rate of ad valorem tax times original price.
SNMR, SNMR', $SNMR_2$: Marginal curves of SNAR, SNAR', $SNAR_2$.

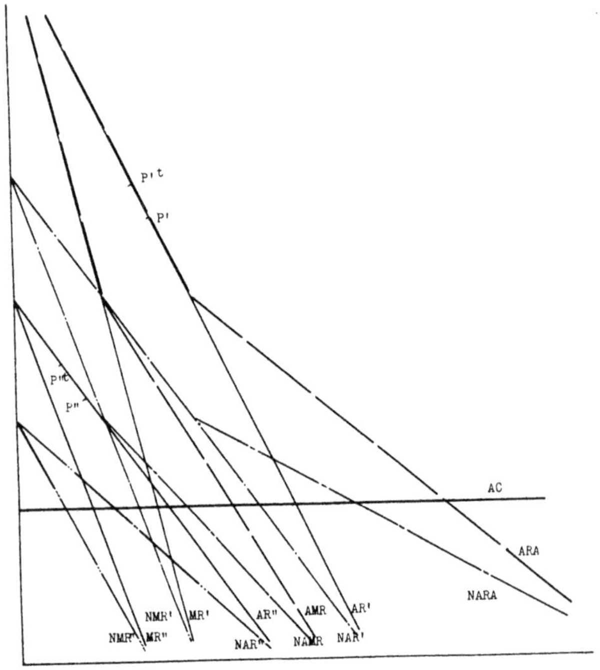

CHART NO. 22

AC : Average cost.

AR' and AR": Average revenue, markets 1 and 2 respectively.
MR' and MR": Marginal curves of AR' and AR".
ARA : Average revenue, both markets.
AMR : Marginal revenue curve of ARA.
NAR' and NAR": Net average revenue after tax, markets 1 and 2.
NMR' and NMR": Marginal curves of NAR' and NAR".
NARA: Net average revenue after tax, both markets.
NAMR: Marginal curve of NARA.

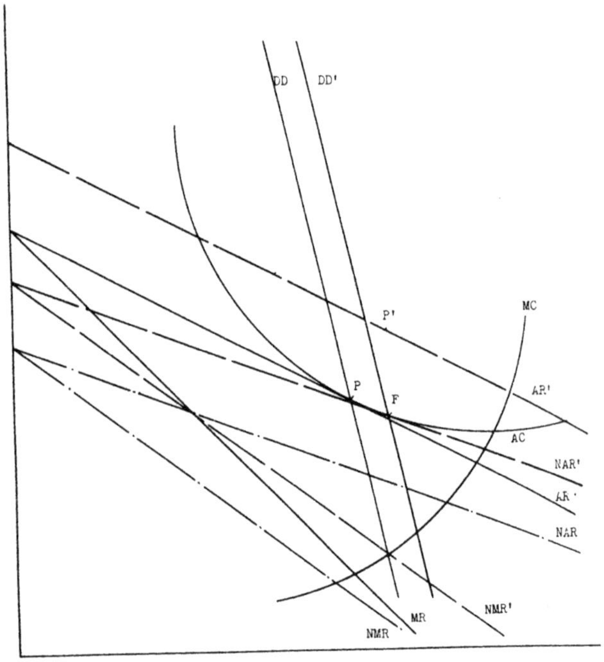

CHART NO. 23

AC : Average cost. MC : Marginal cost.

AR and MR: Average revenue and marginal revenue, before tax.
NAR: Net average revenue, after tax, before readjustment.
NAR': Net average revenue, after readjustment from tax.
AR': Average revenue, after readjustment from tax.
NMR, NMR': Marginal curves of NAR and NAR'.

DD : Average revenue curve, assuming prices of other firms to be identical with prices of this firm.
DD': DD curve after readjustment from tax.

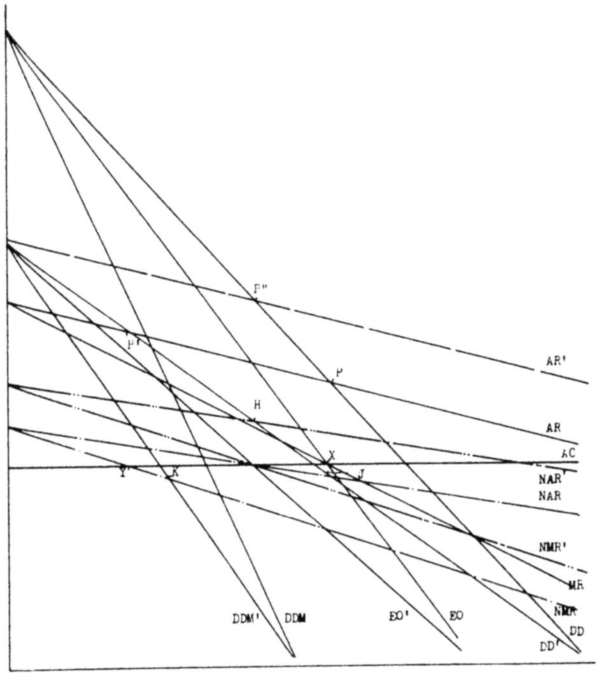

CHART NO. 24

AC : Average and marginal cost.

AR and MR: Average revenue and marginal revenue, before tax.
NAR : Net average revenue, after tax, before readjustment.
NAR': Net average revenue, after final readjustment to tax.
NMR and NMR': Marginal curves of NAR and NAR' respectively.
AR': Average gross revenue, after readjustments from tax.

DD and DD': Average revenue, assuming prices of other firms to be identical to prices of this firm, before and after tax respectively.
EO and EO': Line of equilibrium levels of output, before and after tax.
DDM and DDM': Marginal curves of DD and DD' respectively.

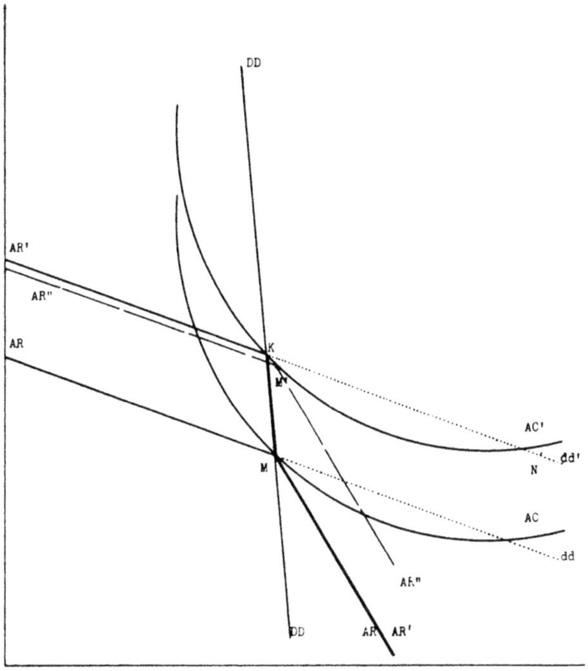

CHART NO. 25

AC : Average cost, before tax. AC': Average cost, after tax.

AR : Average revenue, before tax.
AR": Average revenue, after tax, no increase in oligopoly.
AR': Average revenue, after tax, increase in oligopoly.
DD : Average revenue curve, assuming prices of other firms to be identical with prices of this firm.

dd : Lower portion of AR curve, if other firms left their prices at M while this firm cut its prices.
dd': dd curve after tax, and increase in oligopoly.

NOTE: AR' is identical with DD between K and M, and identical with AR below M.

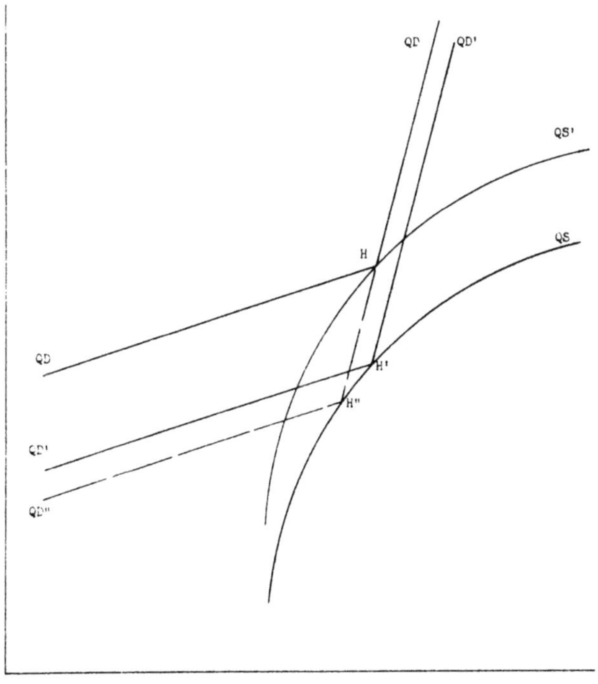

CHART NO. 26

y axis: $ expenditures on quality improvement.
x axis: Number of units of commodity.

QS' and QD: Quality-supply and Quality-demand curves, respectively, before tax.
QS and QD': Quality-supply and Quality-demand curves, respectively, after tax.

QD": Quality-demand curve, when firms realize other firms will also cut quality as a result of the tax.

NOTES

CHAPTER I

1. The most complete historical account of the theory of incidence is to be found in Seligman, E.R.A., *Incidence of Taxation*, 5th Edition, New York, 1927, Part 1.
2. The process by which the final pattern is reached is, of course, a part of the study of incidence, but the latter itself is the pattern or form, not the process by which the latter is reached.
3. Great Britain Treasury, *Report of the Committee on National Debt and Taxation*, London, 1927, (hereafter referred to as the *Colwyn Report*), pp.106-108.
4. Silverman, H.A., *Taxation, Its Incidence and Effects*, London, 1931, pp. 3-4.
5. Formally, a tax levied as a percentage of gross revenue and one levied as a percentage of sale price of goods sold are identical.
6. In England the term *imperfect competition*, as introduced by Joan Robinson, is most commonly accepted. The history of the theory of monopolistic competition is becoming too well known to require special treatment at this point. The beginnings of the analysis are to be found in the work by J.M. Clark, *Economics of Overhead Costs*, Chicago, 1923. This was to a great extent ignored by economic theorists, and the more recent analysis had its genesis in the controversy in the 1920's over the explanation of the existence of decreasing cost conditions in the individual firm. (Note Robertson, D.H., Sraffa, P., and Shove, G.F., "Increasing Returns and the Representative Firm," *Economic Journal*, 40:78-116, March, 1930, for bibliography and summary of the dispute.) The article in this discussion of chief significance for the developments to follow was that by P. Sraffa, "The Laws of Returns Under Competitive Conditions," *Economic Journal*, 36:535-550, December, 1926. Then, shortly after 1930, two books appeared almost simultaneously, one by Edward Chamberlin, *The Theory of Monopolistic Competition*, Cambridge, 1936 (revised), and the work of Joan Robinson, *The Economics of Imperfect Competition*, London, 1933. The latter is essentially an analysis of the individual firm with the use of the marginal analysis and provides little attention to monopolistic competition in the sense of a sphere characterized by both monopolistic and competitive conditions. Since that time numerous articles have appeared; in the Revised Edition of the *Theory of Monopolistic Competition* (1936), Chamberlin gives an extensive list (pp.211-219), and it is unnecessary to repeat them here. Some of the more important articles appearing since 1936 include: Bronfenbrenner, M., "Applications of the Discontinuous Oligopoly Demand Curve," *Journal of Political Economy*, 48:420-433, June, 1940; Cassels, J.M., "Excess Capacity and Monopolistic Competition," *Quarterly Journal of Economics*, 51:426-443, May, 1937; Chamberlin, E.H., "Monopolistic or Imperfect Competition," *Quarterly Journal of Economics*, 51:557-580, August, 1937; Clark, J.M., "Toward A Concept of Workable Competition," *American Economic Review*, 30:241-256, June, 1940; Copeland, M.A., "Competing Products and Monopolistic Competition," *Quarterly Journal of Economics*, 55:1-35, November, 1940; Higgins, Benjamin, "Elements of Indeterminacy in the Theory of Non Perfect Competition," *American Economic Review*, 29:468-479, September, 1939; Kaldor, Nicholas, "Professor Chamberlin on Monopolistic and Imperfect Competition," *Quarterly Journal of Economics*, 52:513-529, May, 1938, and "Reply," by E.H. Chamberlin, pp.530-538; Machlup, F., "Theory of

Monopolistic Competition," *American Economic Review*, 29:227-236, June 1939; Machlup, F., "Monopoly and Competition, a Classification," *American Economic Review*, 27:445-451, September 1937; Robinson, E.A.G., "Monopolistic and Imperfect Competition," *Economic Journal*, 47:169-172, March 1937; Smithies, A., "Equilibrium in Monopolistic Competition," *Quarterly Journal of Economics*, 55:95-115, November 1940; Sweezy, P.M., "Demand Under Conditions of Oligopoly," *Journal of Political Economy*, 41:560-573, August 1939; and Sweezy, P.M., "On the Definition of Monopoly," *Quarterly Journal of Economics*, 51:362-363, February 1937. See also Triffin, Robert, *Monopolistic Competition and General Equilibrium Theory*, Cambridge, 1940.

A very good summary of the theory of value restated in terms of the influence of the work of the above writers is to be found in Meyers, A.L., *Elements of Modern Economics*, New York, 1937, pp.9-162.

7. The value analysis is supplemented by a partial restatement of the problem of distribution, especially by Robinson, *Imperfect Competition*, *op. cit.*, Books VII, VIII, IX. This part of the theory is excluded from the discussion in this study.
8. For the development of this tool, see Robinson, *Imperfect Competition*, *op. cit.*, p.iv.
9. The terms "pure" and "monopolistic" are used in preference to "perfect" and "imperfect" as best signifying the essential elements in the two cases. In this study, the concept of perfection of competition, in contrast to that of pureness, concerns the presence or absence of such factors as complete knowledge, motivation by the desire for highest gain, etc.
10. It must be recognized that there is not one but a series of short run curves, depending on the time elapsed. For simplification of analysis, the intermediate curves will be ignored.
11. The marginal of the total cost curve in this case is the same as that of the prime cost curve, as additions to prime cost and additions to total cost incurred because of increases in output are obviously identical.

    Average cost curves are always intersected by their respective marginal curves at their lowest points. As long and only as long as additional units of output cause an increase in total cost less than the average cost of the preceding unit, the average cost curve must continue to fall.
12. Technically, this statement is not strictly correct, as the points of tangency of the long run curve and the short period curves on which it is based cannot be at the low point of the latter except where the former is horizontal. The statement as given, however, is sufficiently accurate for the purposes of this study.
13. Thus essentially from non-divisibility of certain factors such as specialized management, utilization of by-products, utilization of certain types of machines, etc.
14. The long run average cost curve on Chart 1 is LRAC.
15. It would appear that some firms will be operating at lower average cost than others because of special ability in management or other factors. However, if the payments to these factors are considered as cost, as they must be under competition, the minimum points of all cost curves are located at the same cost level.
16. It must be emphasized that the cost conditions of the industry are distinct from those of the individual firms. The firms can never operate under decreasing cost conditions in pure competition; the industry as a whole, however, may operate under such conditions if increase in total

output of the entire industry lowers the cost curves of the individual firms. The individual firms cannot gain these latter economies by their own individual expansion.

17. The exact nature of pure competition is indicated on page 7.
18. The concept of a supply curve under decreasing cost conditions is not entirely clear; it is used here in the usual fashion, the author recognizing, however, that there are serious difficulties in the concept. With such conditions, the cost curve is the industry supply curve only in the sense that it indicates the amounts that can be supplied at each price with average cost of the firms just equalling that price.
19. This will be the case only when (1) the number of producers in the field is large, (2) the products of each firm are identical. One of the best examples is wheat production.
20. The actual location of the cost curve, under increasing or decreasing conditions for the industry, depends on the total output of the industry at equilibrium.
21. Chamberlin (*Monopolistic Competition*, *op. cit.*, p. 9) restricts the term "monopolistic competition" to situations of differentiation, considering oligopoly as a separate category. In this study, the former term is defined more broadly to include the latter also.
22. That is, that a change in the price charged by the firm does not cause the demand schedule to shift because of changes in price of other firms caused by the first change. A change in price will, of course, cause sales to change.
23. Thus, the firm and the industry are identical.
24. This has been stressed by Triffin, *Monopolistic Competition*, *op. cit.*
25. This does not mean that profits must always come to a normal level in monopolistic competition. Some writers, for example E. A. G. Robinson ("Monopolistic and Imperfect Competition," *op. cit.*, *Economic Journal*, 47:169-172), have confined the term monopolistic or imperfect competition to the situation where all excess profits are eliminated. Because of the unlikelihood of this occurring where reputation is established, where no one producer can get quite close enough to those making excess profits to eliminate all of the latter, to so define the concept would lessen its significance for purposes of analysis. The condition where all excess profits are eliminated is convenient for purposes of exposition, but is not considered the necessary criterion of monopolistic competition.
26. The preceding analysis applies also to the situation considered by traditional monopoly analysis, the action of the firm being regarded as independent of any competition whatsoever.
27. Assuming that the cost conditions would be the same, and that each interprets the demand curve just as a single producer would.
28. Only in this situation will profits be normal.
29. By the term *excess profits* is meant a rate of profits greater than the average return earned in all industries, or in other words, a rate that would draw new firms into this industry provided they can enter.
30. Under some conditions, especially where the advertising cost curve rises from the initial point, it may be unprofitable to advertise at all. The assumption of a declining portion of the curve is not essential to the analysis.
31. A new combined cost curve could also be drawn; for every price there is an optimum selling cost, so for each price the amount supplied must be such that the excess of the selling price

over production cost equals the selling cost optimum for that price. This, however, is unnecessary for purposes of analysis. The analysis in the section above is based on an article of Smith, H., "Advertising Costs and Equilibrium," *Review of Economic Studies*, 2:62-65, Oct. 1934.

32. It should be noted that the existence of selling costs may provide a means of eliminating excess profits as firms spend more and more on advertising; also, on the other hand, advertising may be a factor leading to the genesis of excess profits, in that it aids in the establishment of a reputation for a product which can be broken down by other firms only with difficulty.
33. See Galbraith, J.K., "Monopoly and Price Rigidities," *Quarterly Journal of Economics*, 50:456-475, May, 1936, and Burns, A.R., *Decline of Competition*, New York, 1936, Chapter 5.
34. For discrimination to persist, there must be some sort of a barrier, natural or artificial, between the parts of the market, preventing resale of products or interchange of buyers between parts.
35. See Chart 12.
36. This method of pricing is particularly important in retailing.

CHAPTER II

1. The most thorough analysis is to be found in Brown, H.G., *The Economics of Taxation*, New York, 1924, pp.53-96. See also Seligman, *Incidence*, *op. cit.*, pp.217-255, 339-342, 355-357; Silverman, H.A., *Taxation, Its Incidence and Effects*, *op. cit.*, pp. 91-110, 116-120; *Colwyn Report*, *op. cit.*, pp.209-232; Buehler, A.G., *General Sales Taxation*, New York, 1932, pp.173-178; Buehler, A.G., *Public Finance*, New York, 1936, pp. 229-239, 245-248; Bastable, C.F., *Public Finance*, London, 1917, pp.372-377; Dalton, H., *Principles of Public Finance*, 9th ed., London, 1936, pp. 51-58, 64-70, 72-78; Lutz, H.L., *Public Finance*, New York, 1936, pp. 386-390; Plehn, C.C., *Introduction to Public Finance*, 5th ed., New York, 1926, pp.320-327; Shirras, G.F., *Science of Public Finance*, London, 1936, vol.1, pp.349-354; Shultz, W.J., *American Public Finance and Taxation*, New York, 1931, pp.281-293, 377-379; Robinson, M.E., *Public Finance*, Cambridge, 1922, pp.92-94; Jensen, J.P., *Government Finance*, New York, 1937, pp.186-192.
2. Since this study was completed (April, 1939), one book (Meyers, A.L., *Modern Economic Problems*, New York, 1939,) has appeared which in brief fashion makes use of the individual firm analysis for tax incidence. (Note especially pp.36-53).
3. For purposes of simplification of the analysis, it is assumed in this and the two following chapters that the products are sold by the producer directly to final consumers. In the chapter on retail sales taxes, attention will be given to the problems of the significance of vertical price relationships for incidence. In general, changes in costs of distributors as volume falls and shifts in the degree of competition in these lines will affect the margin between prices at the production level and the retail price. Part of the burden passing off of the producer may be absorbed in excess profits or returns to specialized factors in the distribution units, or additional burden may pass onto the consumer as a result of increase in distribution margins. Any change in the margin will, of course, affect the total sales decline and in turn produce further change in production cost.
4. Actually, something more than average variable cost must be earned, if the plant has any salvage value, either by junking or by converting directly to other uses. If an alternate use of

equal productivity to the original is available, the plant must earn almost the entire fixed cost or it will be turned to the other use. In this case, the short run industry supply curve is of almost as great elasticity, below the old price, as the long run curve.

5. The industry supply curve is the summation of the supply curves of the individual firms; the latter curves are based on the portions of the marginal cost curves of the firms above the average variable cost curves.
6. Regardless of the long run cost conditions of the industry, the short run cost curve under pure competition always slopes upward from left to right. That is, at lower prices, less will be supplied in the short run, although the reduction will not be great so long as the price covers variable cost of the firms. More will be supplied than in the long run at the same prices, since only variable costs need be covered in the former, while all cost must be met in the longer period if the supply is to continue to come forth.
7. One of the most common examples of confusion in the usual treatment of incidence under pure competition is the failure to recognize that price increases in such conditions cannot be made at the will of the firms. A few writers have been careful to stress the fact that the imposition of the tax cannot increase price until supply has been reduced. For example, note Brown, *Taxation*, *op. cit.*, pp. 83-84; Buehler, *Public Finance*, *op. cit.*, p. 235; Plehn, *Public Finance*, *op. cit.*, p. 231. But in many cases the essential nature of the price-determining process under competition is ignored; it is assumed that producers in such circumstances possess some power over price determination, and can thus effect immediate shifting, in part at least. A few illustrations serve to indicate the confusion. Silverman (*Taxation*, *op. cit.*, p. 109), states:

> Should the tax (per unit of output) be of small amount, however, the more profitable concerns (in competitive conditions) may decide to bear the amount themselves, in which event the marginal firms may be driven out of existence.

Even worse is Shultz (*Public Finance*, *op. cit.*, p. 284):

> If a tax proportional to the price of a commodity is based on its production or sale, the initial tendency of the producers or dealers of that commodity will be to add the amount of the tax to the prices they originally charged for the commodity. Since all producers or dealers are called on to pay the tax, there will be no competitive factor to check this tendency to add the tax to the price of the commodity and so to shift it.

Perhaps under certain conditions, but not those of pure competition, which the author is supposedly talking about, would this be true.

Dalton slips in a similar manner (*Public Finance*, *op. cit.*, p. 54):

> For, the more elastic the demand, the more the demand will fall off, as a result of a given rise in the price of the object, and the less therefore will it be worthwhile for sellers to raise the price.

Lutz also confuses the demand curve for an individual firm with that for an industry in indicating that where demand is elastic, sellers under conditions of competition will not find it profitable to raise prices (*Public Finance*, p. 386).

Plehn, on the very same page on which he indicates that sellers cannot add to the price at will, says, as far as a tax on candy, produced competitively, is concerned, that the initial reaction will be for all producers to raise prices, the lessened demand then resulting in failure of the marginal firms (*Public Finance, op. cit.*, p.321). Finally, M E Robinson indicates that sellers in competition often will not raise prices when a tax is imposed, because to do so would cause them to suffer still greater losses in profits from reduced demand (*Public Finance, op cit* , p. 92)

Actually, under conditions of pure competition, no seller could gain anything by failing to raise his prices as the market level rose; since his market is unlimited at the market price, and no one could take the initiative in raising prices without losing his entire volume of sales. It is an essential feature of pure competition that each is producing so small a part of total output that he cannot affect price in any manner by his own action, no amount of desire on the part of producers to get higher prices will enable them actually to realize greater receipts.

8. Thus, the short run supply curve can be considered as a straight vertical line. Where sellers are not entirely rational, or lack information, the supply curve is not necessarily identical with the cost curve.
9. If the firm does not leave the industry, operation will be carried on at the optimum again when a new permanent equilibrium is reached. If capacity has been reduced, it must be restored back to the old level (assuming constant technological conditions).
10. The only reason that there is a difference between long run and short run is because some or all factors are not completely mobile.
11. The larger the ratio of mobile to immobile factors, the higher the percentage of variable to total cost, and the greater the likelihood of rapid attainment of final readjustment.
12. The traditional analysis of incidence usually gives brief mention to short run incidence, the writers recognizing that the immediate incidence is not necessarily the same as the final. They point out that, in general, less is shifted immediately because of the relative inelasticity of supply, produced by immobility of certain factors, especially invested capital, in a short period of time. Thus the initial effect would be a reduction in return to those factors which are least mobile. Eventually, as capital wears out, and skilled labor shifts, full price increase will occur. Note Brown, *Taxation, op. cit.*, pp. 81-86. In August 1939, Fagan and Jastram, in an article entitled "Tax Shifting in the Short Run," *Quarterly Journal of Economics*, 53 562-576, provided the first careful treatment of the problem to appear in print.
13. As time passes with a given plant, more and more of the costs become variable and thus the average variable cost curve rises.
14. If dynamic elements are considered, it will be seen that economic obsolescence from technological change intensifies the difference between old and new plants.
15. The traditional concept of the "marginal" firm leaving the field is inadequate as it emphasizes that the ones whose average cost, exclusive of profits, including in the latter wages for specially capable management, is highest are those which go out first. This approach stresses only one "compressible" return, ignoring the fact that under certain circumstances the other shares which are part of long run cost can likewise be reduced. Thus the possibility that the firm making particularly great use of specialized factors, while having high average cost exclusive of profits

initially, experiences a considerable cost reduction as the demand for the specialized factors fall, is neglected. Also, the firms having high fixed cost will remain longer, because these fixed costs can be compressed, whereas variable costs per unit of output can be reduced much less easily. By including profits from special management ability with the costs, similar treatment is given to all compressible items.

16. Attention must be called again to the fact that Chart 2 is based on the assumption of a constant cost industry.
17. The traditional analysis of the problem indicates that the tax represents an addition to cost and accordingly must force prices up in general by the amount of the tax, or the supply will disappear. Note references at the beginning of the chapter.
18. That is, to individuals in their capacities as consumers rather than as producers. The two groups, of course, are not distinct, but are in general composed of the same persons; nevertheless in some cases persons bear taxes because of their activity as producers, in other cases because of their activity as consumers; the allocation of burden as between individuals, and the reaction of the latter to the burdens, will differ in the two cases.
19. It is questionable whether decreasing cost from external economies is of much general significance. Nevertheless the possibility exists. It must be emphasized that a fall in cost from technological developments represents not a characteristic feature of a supply curve, but the movement of a curve over time. If a machine which will lower cost is available, it is within the power of the individual firms under pure competition, with unlimited markets, to gain advantage of it. External economies could be due to technological factors only when, in subsidiary industries not operating in pure competition, larger output would allow use of improved techniques.
20. Seligman, *Incidence*, *op. cit.*, pp. 233-248, by considering differential advantages of producers as something apart from the case of increasing cost conditions, introduces a useless and confusing division.
21. A smaller number of firms will leave the field than under other cost conditions. Under decreasing cost conditions, the number of firms leaving the field would be the greatest.
22. The various writers mentioned at the beginning of the chapter take into consideration the manner in which modifications in cost from output reduction influences the final price rise. (Note especially Brown, *Taxation*, *op. cit.*, pp.59-94, and Jensen, *Government Finance*, *op. cit.*, pp.186-188). The analyses, however, run almost entirely in terms of industries, without reference to individual firms. The conclusions as to constant cost and increasing cost conditions are the same as those indicated above. In the case of the latter, it is pointed out that the marginal or high cost firms are those which are forced out, the production remaining in the hands of firms possessing special ability to turn out goods at lower cost, either because of special capacities of management or possession of specialized resources of superior quality. In the case of decreasing cost, the treatment is very unsatisfactory. The conclusion usually reached is that indicated above, that price will rise by more than the tax because of higher production cost at reduced volume of output. However, the analysis by which the conclusion is attained in most cases fails to recognize the fact that with pure competition, firms cannot be operating under conditions of decreasing

cost produced by internal economies. For example, W.J.Shultz, in *American Public Finance*, (*op. cit.*, pp.280-281), indicates:

> If the taxed commodity is produced (under competitive conditions) at decreasing cost, as is the case with most standardized machine-made commodities when large output permits economies of production and distribution by the individual producers, the reduction in output (from higher prices) will cause the reduced supply to be placed on the market at a higher cost per unit than the original supply, ...

Likewise, Lutz indicates that as output declines in decreasing cost industries, less internal and external economies can be utilized. (*Public Finance*, *op. cit.*, p.390). He points out further that the determining influence on price on the cost side, under decreasing cost conditions, is the most capable and efficient producer, rather than the least efficient one as under increasing cost situations, and implies, although he does not say, that a tax under such conditions raises price by more than the amount of the tax by driving out the most efficient producer and leaving the market to be supplied by the less efficient ones.

Seligman recognizes that the condition of decreasing cost from internal economies is unstable in competition, and deals with it as a transitory phenomenon. However, he ignores the case of external economies, and confuses the whole problem by introducing dynamic considerations into an analysis in which they will not fit. (*Incidence*, *op. cit.*, pp.240-247.)

Brown is aware of the internal-external distinction, but apparently considers the latter of little importance. (*Taxation*, *op. cit.*, pp. 86-95.) One of the few clear discussions is the brief analysis in Marshall. (*Principles of Economics*, 8th ed., London, 1923, p.469.) Some of the recent text writers avoid entangling themselves in the difficulty by merely talking of decreasing cost in general without explaining why it exists. (See Jensen, *Government Finance*, *op. cit.*, pp.186-188; Buehler, *Public Finance*, *op. cit.*, p. 246.) Meyers, (*Economic Problems*, *op. cit.*), who never makes use of the concept of an industry of decreasing cost in pure competition, does not treat the problem at all.

23. In regard to this problem, it must be noted that elasticity is likely to be different in the long run than in the period immediately after the imposition of the tax. The latter may lead to a change in tastes over a period of time, in that the higher prices in this line may encourage development of new substitute products. In this case long run elasticity would be greater than that in the short run.

24. With the exception of that in Dalton's 9th edition, all treatments of incidence which deal with the effect of different elasticities generalize the rule that the more elastic the demand the less that will be shifted. Dalton (*Public Finance*, *op. cit.*,) accepts the generalized rule (pp.53-54); then in the mathematical note (p.78) he qualifies it as far as decreasing cost conditions are concerned. For the usual position note Seligman, *Incidence*, *op. cit.*, pp.229-232; Silverman, *Taxation*, *op. cit.*, pp.102-103; Buehler, *Public Finance*, *op. cit.*, p.235.

25. The significance of shifts in demand for incidence is developed by Kendrick, M.S., *Taxation Issues*, New York, 1933, pp.122-129. See also Black, D., *The Incidence of Income Taxes*, London, 1939, pp.134-156.

26. This problem is considered in detail in subsequent sections.

27. The problem of incidence is treated by one writer, Antonio De Viti De Marco (*First Principles of Public Finance*, New York, translation, 1936, pp. 141-165) entirely in terms of demand. In the first place he assumes away the problem of the effect of a sales tax on cost of production by maintaining that any price increase resulting from the tax does not involve tax shifting at all, since no economic forces are involved. Instead, the process represents merely advancement of the tax by the manufacturer for the consumer onto whom the levy is passed directly (p. 160). This, of course, involves very peculiar definitions of both shifting and incidence and economic forces. He discusses incidence solely in terms of demand changes. He points out that the state spends the tax money for different articles than the tax payers would have; accordingly shifts in demand occur, affecting prices, and distributing burdens accordingly. The treatment, in general, is extremely unsatisfactory; he implicitly defines incidence in the early part of the chapter in the usual fashion, but in the analysis uses the term to refer solely to price changes resulting immediately from shifts in demand. He fails to explain the manner in which the burden is finally distributed, despite the fact that he sets this out as the problem requiring solution. Any attempt to do this without considering the influence of cost changes, both those resulting immediately from the tax, and those produced by the demand shifts, cannot hope to succeed, since these elements play a fundamental part in determining the groups upon whom the tax finally rests.

28. When subsidiary industries are subject to monopoly conditions, the use of technological methods in these fields will be affected by output change in the industry in question.

29. It is the possibility of variation in prices of specialized factors which is one of the elements allowing cost reductions at reduced output under increasing cost conditions. The distinction between specialized and general factors is, of course, somewhat arbitrary, but is useful for purposes of analysis. Any declines in prices of the general factors could be considered as elements making for increasing cost conditions.

30. The spending of the tax money by the government does not restore output and employment to the original level; this spending merely replaces the spending that would otherwise have been done by those now suffering reduced purchasing power because of the existence of the tax. The check on employment caused by the cost increase remains. There may be, of course, a change in average propensity to consume; this will be considered below.

31. The possibility of changes in factor prices resulting from the tax has for the most part been ignored, despite the fact that in terms of orthodox value analysis the incidence would be modified significantly by changes along these lines. This problem was considered by Brown in his *Economics of Taxation*, (*op. cit.*, pp. 62-67), and in an article appearing just after this study was originally completed ("The Incidence of a General Output or a General Sales Tax," *Journal of Political Economy*, 47:254-262, April, 1939), he gives careful treatment to the problem; the conclusions are substantially the same as those indicated in the above section. The problem has been under consideration for some time also by Professor Earl Rolph of the University of California.

32. The problem of the relation of changes in money wages to the volume of employment has received extensive treatment in recent years. Note especially Keynes, *General Theory, op. cit.*, pp. 257-279; Champernowne, D.G., "Unemployment, Basic and Monetary: the Classical Analysis and the Keynesian," *Review of Economic Studies*, 3:201-216, June, 1936; Von Habeler, Gottfried, *Prosperity and Depression*, Geneva, 1937, pp. 292-301; Pigou, A.C., "Real and Money Wage Rates in Relation to Unemployment," *Economic Journal*, 47:405-422, Sept., 1937, and "Money Wages in Relation to Unemployment," *Economic Journal*, 48:134-138, Mar., 1938.
33. See Keynes, *General Theory, op. cit.*, pp. 175-193.
34. In brief, the interest rate is determined by the relation of the supply of money, broadly defined to include demand deposits, to the demand for money for purposes of carrying on business transactions and for purposes of liquidity. The latter involves the desire to be in a position to take advantage of expected future interest rate changes. The demand schedule is of normal nature, more being desired at lower rates than at higher, since with the former, less loss in returns is suffered as a result of holding cash and there is greater likelihood of interest rate increases in the future. The supply is more or less fixed at any time; the interaction of the two determines the interest rate. If the interest rate is too high, people will not wish to hold all the money in existence; in attempting to get it out of their hands, they will buy bonds and other securities. Bond prices will rise, and thus the current interest rate will fall. If the rate temporarily is too low, the attempt of people to exchange securities for cash will cause a fall in security prices and thus a rise in the rate of interest. The rate thus determined is subject to one limitation: given the demand for money to hold, the supply of money must not be greater than that to allow an interest rate equal to marginal productivity of capital with the amount of savings that is available with full employment of resources; otherwise price inflation will occur. See Keynes, *General Theory, op. cit.*, pp. 165-244, and Curtis, M., and Townshend, H., *Modern Money*, New York, 1938, pp. 132-173.
35. Some writers have considered also the possibility of long run changes in supply prices of the factors arising out of the effect of commodity price increases upon the supply of the factors. In particular, those in the English classical tradition maintained that at least part of the tax falling on those consumers who were workers would pass on to nonlabor classes. The higher prices of necessities would reduce real income below subsistance, reduce the population and supply of labor, and raise wages. This position is taken by Adam Smith (*Wealth of Nations*, London, 1776, Book V, Chap. 2, Part 2, Article 4, Rogers Ed., Oxford, 1880, vol. 2, p. 467), Ricardo (*Principles of Political Economy and Taxation*, London, 1816, p. 285); and John Stuart Mill (*Principles of Political Economy*, London, 1886, Book V, Chap. 3, Ashley Ed., London, 1929, pp. 839-840).

A somewhat similar position is taken by John A. Hobson in *Taxation in the New State*, (London, 1919, Part 1, Chap. 3) as to that part of the tax which rests upon elements of income necessary to cover the cost of producing the laborer. In general, however, this thesis in rigid form has been abandoned with the decline of the subsistance law of wages. However, it is the belief of the Colwyn Committee that excises lead to some wage increases when price indices are used as a basis of wage determination in arbitration. *(Colwyn Report, op. cit.*, pp.214-217.)

Some writers, (see Dalton, *Public Finance, op. cit.*, pp.64-65), following in the lines of Adam Smith, *(Wealth of Nations, op. cit.*, Book V, Chap.2, Part 2, Article 4, vol.2, p.355, Cannan Ed., 1904), have maintained that prices will, under constant cost, rise by more than the tax, to compensate producers for the additional capital required because of the tax paid. In case of other cost conditions, following the same line of analysis, the price will be forced up by more than it would have been in the absence of this factor. This is denied in part by Seligman on the grounds that the concept is based on the doctrine of normal profits; actually, according to him, in each case there is some seller, making no profits, who will not have anything to pass on. Thus, prices will rise only by the amount of the tax. He grants the argument as to interest charges on the capital, but claims that the amount would not be significant. *(Shifting and Incidence, op. cit.*, pp.352-355.)

36. In the case of goods produced outside the country, it is assumed that a tariff is levied at rates imposing similar burden to that of the tax on domestic producers.

37. If government revenue is raised in the other areas by levies of a different nature placing comparable burden on the industry in question to that imposed by the sales tax in the home area, there will be no advantage of lower cost to the outside industries. When different means of raising revenue are used by the various government units, however, some industries will be burdened more heavily in some localities than in others, and the differential will cause the difference in cost as indicated above. The same is true when different amounts of revenue are raised.

38. Where transportation costs do exist, some production may remain in the taxed area; whether the latter occurs or not prices will be higher in the taxed area, and consumers will be paying more for the commodity despite the fact that there may be no revenue collected as a result of the tax.

39. The most complete discussion of the problem of taxation by limited jurisdictions is to be found in the National Industrial Conference Board study, *General Sales or Turnover Taxation*, New York, 1929, pp.30-38.

40. For example, production of diverse agricultural products which are planted and harvested at different seasons allows fuller utilization of capital equipment and labor.

41. In many fields, where no close calculation of costs and revenue is made, no output reduction at all will occur.

CHAPTER III

1. The sales are, of course, affected by a price adjustment, but not the location of the demand curve itself.

2. *Op. cit.*, pp.76-82. For other analyses of incidence under monopoly, see Edgeworth, F.Y., "The Pure Theory of Taxation," *Economic Journal*, 7:226-238, June, 1897; "Professor Graziani on the Mathematical Theory of Monopoly," *Economic Journal*, 8:234-239, June, 1898; "Professor Seligman on the Mathematical Method in Political Economy," *Economic Journal*, 9:286-315, June, 1899; "The Pure Theory of Monopoly," in *Papers Relating to Political Economy*, London, 1925, pp.11-142; Cournot, A., *Recherches sur les Principes Mathematiques de la Theorie des Richesses*, Paris, 1838, Chap.6 (pp. 67-78 in the translation *Mathematical Principles of the Theory of Wealth*, New York, 1927); Seligman, E.R.A., *The Shifting and Incidence of Taxation*, 2nd Edition, New York, 1899, pp.204-212, 273-292; 3rd Edition,

New York, 1910, pp. 247-248, 339-358; 5th Edition, *op. cit.*, pp. 226-228, 247-248, 342-349; 356-358; Adams, H.C., *Science of Finance*, New York, 1898, pp. 393-398; Wicksell, Knut, *Zur Lehre von der Steuerincidenz*, Upsala Universität, Dissertations, vol. 21, No. 5, 1895, pp. 10-21; Plehn, *Public Finance*, *op. cit.*, pp. 324-327; Bastable, *Public Finance*, *op. cit.*, pp. 374-375; Dalton, *Public Finance*, *op. cit.*, pp. 59-61; Silverman, *Taxation*, *op. cit.*, pp. 111-114; Shirras, *Public Finance*, *op. cit.*, pp. 324-327; Brown, *Taxation*, *op. cit.*, pp. 97-140; Jensen, *Government Finance*, *op. cit.*, pp. 189-192; Shultz, *American Public Finance*, *op. cit.*, pp. 293-295; Lutz, *Public Finance*, *op. cit.*, p. 388; Buehler, *Sales Taxation*, *op. cit.*, p. 178; *Public Finance*, *op. cit.*, p. 236; Nelson, C.L., et. al., *Sales Taxes*, Minneapolis, (League of Minnesota Municipalities), 1935, pp. 61-62.

All subsequent references to Seligman, *Incidence*, refer to the 5th edition unless otherwise indicated. Cournot's work, largely mathematical, is apparently the first dealing with the problem. This provided the basis for Edgeworth's analysis. Seligman's conclusions on the problem are quite different in the later editions of his work than in the second, as he was forced to recognize the validity of several attacks made by Edgeworth. Further references will be found in Edgeworth's articles, and in Seligman, especially as to the Italian tax writers who devoted much attention to the problem around the turn of the century. The most complete of the more recent analyses is to be found in Brown.

Meyers, in *Economic Problems*, *op. cit.*, which, as indicated, appeared after this study was completed, applies the marginal analysis to incidence under monopoly. See pp. 36-43.

3. That is, if for each unit of output increase AR falls one price unit, MR must fall two price units per unit of output. For geometric proof see Robinson, *Imperfect Competition*, *op. cit.*, p. 50.
4. Proof in terms of the areas method is to be found in Wicksell, *Steuerincidenz*, *op. cit.*, p. 17; Brown, *Taxation*, *op. cit.*, p. 105; Jensen, *Government Finance*, *op. cit.*, pp. 189-190.
5. The term "slope" is used instead of "elasticity" for greater accuracy in statement. In general, however, by the term slope is meant approximately what most writers in the field of incidence have meant by the term elasticity.
6. The problem as to whether or not incidence is the same regardless of elasticity of demand attracted much attention near the turn of the century. Seligman took the position that in the case of a more inelastic demand - one with a steeper curve - a greater part of the tax would be shifted, as there would be less reduction in sales as a result of a given price increase. (*Incidence*, *op. cit.*, pp. 346-348.) The same position was taken by Graziani, who maintained that when demand is inelastic, an increase in price will cause less loss in sales, and thus a greater net profit from the price increase than in the case of a less elastic demand; accordingly the output reduction would be carried farther in the first case. (Quoted by Edgeworth, "Mathematical Theory," *Economic Journal*, *op. cit.*, 7:228). Edgeworth denied the validity of the position, denying that the conditions which favor original elevation of the price also favor additional elevation after the tax. He maintained rather that the reverse was true: that the more inelastic the demand, the less that will be shifted. His proof is the mathematical treatment advanced by Cournot. Actually, as indicated above, under constant cost conditions the elasticity is of no significance, so long as the curves are straight lines. The source of Edge-

worth's error is not clear. In a later article in the *Economic Journal* ("Seligman on Mathematical Method," *op. cit.*, 9:313), he points to an error in his mathematical method in the "Pure Theory," and grants that under decreasing cost, greater elasticity likely involves greater ability to raise prices. But he does not reconsider constant cost conditions. Seligman, as Edgeworth pointed out, was really referring to a condition where the demand curve becomes more steep above the old price, rather than to different positions of straight line demand curves. See Seligman, *Incidence*, *op. cit.*, p.346; Edgeworth, "Seligman on Mathematical Method," *Economic Journal*, *op. cit.*, 9:307-308.

7. This situation will occur when a good is sold to two groups of buyers, a wealthy group, not influenced to any extent by price changes within ordinary limits, and a poorer group which will buy only below a certain point. For example, the demand for railway tickets, given the level of motor transportation fares, would likely be of this nature.
8. See Robinson, *Imperfect Competition*, *op. cit.*, pp.79-80. Her analysis deals with a demand curve which is concave throughout, but the result is substantially similar to that reached here.
9. For a somewhat similar analysis, see Brown, *Taxation*, *op. cit.*, pp.98-99.
10. See Robinson, *Imperfect Competition*, *op. cit.*, p.81. This problem of whether or not a situation can arise in which there will be no shifting of the tax per unit of output was disputed by Seligman and Edgeworth some years ago. Edgeworth, following Cournot, maintained and demonstrated mathematically that the only cases where shifting would be absent were those in which the monopolist could not change the volume of his output, and where the monopolist is a sole buyer and the supply of the article bought is fixed. See "Pure Theory," *Economic Journal*, *op. cit.*, 8:237. The argument is based on an assumption of a straight line demand curve, and is valid for this condition. Seligman took the position, assuming a change in elasticity, that occasions would arise where there would be no shifting since any price rise would lead to a great reduction in sales. (*Incidence*, *op. cit.*, p.345.) See also Brown, *Taxation*, *op. cit.*, pp.97-98. Wicksell took the same position as Edgeworth (*Steuerincidenz*, *op. cit.*, p.11).
11. That is, at the point of maximum profits, marginal cost is declining.
12. That is, because of the ability to produce at lowest cost.
13. Brown, (*Taxation*, *op. cit.*, p.129) reaches the same conclusion, but explains the result in different terms: "Expressing the matter in other words, we may say that a monopoly is more likely to raise its price or is likely to raise it farther because of a tax proportional to output if it produces under conditions of decreasing than if it produces under conditions of constant cost. For by raising its price it gains as much on each unit of business still done as if it operated under conditions of constant cost; while its loss on the business cut off is less since the cost of this business (except for the marginal unit or units) is greater than in the case of constant cost."

    H.C.Adams (*Finance*, *op. cit.*, p.398) reaches exactly the opposite conclusion:

    > To express this in another way, such an industry (of increasing returns) will not only suffer in the reduction of sales should it add the tax to the price, but by virtue of its reduced sales, will also suffer in the reduction of the rate of profit upon such

sales as it retains. This being the case, an industry administered under the law of increasing returns is less able to throw off the tax imposed upon it than an ordinary legal monopoly (that is, one of increasing or constant cost, not regulated as to rates).

It is true, of course, that under decreasing cost, as output is reduced, there is more loss to the monopolist (compared with the situation where no output reduction was necessary) than if costs were constant, but it does not follow from this that output will not be reduced as far. As long as MR is below MC, output will be lowered, and this process must go farther, with a greater price rise, when MC is rising (at smaller outputs) than when it is constant. If output were not reduced as far, losses would be still greater. Seligman, in his 1899 edition, maintained, as Adams, that under decreasing cost, less would be shifted than under constant cost. *(Incidence*, 2nd edition, *op. cit.*, pp. 202-212.) The reasoning is similar to that of Adams, but is more lengthy, and graphic proof is advanced. The error in his reasoning was pointed out by Edgeworth ("Seligman on the Mathematical Method," *Economic Journal, op. cit.*, 9:293-302), who showed that he had assumed that under all cost conditions, that with a given price, the total costs would be the same before the tax, an obvious impossibility. In the third and subsequent editions, Seligman acknowledges the error in a footnote (3rd edition, *op. cit.*, p. 247n). His explanation of the validity of the Edgeworth proposition is not very satisfactory:

> In the case of monopoly there is indeed no marginal producer, but the influence of diminishing and increasing returns is apt to be similar to that in the case of competition. For if a monopolized article is the product of an industry which obeys the law of increasing returns, ... then as compared with an industry subject to the law of constant returns, the price of the article before the imposition of the tax will be apt to be lower, if the total cost remains the same. That is, other things being equal, the point of maximum monopoly revenue will be reached at a lower price (which means a greater output) in the case of an industry of increasing return than is the one of constant return. But if the price before the imposition of the tax is less, it follows that, after the tax is imposed and given the same degree of elasticity in both cases, the monopolist under conditions of increasing return will have more of a margin within which he can profitably raise the price than under conditions of constant return. The tendency will thus be that, as in the case of competition, he will add more of the tax to the price. *(Incidence, op. cit.*, p. 247.)

To say the least, this is not very enlightening.

Edgeworth provides brief mathematical treatment in *The Pure Theory of Taxation*, *(Economic Journal, op. cit.*, 7:237), and reaches the conclusion accepted above. His explanation in non-mathematical terms *(ibid.* 237n) is very difficult to understand. Edgeworth's conclusion is accepted by Shirras, *Public Finance*, *op. cit.*, p. 356, and Bastable, *Public Finance*, *op. cit.*, p. 375, but without any complete explanation.

14. For more elaborate geometric proof, see Robinson, *Imperfect Competition*, *op. cit.*, p. 78. With such a cost curve, under pure competition, price would rise by twice the tax, as

equilibrium would be reached only after twice as great an output reduction as under constant cost, and thus twice as great a price increase.

15. Actually, where this relation does exist, equilibrium will be reached on the increasing cost portion of the cost curve. An equilibrium is inevitable somewhere so long as MR is above MC, as the cost curve must eventually turn up, while the demand curve must approach the X axis.

16. Note Wicksell:

> The growth or decline of net profits in the immediate neighborhood of the theoretically most advantageous selling price is very small. This feature is common to all real maximization, ... It is therefore largely a matter of indifference to the monopolist whether his price is a little above or a little below that which is theoretically the best - however important the matter may be to the consumer. *Lectures on Political Economy*, translation, New York, 1934, vol. I, p. 96.

17. Under decreasing or increasing cost, the average cost of the greatest amount which can be sold with price covering average cost: where AR and AC intersect.

18. This chart is based on that given by Robinson, *Imperfect Competition*, *op. cit.*, p. 183.

CHAPTER IV

1. This problem has been almost entirely neglected up to the present time. Nothing more than a few very brief suggestions as to the effect of monopolistic competition on incidence and a few references to the need for exploring this field are to be found. R.M. Haig, in the article on taxation in the *Encyclopedia of Social Sciences* points out the need for extension of the theory of incidence:

> Pure monopoly and free competition are not often encountered in modern business life. . . . The discussions of shifting and incidence in the literature of Public Finance have only slightly been affected by the recent work of economists in the field of prices. It even seems doubtful whether the implications of the writings of Alfred Marshall have been given the consideration they deserve. The studies of supply and demand curves by statisticians, such as Ezekiel and Shultz, the conception of the bulkline producer developed by Taussig and Secrist, the importance of overhead costs as a factor in price determination emphasized in the writings of J.M. Clark, and the new studies of imperfect and monopolistic competition are full of suggestions for the student of public finance. (New York, 1934, vol. 14, p. 537.)

In the pamphlet entitled, "Sales Taxes," published by the League of Minnesota Municipalities, brief treatment of the problem, with no analysis of the means by which the conclusions are reached, is presented:

> More common than either perfect competition or complete monopoly is the situation where several large producers control the market. This partial monopoly, or monopolistic competition, has only recently been the subject of extended analysis. Although there are various situations, generally the price increase will be somewhat less than under monopoly. The greater the number of producers in the market, the more will the changes approximate those which occur under competition. *(Sales Taxes, op. cit.*, p. 62.)

E.D. Fagan stresses more strongly the inadequacy of present incidence theory:

> This assumption (of free competition) must be abandoned or significantly modified if our conclusions are to be of value as guides to fiscal policy. One must include both the competitive and non-competitive elements affecting the particular as well as the general supply and demand schedules. This cannot be done satisfactorily by shifting from the assumption of free competition to that of pure monopoly. ("Tax Shifting and the Laws of Cost," *Quarterly Journal of Economics*, 47:690.

In this article, rather than attempting to develop any theoretical analysis, Fagan concludes:

> Conclusions applicable to policy can be deduced only from a realistic study of the forces which determine the elasticity of demand and of supply in the actual market to which they really belong. *(Ibid.)*

In an article appearing in the August, 1939, *Quarterly Journal of Economics*, ("Tax Shifting in the Short Run," *op. cit.*, 153:576-589), Fagan, in conjunction with Roy Jastram, considered the problem in some detail, but only for short run incidence.

Meyers, in *Modern Economic Problems*, (*op. cit.*, pp.44-50) treats the problem briefly; the essential part of his discussion is to be found in the following paragraph (p.47):

> A tax per unit of output on the firms operating in an industry under conditions of monopolistic competition constitutes an addition to marginal cost. Here again, however, we must consider the most likely changes in demand as well as the change in cost, so that the analysis that we made for this type of tax on perfect monopoly is no longer applicable. All we can say definitely is that because the individual firm's demand curves will be shifted somewhat (as all firms attempt to raise prices to shift the tax), the proportion of the tax shifted will tend to be somewhat greater than it would be in the case of a perfect monopoly. We cannot assume, however, that each firm's demand curve will be shifted by the amount of the tax, particularly if the competing products sold at different prices before the tax was imposed.

Likewise Dalton, Bastable, and Buehler indicate the need for modifying the theory of incidence in the light of conditions characterized by the presence of elements of both monopoly and competition. In "Public Finance," Dalton points out:

> The argument of the preceding chapter regarding the incidence of taxes on a monopolist must be applied with discretion to practical problems. In reality, perfect competition is rare, and perfect monopoly is still rarer. Some element of monopoly enters into the determination of nearly all prices, and fear of competition, actual or potential, actuates nearly all apparent monopolists. Price may be influenced by the exercise of monopoly price as soon as a single seller, or group of sellers acting in combination, controls a considerable proportion of the commodity to be sold. But where monopoly power exists, though we may assume that it is seldom neglected, yet it is not always fully exercised. *(Public Finance, op. cit.*, p.67.)

In his "Public Finance," Bastable states:

> But the theoretical concept of a pure monopoly is of little direct service in dealing with the question of incidence; for in very few cases is a monopoly strictly so called to be found. There is in truth rather a number of limited or qualified monopolies, arising in part from natural, in

part from legal limitations. Both monopoly and competition have to be considered, and in particular the interaction of these opposed conditions, as well as the effect of financial change, in readjusting these areas. (*Public Finance, op. cit.*, p. 375.)

Finally, Buehler, in *General Sales Taxation:*

The problem here would be greatly simplified if every case could be treated as one where free and unrestricted competition or complete monopoly prevailed, but unfortunately the conditions of conducting business are subject to varying degrees of competition and monopoly. For the sake of our theoretical discussion, it may be assumed, however, that either free competition or complete monopoly prevail. (*Op. cit.*, p. 178.)

And in his more recent *Public Finance:*

In the business world competition is seldom free and monopolies are seldom absolute, but there exists a regulated competition, which may be a mixture of competition and monopoly. Because there are all degrees of competition and monopoly, theories of tax incidence must be modified according to the conditions prevailing in each case. (*Op. cit.*, p. 236.)

2. The DD curve indicates the amounts that can be sold at each price level, provided the prices of other firms in the industry are the same as those of the firm in question. AR indicates the amounts that can be sold at the various levels assuming that the prices charged by the other firms remain unchanged at the figure at which the curve is intersected by DD.
3. It would seem as if the price rise resulting from the initial action of the firms would be to PX instead of P_n. This would be the case if the firms adjusted output to the level which would be the optimum, and then sold it at the price which could be obtained. Actually, however, under monopolistic competition the technique is characteristically that of setting the price and selling the amount that can be disposed of at that price; under such conditions the result will be as indicated. The final result will be the same; if price did go up to PX, it would be at once profitable for each firm to start cutting prices, as MR would greatly exceed MC; this would take place until price falls to the level indicated above.
4. The firm's AR curve is now AR'.
5. For detailed explanation of the relation of DD and AR, see Chamberlin, *Monopolistic Competition, op. cit.*, pp. 92-93. This is a very difficult matter to express in words.
6. Thus on Chart 13, the marginal revenue curve would be the marginal curve drawn to curve DD.
7. This is based on the analysis of significance of different slopes of demand curves presented in Chapter III.
8. Comparable to AR on Chart 13.
9. Assuming that the inflow will not reduce too greatly the strength of the oligopoly elements.
10. Provided that pure competition exists after the tax as well as before.
11. Often the plants would still be operated under new owners; the loss is borne by the old owners who lose their investment. To the extent that the old plants still operate under new owners there is less chance of price increase, and delay of establishment of a new equilibrium.
12. This is, of course, the demand curve for the product of the firm, with, at each price, the optimum sales expenditure for that price.
13. For brief reference, see Smith, H., "The Imputation of Advertising Costs," *Economic Journal*, 45:684, December, 1935, and Lerner, A.P., "Concept of

Monopoly and the Measurement of Monopoly Power," *Review of Economic Studies*, 1 173-175, June, 1934.

14. For a discussion of means of determining the size of the advertising budget, see Sandage, C.H., *Advertising Theory and Practice*, Chicago, 1936, pp.555-556.
15. There may be some burden on the consumer if the advertising has been of benefit to the latter.
16. This situation may be produced by legal limitation of entry, exclusive possession of raw material sources, reputation from advertising, etc.
17. The nature of the DD curve is the same as on Chart 13.
18. The reason for the smaller price rise under conditions discussed in this section than with pure competition can be stated somewhat differently. For each equilibrium output in the former, price exceeds that of pure competition for the same cost curve by the excess of average revenue over marginal revenue. At each successively lower output this excess lessens, since marginal revenue draws nearer average revenue. Thus after the tax the price is somewhat less above the new competitive price than before.
19. *Monopolistic Competition*, *op. cit.*, pp.52-53.
20. The effect of a tax under conditions of the special cases of duopoly developed by Cournot and Edgeworth could be analyzed; since these are essentially special cases, they will be ignored in this study.
21. That is, those enjoying excess profits. The term "marginal" is used to refer to those firms having only normal profits, and thus in a somewhat different sense than in previous chapters.
22. The technique developed in Chapter VII is applicable to the present problem. Because of the particular significance of the technique for the subject of Chapter VII, the analysis is introduced in the latter.
23. See Silverman, *Taxation*, *op. cit.*, pp.96-98.
24. That is, those costs for which no one product is responsible.
25. That is, those costs for which the product is directly responsible, in the sense that they would not be incurred if this product were not produced.
26. Thus there is no true average cost for each good.
27. In one sense this does not necessarily involve departure from marginal pricing, if the firm takes into consideration in calculating marginal revenue the secondary reactions produced by the action of the competitors in response to the firm's own action. However, general acceptance of the average pricing method tends to divert the attention of the firms from consideration of marginal revenues and marginal cost, and leads to the establishment and maintenance of prices which would not be justifiable on the latter basis.

J.M.Clark (*Overhead Costs*, *op. cit.*), provides the most complete discussion of the relation of overhead and joint costs to price. He emphasizes the attention business men give to average cost as a basis for price setting, to the attempt to allocate total cost as among products in such a way as to insure that they will all be covered. He gives specific reference to the manner in which cost accounting practices serve to check destructive competition under conditions of excess capacity, indicating:

> Another very important check (to price cutting), mentioned in an earlier chapter, is cost accounting. Within what Professor Taussig has called the "penumbra" of supply and demand, cost accounting can and does frequently govern price policy. A 'standard burden rate,' including interest on investment, is a very powerful check

on price cutting. (p.435.)

Note also pp. 64-65, 206-207, 216-257, 434-450.

The significance of average cost pricing has been emphasized by J.K. Galbraith, in "Monopoly Power and Price Rigidities," *Quarterly Journal of Economics*, 50:470-472, May, 1936.

28. See Pribram, K., *Cartel Problems*, Washington, 1935, pp. 31-34, 211; Burns, *Decline of Competition*, *op. cit.*, p. 50; Federal Trade Commission, *Open Price Trade Associations*, Washington, 1929, pp. 192-193; Bureau of Foreign and Domestic Commerce, *Trade Association Activities*, Washington, 1927, pp. 55-61.
29. The part of the tax not shifted is, of course, borne by the profit receivers.
30. Unless oligopoly elements are strengthened.
31. If new firms specializing in these non-taxed lines arise to take advantage of the higher prices, or if firms in other lines add these for the same reason, the exodus of the firms in the field will be greater and the price rise greater. The less important is the product taxed in relation to the total profit of the firm, the more significant will the offsetting factor mentioned in the context be. If a large number of the non-marginal lines are taxed, it will be of very little importance.
32. It is difficult to see how there could be any actual reduction in the price of the taxed article. Edgeworth maintained, in connection with a tax on railway tickets, that a tax on one class might cause the price of both to fall. ("Pure Theory," *Economic Journal*, *op. cit.*, 7:46; and "Mathematical Method," *Economic Journal*, *op. cit.*, 9:290-292.) It is clear that under decreasing cost conditions the price of the untaxed line would fall, but only with very peculiar asymmetry of cost and demand curves could the price of both possibly fall. There is no decrease in demand in the market sense comparable to the increased demand for the substitute, but merely a decrease in the sense that less will be taken at higher prices. This phenomenon seemingly would never lower prices no matter how steeply cost is of increasing nature. Rather, only a small part of the tax will be added to price. See also Hotelling, H., "Edgeworth's Taxation Paradox and The Nature of Demand and Supply Functions," *Journal of Political Economy*, 40:577-616, October, 1932.
33. This type of reaction in itself shows the presence of oligopoly.
34. Probably by more, since the percentage figure designed to supply the profit is applied to a larger base.
35. Unless, of course, the firms run at a loss because of the excessive price increase.
36. The question may well be asked, as to why it is assumed that the business man will be sufficiently rational to drop an unprofitable line, yet follow pricing practices which do not lead to maximum profits. In the first place, as previously indicated, under a multiple line situation, average cost pricing is not so irrational, from a long run view, as it might seem, and is in fact almost inevitable. Secondly, it is very much easier to find out whether a particular line is profitable or not than to determine if the price being charged is the optimum one.
37. Unless, of course, the tax is relatively very high.
38. When demand is so elastic, despite the oligopoly elements, that average revenue increases (at smaller volumes of output) less rapidly than average cost, obviously increases of this nature will not occur; there may be no price rise at all.

APPENDIX TO CHAPTER IV

1. The conclusions, accompanied by sta-

tistical evidence, were published by the U.S.Treasury Department, Bureau of Internal Revenue, for the U.S.Department of Agriculture, Bureau of Agricultural Economics, entitled, *An Analysis of the Effects of the Processing Taxes Levied Under the Agricultural Adjustment Act*, Washington, 1937.
2. *Ibid.*, p.12.
3. *Ibid.*, p.75.
4. *Ibid.*, pp.21-22.
5. *Ibid.*, p.27.
6. *Ibid.*, p.28.
7. *Ibid.*, p.30.
8. *Ibid.*, p.39.
9. *Ibid.*, p.94.
10. *Ibid.*, p.48.
11. *Ibid.*, p.101.
12. *Ibid.*, p.56.
13. *Ibid.*, p.103.
14. *Ibid.*, p.60.
15. *Ibid.*, p.61.
16. The period of readjustment would be lengthened, if not made indefinite, by the payment of the benefits provided under the act. Where no reduction in price to basic producers occurs, the payment of the benefits could not act to increase supply and lower price, since they are paid only for acreage reduction, on the basis of quotas depending primarily on past output. See Nourse, E.G., Davis, J.S. and Black, J.D., *Three Years of the Agricultural Adjustment Act.*, Washington, 1937, pp.90-91.
17. Bureau of Agricultural Economics, *Processing Taxes*, *op. cit.*, p.5.
18. *Ibid.*, p.10.
19. *Ibid.*, p.12.
20. *Ibid.*, p.21; pp.27-28.
21. *Ibid.*, p.29.
22. *Ibid.*, pp.37-43.
23. *Ibid.*, p.54.
24. *Ibid.*, p.65.
25. *Ibid.*, p.5.
26. *Ibid.*, p.18.
27. *Ibid.*, p.32.
28. *Ibid.*, p.64.
29. *Ibid* , p.5.
30. *Ibid.*, p.5.
31. *Ibid.*, p.5.
32. *Ibid.*, pp.44-47.
33. *Ibid.*, p.6.
34. *Ibid.*, pp.6-7.
35. *Ibid.*, p.35.
36. *Ibid.*, p.9.
37. *Ibid.*, pp.18-19.

CHAPTER V

1. Brown, *Taxation*, *op. cit.*, p.135, treats the problem very briefly, concluding that under competition there is no essential difference in results as between the two types of levies. Silverman's discussion of the difference between specific and ad valorem levies (*Incidence*, *op. cit.*, pp.96-97) centers around the shifting of demand as between grades. Up to the time this study was near completion no careful analysis of the problem had been made. Then, in February, 1939, an article by D.W.Gilbert, entitled "The Shifting of Sales Taxes," appeared in *The Quarterly Journal of Economics*, (53:275-285). Gilbert makes use of the same technique of analysis as used in this study, but reaches somewhat different conclusions because of a different concept of incidence, and a different assumption as to the way in which ad valorem taxes are levied. Then in the August, 1940 issue of *The Quarterly Journal of Economics*, (54: 665-693), three short articles appeared in discussion and criticism of Gilbert's original article. These included "The Incidence of Sales Taxes," by Benjamin Higgins, "The Shifting of Sales Taxes," by R.W.Jastram, and "Ad Valorem and Specific Taxes," by the present author, in which was presented some of the analysis contained in this chapter. These were followed by a "Rejoinder" by Professor Gilbert.
2. Similar technique has been used by both Gilbert (*op. cit.*) and Fagan and

Jastram ("Tax Shifting," *Quarterly Journal of Economics*, *op. cit.*, 53: 582-585); it was developed independently by the present writer, however, in the fall of 1938, when this section was first written.

3. Note, for example, the provision in the Ohio Retail Sales tax law: "The tax collected by the vendor from the consumer under the provisions of this act shall not be considered as a part of the price. . . ." (Ohio General Code, Sec. 5564.)

   Some ad valorem taxes are imposed, however, on price or gross receipts including the tax; reference will be made to this type of levy in subsequent footnotes.
4. Not, of course, net of production cost.
5. If the tax is based on the price including the tax, the NAR curve would diverge more rapidly than in the case in hand (NAR_z on Chart 17).
6. If a specific levy were plotted in this manner, the NAR curve would be parallel to the AR curve, and their marginals would be parallel.
7. The same conclusion applies if the tax is levied on the price including the tax; on Chart 17, the tax and price are both MN.
8. With a tax levied on price including the tax, the price rise is substantially greater (with the same rate). But the amount of the tax is greater also; the incidence is the same in the two cases.

   Gilbert indicated that the price rise was greater than with a specific tax of a rate equal to the ad valorem rate times the old price, and concluded from this that there was a greater burden on the consumer from the ad valorem than from the specific levy ("Sales Taxes," *Quarterly Journal of Economics*, *op. cit.*, 53: 276-278). He ignores the fact that the revenue to the government is greater also in the former.
9. See paragraph 2 of footnote 10.
10. The price rise would be greater with the ad valorem than with the specific if the former were levied on price including the tax, since in this case the size of the base on which the rate is applied rises as the price rises because of the tax; when equilibrium is again reached, the base to which the 50% is applied is greater than the original price. (Thus on Chart 17, price, with NAR_z, rises from P to N, instead of to P', as with the specific.) This is the same conclusion as that reached by Gilbert (*op. cit.*, pp. 277-278).

    The conclusions of the comparison made in the context of this paragraph apply also, in the case of an ad valorem tax levied on price including the tax, to the question discussed in the previous paragraph of the context, as to the relative price increases in the case of the two levies imposing the same burden at the old level of output. With this type of ad valorem levy, a 50 cent specific and 50% ad valorem levy involve the same burden at the old level of output; the NAR curves cross directly below the old price.
11. With a tax levied on price including the tax, this tendency will be even more pronounced since a still greater output reduction is necessary.
12. Less than one hundred per cent.
13. This conclusion applies also with an ad valorem tax levied on price including the tax, since the same reasoning applies as in the case under consideration in the context.
14. The reason for this is that, so long as AR and AC are straight lines, the distance between them will at any level of output be the same percentage of the distance between AR and a line horizontal to the old AR-AC intersection as at any other level.
15. For an ad valorem tax applied to price including the tax, the conclusions for the comparisons being made in this

paragraph are the same as those to be found in the next paragraph below.

16. This conclusion applies also to the question of the relative increase from a specific tax and an ad valorem tax applied to the price including the tax, imposing the same burden at the old price level. For the type of comparison considered in this paragraph, the same conclusion applies for either type of ad valorem; the difference is greater in the case of the levy on price including tax.

Gilbert's conclusion differs from this; he maintains that which tax yields greater price increase depends on the elasticity of demand *(op. cit.*, pp. 281-282). Jastram ("Shifting of Sales Taxes," *Quarterly Journal of Economics, op. cit.*, 54:675-677) indicates that Gilbert's conclusion is erroneous. The source of Gilbert's error is not clear.

17. With an ad valorem levy imposed on price including the tax, the conclusion is the same. On Chart 20, compare price rise from P to P'' in the case of the ad valorem, and to P''' in the case of the specific; or from P to P' in contrast to P to P'''' with the type of ad valorem considered in the context.

18. With the ad valorem levy imposed on price including tax, the conclusion is the opposite; in this case, the NAR curves cross directly below the old price, and thus the price rise is greater with the ad valorem. (Compare the increase from curves NAR_2 and $SNAR_2$ on Chart 20.

This conclusion is reached also by Gilbert *(op. cit.*, p. 279-280).

19. These general conclusions are the same if the tax is levied on price including the tax; the NAR curve would be lower at the Y axis, and the price increase and the tax somewhat greater.

20. The same analysis applies to firms in monopolistic competition in the short run.

21. With straight line curves, the AR curves and the MR curves must cross at the same price level and, since when the ARs are equal, the MRs, which under the conditions are equal to one half of their respective ARs, must be also.

22. The conclusions of this paragraph also apply to the problem of the comparison of a specific tax and an ad valorem levy at a rate of the ratio of the specific levy to the old price, the ad valorem being levied on price including the tax.

With increasing cost, the marginal curve slopes upward from left to right, and the point of intersection of the two marginal net revenue curves is more likely to be at a higher price level than the level at which they intersect the marginal cost curve than in the case (decreasing cost) in which the cost curve is sloping downward from left to right.

23. Gilbert ("Sales Taxes," *Quarterly Journal of Economics, op. cit.*, 53: 282) errs in saying that the rise will always be greater with a specific levy.

24. This is similar to the comparison made by Brown, *(Taxation, op. cit.)*, in the first part of his discussion of the problem, (pp. 135-138). However, he considers the ad valorem tax as applied to the price plus the tax; in his example (p. 138), if he had applied the ad valorem tax to the price net of the tax, his result, as to which levy causes the greater rise, would have been the reverse of that which he reached. Furthermore, he is unable to explain why in some cases an ad valorem tax, in others a specific tax, will cause a greater rise. He then turns to a comparison comparable to that in the paragraph preceding the one to which this note refers, except that again he applies the ad valorem rate to the gross

price (pp. 138-140). He does not discover that even with this comparison, at times the ad valorem levy will cause a greater increase.

25. Thus, since the comparison made with an ad valorem levied on price including the tax is equivalent to the comparison made in the previous paragraph, there is less likelihood of a greater rise with an ad valorem levied on price net of the tax type than with the other.

26. Brown's reasoning on this problem is to be found on pages 135 and 136 of his *Taxation, op. cit.*, as follows:

> But there is some ground for making a distinction in the case of monopoly, and the conclusion appears to be that a tax on gross returns is likely to cause price to rise less than a tax on output. The general reasoning by which this conclusion is arrived at is certainly plausible and should perhaps be convincing. It is based on a comparison between gross returns and gross output. An increased price will decrease demand and, therefore, appreciably curtail output. But gross returns are figured by multiplying gross output and price. And, since the decline in output, in case there is an attempt to shift or partly shift a tax, is consequent on a rise in price, the product of output and price will not decrease in as rapid proportion as will physical output. It appears to follow that a tax in proportion to output is likely to cause a greater rise in price than a tax according to gross returns. For a tax according to output decreases as output decreases and a tax according to gross returns decreases only as gross returns decrease. And, therefore, a tax according to output is cut off to a larger extent by a rise of price which results in decreased output than is a tax according to gross returns.

Unfortunately, his first example does not bear out his reasoning, but he does not know exactly why. If this reasoning were valid, it is difficult to see why it would not apply in all cases. Actually, it is very similar to the line of reasoning which led several writers to err on the significance of decreasing cost conditions, and of elasticity of demand, for incidence. It is true that as output is reduced, tax per unit rises with an ad valorem levy and not with a specific levy, but the conclusion does not follow that reduction will not be carried as far in the former case. Furthermore, the essential problem in incidence analysis is the question of the proportion of tax added to price in different conditions.

Seligman originally maintained (*Incidence*, 1st edition, *op. cit.*, p. 162) that a tax on gross receipts would never cause a monopolist to raise his price. The error in this position was pointed out by Edgeworth ("Pure Theory," *Economic Journal*, *op. cit.*, 7. 228), and others, and acknowledged by Seligman in the second edition (p. 286n). In later editions he deals with gross receipts in a similar manner as output levies, and does not consider the difference in incidence in the two cases (5th edition, pp. 355-358). Wicksell deals with an ad valorem and a specific tax which yield the same revenue, and comes to the conclusion that the gross revenue tax will always add less to the price. He does not, however, provide any detailed analysis of the problem. (See *Steuerincidenz*, *op. cit.*, p. 14.) As far as monopoly is concerned, the problem is ignored by the other discussions of incidence previously mentioned.

Fagan and Jastram ("Tax Shifting," *Quarterly Journal of Economics*, *op.*

cit., 53:584) recognize that the rise may be greater with specific but do not explain in detail why this is the case.

Gilbert, "Shifting of Sales Tax," *Quarterly Journal of Economics, op. cit.*, 53:282) maintains:

> Thus the price rises less with a sales tax than with the equivalent specific tax on original production. The consumer is therefore harmed less through price rise or curtailed consumption, while the government receives $900 rather than $500 of tax revenue. In the extreme case of a demand which is nearly inelastic, the two types of tax may produce the same price change, so that it is a matter of indifference which is used, but this is the exception and, generally speaking, monopolists should be taxed with sales value taxes rather than with taxes per unit of physical output or sales.

27. The same conclusion applies in the case in which the tax is levied on price including the tax.
28. The burden is really borne by factors losing employment in the industry.
29. The same reasoning applies if the tax is levied on price including the tax; the same is true in regard to the comparison in the next paragraph.
30. If the net curve with such a specific levy were drawn on Chart 24, it would intersect NAR at J.
31. This result is different from that in the preceding paragraph (where percentage of tax added to price is considered), because the point of intersection of the two NMR curves must always be above cost in the former case, or production will cease.
32. That the new EO curve is of this nature can be proven easily by determining equilibrium outputs with a given tax rate with different cost curve locations.
33. Even if these requisites are met, if comparison is made between a particular industry with selling costs, and the same industry, cet.par. without, the price increases will be different since the location of the cost curve is different. But in this case selling costs can be treated simply as an addition to production costs, and so the formal analysis is the same as if they did not exist. Where the requisites are not met, they cannot be so treated.
34. When the tax is levied on price including the tax, a further readjustment is required because the tax per unit rises as the price rises. With a low tax rate, this readjustment would be so minute that in practice it would not ordinarily occur.
35. That is, lower than that which would yield maximum profits.
36. This tendency will be even greater, of course, if the tax is levied on price including the tax.

CHAPTER VI

1. The manufacturers' sales tax, as used in Canada and other countries, and proposed many times in the United States, is an example of this type of levy. Note Buehler, *General Sales Taxes, op. cit.*, pp. 116-130, and National Industrial Conference Board, *General Sales or Turnover Taxation*, New York, 1929, pp. 180-194.
2. The literature on incidence of the manufacturers' sales tax is extremely brief. Buehler's discussion (*General Sales Taxation, op. cit.*) is primarily concerned with sales taxes on particular lines; some reference to the significance of the general feature of the tax is given on pp. 180-181. Brief reference is to be found in Nelson, *Sales Taxes, op. cit.*, p. 60; National Industrial Conference Board, *General Sales or Turnover Taxation*, New York, 1929, pp. 9-17, National Industrial Conference Board, *Sales Taxes, General, Selective and Retail*, New

York, 1932, pp.38-44; Ricardo, *Political Economy, op. cit.*, pp.227-228, (Chapter 17); Shoup, C., *The Sales Tax in France*, New York, 1930, p.837; Mill, J.S., *Principles, op. cit.*, pp. 271-276; Jensen, *Government Finance, op. cit.*, p.196; Shultz, *Public Finance, op. cit.*, pp.296-297; Hayes, Gordon, *The Incidence of a Sales Tax, Annals of American Academy of Political and Social Science*, 95:210-211, May, 1921; Orcutt, B.S., "Why a Sales Tax?" *Administration*, 1:658-666, May, 1921 (the typical view of the business writer); Paton, William A., "The Pro and Con of a Sales Tax," *Administration*, 2:367-372, September, 1921; Owen, Lyle, "Who Pays the Taxes?" *Tax Magazine*, 15:83-84, February, 1937; Lord, Charles E., "Will the Sales Tax Solve the Problem?" *Congressional Digest*, 2:347, September, 1923. One paragraph of the latter serves to illustrate the feeling of many business writers on the subject:

> It ought to be evident that a tax that is uniform and of low rate and applies to everything has no bearing whatever on profit. A tax that applies to everybody in business becomes an absolute negligible element in commercial transactions and will have no bearing on commercial transactions.

Further references, especially to foreign works are given in Buehler, *Sales Taxation, op. cit.*, pp.329-331. Of those which are accessible, no discussions of importance of the significance of the general nature of gross revenue taxes are to be found, so no mention is made here of them.

After this study was originally completed H.G.Brown's article on the subject appeared, entitled, "Incidence of a General Sales Tax," *Journal of Political Economy, op. cit.*, 47:254-262.

3. J.S.Mill's denial of the possibility of a general rise in prices (*Political Economy, op. cit.*, p.837) was based on an assumption of a given level of income and output, which is an integral part of the classical theory of distribution. The same is true of Brown's analysis ("Incidence of a General Sales Tax," *Journal of Political Economy, op. cit.*, 47:255).
4. Attention must again be called to the fact that the analysis is based on the assumption that the government spends the tax money in substantially the same way that the private individual would otherwise have done. Any deviations from this would produce price changes under other than constant cost conditions. If the government did not spend the money at all, further reductions in employment would occur beyond that occuring from output reduction and exodus of firms due to the tax itself.
5. For a clear statement, see Garver, F.B., and Hansen, A.H., *Principles of Economics*, New York, 1937, Chapter 26, pp. 438-462.
6. The question of the relation of the rate of interest to the volume of savings has received extensive attention in classical economics. Among the more complete discussions are those to be found in Marshall, *Principles, op. cit.*, pp.230-236; Cassel, G., *Theory of Social Economy*, New York, 1932, pp. 232-246; *Colwyn Report, op. cit.*, pp. 136-140; Pigou, A.C., *A Study in Public Finance*, London, 1928, pp.77-82; Brown, *Taxation, op. cit.*, pp.186-198; Seligman, *Studies in Public Finance, op. cit.*, p.78; Mill, J.S., *Principles, op. cit.*, pp.824-827. For the latter, the fact that the tax checks accumulation brings the economy to a stationary state earlier than otherwise. Since, however, profits would fall to a rate bringing this state eventually anyway, in the long run the existence of the tax does not affect the distribution of the tax burden as between workers and capital owners.
7. Brown in his recent *Journal of Political Economy* article, ("Incidence of a

General Sales Tax," 47:254-262), is one of the few writers to emphasize this reaction.

8. J.M.Keynes, *General Theory, op. cit.*, pp.175-193.
9. *Ibid.*, pp.165-244. See also pp.25-27 of this study.
10. The actual gross interest rate varies between lines according to special risks involved. The above analysis runs in terms of a "standard" rate of interest, with "normal" risk involved.
11. The interest rate cannot remain below the level at which investment is equal to the volume of savings with full employment of resources, or inflation will occur. Thus in a rapidly expanding economy, the rate must be relatively high to hold investment in check; a small reduction in the rate would substantially increase investment and eliminate the unemployment.
12. See Keynes, *General Theory, op. cit.*, pp.202-204.
13. This is recognized by Brown, "Incidence of General Sales Tax," *Journal of Political Economy, op. cit.*, 47: 261-262.
14. See Clark, J.M., *Economics of Overhead Costs, op. cit.*, pp.437-439.
15. Before wage changes occur.
16. See Brown, "Incidence of a General Sales Tax," *Journal of Political Economy, op. cit.*, 47:254-257.
17. The readjustments of production as among various lines, produced by the factors discussed above, would cause some changes in total volume of output apart from changes in supplies of factors.
18. This is less likely to be true in the case of unskilled workers; the growth of industrial unions, however, greatly increases the number of cases in which reductions will be checked.

    One type of labor - paid management officials - seems especially likely to experience reduced incomes, as these men are often part owners and will accept smaller salaries in order to avoid failure of the firms and complete loss of their jobs.
19. In the case of those groups of workers whose wages are cut, the members of the groups may escape unemployment, but unless the demand for these workers is elastic, their total purchasing power will be reduced, and unemployment of other workers increased.
20. See p.26, and p.216(32).
21. This problem receives brief attention in the National Industrial Conference Board's *General Sales or Turnover Taxation, op. cit.*, pp.12-13.
22. In addition, further modifications may be produced by shifts in elasticity of demand for goods produced by changes in the prices of other goods.
23. The limitations of particular equilibrium analysis render difficult a complete description of demand interrelationships. The alternative approach to the problem - general equilibrium analysis - allows consideration of all interrelationships, but involves the creation of a formal system of such nature that the significance of the results cannot easily be obtained. For an attempt to use this approach to the theory of incidence, see Webb, Ursula, "Taxation and Production," *Review of Economic Studies*, 2:18-30, October, 1934.
24. There is, in addition, burden on certain groups of other factors, especially if total output falls, and, even when the latter does not occur, on specialized factors in certain particular lines.

CHAPTER VII

1. A summary of the parts of this chapter dealing with the incidence of a general retail sales tax appeared in the *National Tax Association Bulletin*, 25:226-230, May, 1940, under the title of "The Incidence of Retail Sales

Taxes"; the section dealing with retail price determination appeared in the February, 1941 issue of the *Southern Economic Journal*, (7:380-397) under the title of "A Theory of Retail Price Determination."

2. Extremely few analyses of the incidence of retail sales taxation are available; further, without exception they consist either of summaries of empirical investigation, or of brief reference to the problem of shifting of such levies, without detailed consideration. One of the most useful of the latter is that of Willemsen, A.C., "Operating Aspects of the Retail Sales Tax," *Harvard Business Review*, 11:107-114, October, 1932. H.G. Brown, in his article, "The Incidence of a General Sales Tax," *Journal of Political Economy*, *op. cit.*, 47:257-267, gives more attention than most writers have. Other brief discussions include: Blakey, R.G., "The Sales Tax," *Tax Magazine*, 13:63-70, February, 1935; Buehler, A.G., "Distribution Groans Under Increasing Taxation," *Advertising and Selling*, 21:24-25, 38-40, October 12, 1933; Carver, T.N., "The Shifting of Taxes," *Yale Review*, 5:267, November, 1896; Caverly, H.L., "Scope and Problem of State Sales Taxation," *National Tax Association Proceedings*, 1935, 28:145-161 (especially 159-160), Columbia, S.C., 1936; Jacoby, Neil H., *Retail Sales Taxation*, Chicago, 1938, pp.299-330; Jensen, *Government Finance*, *op. cit.*, pp.196-197; Kansas Legislative Council, Research Department, *The Sales Tax*, 1934, pp.67-71; Leroy-Beaulieu, Paul, *Traite de la Sciences des Finances*, Paris, 1912, vol.1, p.504; Lutz, *Public Finance*, *op. cit.*, p.404; Mangold, W.P., "Who Pays the Sales Tax?" *Advertising and Selling*, 18:24-25, March 16, 1932; McEachern, Justin W., "A Retail Sales Tax and the Retail Merchant," *National Tax Association Bulletin*, 11:205-208, April, 1926; Nelson, *Sales Taxes*, *op. cit.*, p.62; Riley, H.E., "State Sales Taxes and the Cost of Food," *Monthly Labor Review*, 44:241-245, January, 1937; Shirras, *Public Finance*, *op. cit.*, p. 614; Shoup, Carl, "The Sales Tax," *Annals of the American Academy of Political and Social Sciences*, 183:105-107, January, 1936; Walker, Mabel, *Where the Sales Tax Falls*, New York, (General Welfare Tax League), 1934, pp.1-3; Walker, Mabel, *The General Sales Tax*, New York (General Welfare Tax League), 1933, pp. 1-3; Editorial, "What to Do With the Excise Levies," *Advertising and Selling*, 19:15, June 23, 1932.

There have been three empirical studies of the incidence of the retail sales tax, in which attempts were made to determine whether or not retailers thought they were passing on the tax. These include the University of Mississippi, School of Commerce and Business Administration, *Mississippi's General Sales Tax*, University of Mississippi, January, 1933, pp. 14-29; Haig, Robert H., and Shoup, Carl, *The Sales Tax in the American States*, New York, 1934, (summary pp.61-80); Shoup, Carl, "The Experience of 2000 Retailers Under New York City's Sales Tax," *N.T.A. Bulletin*, 21:98-114, January, 1936. There are two references to the incidence of income taxes on retailers which have some bearing on the present problem: *Colwyn Report*, *op. cit.*, pp. 116-117, and Silverman, *Taxation*, *op. cit.*, p.152. The descriptive material on the retail sales tax is very great; among the most complete bibliographies are two by the U.S. Library of Congress, entitled *Sales Taxation in the United States*, Washington, 1934, and 1935, and ones by Chernin, M., *The General Sales Tax in the United States*, Berkeley, (Bureau of Public Administration), 1936 (Unpublished), and Bloomfield, Daniel, *Sales Taxes*, New York, 1934, pp.21-31.

3. Note Baker, H.A., *Principles of Retail Merchandising*, New York, 1939, pp.162-184; Barker, C.W., and Anderson, I.D., *Principles of Retailing*, New York, 1935, pp.163-177; Brisco, N.A., *Retailing*, New York, 1935, pp.225-230; Doubman, J.R.,

Principles of Retail Merchandising, New York, 1936, pp.147-151; Neal, L.E., *Retailing and the Public*, London, 1933, pp.89-101; Nystrom, Paul, *Economics of Retailing*, 3rd Edition, New York, 1930, vol.2, pp.461-483; and U.S.Federal Trade Commission, *Chain Stores; Chain Store Price Policies*, Washington, 1934, pp.2-119.

4. The inadequacy of contemporary analysis of retail price determination has been indicated above. One of the most complete analyses at the present time is to be found in the recent book by Henry Smith, entitled *Retail Distribution* (London, 1937); this book represents a definite contribution to the problem but fails to give as clear a picture of retail pricing as is desirable. In Professor Grether's new book, *Price Control Under Fair Trade Legislation*, New York, 1939, pp.225-235, some attention is given to the problem. The book, of course, deals primarily with price control legislation rather than with retail price determination itself.

   In the April, 1940 issue of the *Journal of Marketing*, E.R.Hawkins, in an article entitled "Marketing and the Theory of Monopolistic Competition," (4:382-389), carried the analysis farther than had previously been done; Dr. Hawkins shows the relevance, yet inadequacy of the theory of monopolistic competition for the explanation of retail price, and gives some consideration to the latter problem. In the unpublished thesis of the same author, entitled *Vertical Price Relations Under Conditions of Monopolistic Competition*, in the University of California Library, he analyzes the problem in more detail.

   The essential features of the parts of this chapter dealing with retail price determination were presented in an article in the *Southern Economic Journal*, entitled "A Theory of Retail Price Determination," 7:380-397, January, 1941.

5. See Beckman, T.N., and Nolen, H.C., *The Chain Store Problem*, New York, 1938, p.147.
6. The Federal Trade Commission Report (*Chain Stores: Price Policy, op. cit.*, pp.19-20) indicates the importance "meeting competition" plays in chain store price policy.
7. After this section was originally written, this type of demand curve for industry in general was indicated by P.M.Sweezy of Harvard, in a *Journal of Political Economy* article entitled "Demand Under Conditions of Oligopoly, (47:568-570, August, 1939). Sweezy calls the demand curve an "imagined" demand curve to distinguish it from the usual demand curve. Professor E.T. Grether (*Price Control Under Fair Trade Legislation, op. cit.*, p.231n) indicates the likelihood of this situation being found in retailing.
8. See Chamberlin, *Monopolistic Competition, op. cit.*, pp.103-104.
9. A unit of retail service consists of all the service performed in the transference of one physical article from the person from whom the retailer buys to the one purchasing from the latter.
10. On this chart, the new cost curve is drawn, for simplification, for a specific tax instead of an ad valorem levy. The difference in the two cases is ordinarily relatively unimportant, as previously indicated.
11. On production cost exclusive of the tax
12. See Beckman, T.N. and Engle, N.H., *Wholesaling*, New York, 1937, pp.480-502; p.506. The figures for all product show the average retail margin to be 28%, the average wholesale margin 11%. Variations among lines are considerable
13. The term "joint cost" is avoided sinc many writers confine the latter to cost in a situation in which two or more products must be produced together for physical reasons.
14. This is recognized by Hawkins, in his *Journal of Marketing* article (*op. cit.*, 4:382-383).

15. Apart from the realization by experience that abandonment of this method of pricing leads in the end to disaster, the chief factor in the retention of the method is the relative ease of finding average cost in contrast to the extreme difficulty of ascertaining marginal cost. The method arose apparently as a simple way of attempting to insure that prices were being set high enough to cover the total overhead.
16. The use of price lines is developed in detail by Baker, *op. cit.*, pp. 163-170.
17. See Grether, *op. cit.*
18. It is interesting to note that in the railroad field, also characterized by a high percentage of overhead cost, stability of rates was obtained only by government regulation. Pricing policy is essentially marginal; prior to the days of regulation, except for short periods of agreements, rate wars were frequent occurrences. Average cost rate making would have prevented these, but not only was this obviously less profitable in the short run, but it was contrary to established rate making policy, in contrast to the situation in retailing.
19. Professor Hawkins indicates the significance of the attention given by merchants to overhead costs as one factor encouraging the use of the markup method. (*Journal of Marketing*, *op. cit.*, 4:384-385.)
20. The practice of stores of watching their competitors' prices tends to make variations in markup less than those in cost.
21. In 1939, 22 states had sales-below-cost legislation (Grether, *op. cit.*, p. 33); 43 states had resale price maintenance laws (*ibid.*, p. 19). Since the time Dr. Grether's book appeared, 5 states have enacted sales-below-cost laws, and the Nebraska law was declared unconstitutional; thus 26 states now have such laws. One additional resale price maintenance law has been passed.
22. *Chain Store Price Policies*, *op. cit.*, p. 23.
23. *Ibid.*, p. 6.
24. The term "average revenue" excludes indirect contributions to revenue unless otherwise specified. The significance of these special contributions will be introduced later.
25. Otherwise readjustments would have occurred before the imposition of the tax.
26. In the case of products of this type, AC is virtually horizontal rather than as indicated on the chart. As a result of the imposition of the tax, and the knowledge that other firms will boost prices, the inelastic portion of the demand curve now extends to a higher level than before. The location of the new point of change in slope depends upon the amount of price increase which other firms are expected to make. The latter is ordinarily the amount of the tax plus some additional amount for higher cost of operation per unit.
27. It is unlikely that this increase would be very great, since no item of common cost, which includes those items most likely to remain constant as output falls, is included.
28. This process is explained in detail in Willemsen, "Retail Sales Tax," *op. cit.*, *Harvard Business Review*, 11:108, October, 1932. This will occur both in cases without excess profits and in ones with the latter where the higher return has come to be accepted as "desirable and obtainable" by all firms in the industry. The presence of a few non-profit making firms which follow the prices of the others does not interfere with this process.
29. Chart 25 serves to indicate price increase in this case also, except that the cost curve now includes some contribution to overhead, and should be of steeper slope than in the previous case. The price increase in this case is likewise to K.
30. The greater importance of average cost

pricing in retailing than in manufacturing strengthens this tendency.

31. This problem receives further attention in the course of the chapter.

32. Actually, even though not required by law, the tax may be quoted as a separate item over and above the original sale price. This is indicated, for example, in the study of Haig and Shoup of shifting under the Michigan Law. (*Sales Tax*, *op. cit.*, p.75). In this case, the original markup is supplemented by an additional markup, rather than being readjusted itself. In general, there appears to be little difference for incidence if this method is used, except that buyers can determine somewhat more easily which stores are absorbing the tax, and thus there may be more incentive to fail to raise prices. The buyers may, of course, be deceived, if the basic price is raised and the tax not quoted separately. This would, of course, injure the sales of the firm pretending to absorb if prices are advertised net of the tax when the latter is added separately. Where the tax is quoted separately, and reduced volume affects cost of operation, the basic markup will eventually be readjusted.

33. In the case of lines making no contribution to overhead, it is not clear that price will rise by more than the tax. It is, in general, not special but rather overhead which rises per unit as output falls, since the latter consists to a large extent of fixed cost. Thus, if the line contributed nothing to overhead before, it will likely rise in price only by the amount of the tax.

34. See Willemsen, "Retail Sales Taxes," *Harvard Business Review*. *op. cit.*, 11:108-109.

35. Note Shoup, "The Sales Tax," in *Annals*, *op cit.*, p.106; Haig and Shoup, *Sales Tax*, *op. cit.*, pp.30-31; Institute of Distribution, *Manual of Taxes*, *op. cit.*, pp.7-15. As indicated in the latter, seventeen of the twenty-four state laws in 1937 had provisions of one sort or another designed to force shifting.

Note also Willemsen, "Sales Taxes," *Harvard Business Review*, *op. cit.*, 11: 109-114.

36. This condition could be included in the discussion of the significance of different demand elasticity, but is of sufficient importance to warrant separate mention.

37. Of course, the desire to get retailers to push the article does influence in this direction.

38. On Chart 25, at the old price M, provided other firms increase price to K, the possible sales of this firm would be extremely great (ON).

39. In other words, at the point at which the real AR curve changes slope.

40. Multiple line stores are likely to experience different reactions on the part of competitors in different lines. A department store, for example, will suffer severe competition from cut-rate specialty shops in certain lines, and will be virtually free of such competition in other lines. Accordingly, price increases will be greater in the latter lines, and the tax burden on all of the goods may pass on to the consumers of these articles.

41. See Willemsen, "Sales Taxes," *Harvard Business Review*, *op. cit.*, 11:109-110.

42. The influence of the separate charging provisions along these lines may be of more significance than would at first appear. The realization of the consumer that he is paying the tax may cause him to cut down on his expenditures more so than if he simply pays a higher price for the goods because of the tax, and may thus prevent as great an encroachment on savings as occurs in the latter case. The difference in change in propensity to consume in the two cases will affect the total change in output, in factor prices, and in com-

modity price.

43. Virtually the same conclusion is reached by Haig and Shoup, (*Sales Tax, op. cit.*, p.30).

> To the economist accustomed to think in terms of impersonal forces operating over long periods of time, such an attempt to control the incidence of the tax without involving price fixing seems at first sight naïve. Closer study, however, with special reference to the period of six months or a year following the introduction of a sales tax, creates both an understanding of, and to some extent a belief in, the claims made by retailers for the mandatory shifting provisions.

Carl Shoup, in "Sales Tax," *Annals, op. cit.*, 183:107, points out that shifting is not insured by such provisions, but that the psychological effect of the law will be to increase the efforts of merchants to shift it. Also in his study of the New York City sales tax, "The Experience of 2000 Retailers Under New York City's Sales Tax," *N.T.A.Bulletin, op. cit.*, 21:98-114, he concludes that the separate charging provisions played an important part in aiding the shifting of the tax. A similar position is taken by Lutz, *Public Finance, op. cit.*, p.404, and Jacoby, *Retail Sales Taxation, op. cit.*, pp.304-316. On the other hand, H.L.Caverly, in "State Sales Taxes," *N.T.A.Proceedings*, 1935, *op. cit.*, p.159 maintains:

> In view of the practical certainty that a retail sales tax will be shifted to consumers, the efforts of a number of state laws to provide the means and mechanism for the collection of the tax from buyers are, in my opinion, of less importance than has sometimes been accorded them. At the most, a provision permitting the dealer to pass the tax on, or even requiring him to do so, or providing a scale or bracket system of charges for his use, merely assists and hastens an adjustment which, in any case would rather promptly take place.

Jensen (Kansas Legislative Council, *The Sales Tax, op. cit.*, p.67), Walker, (*Where the Sales Tax Falls, op. cit.*, p.2), and Riley, "State Sales Taxes," *Monthly Labor Review, op. cit.*, 44:242) also question the significance of such laws for incidence.

44. On Chart 25, if segment MK of AR' were of greater elasticity, obviously the tangency with AC would be farther to the left, and the price increase greater.

45. In this case, on Chart 25, MK would be of such great elasticity that there would be no point of tangency with AC'.

46. This is, of course, not strictly correct, as under the circumstances, an ad valorem levy causes production to be carried on nearer the optimum. In order to simplify exposition, this is ignored in the context.

47. For a discussion of cost conditions in retailing, see Clark, F.E., *Principles of Marketing*, New York, 1932, pp.605-611.

48. In Ricardian terms, it is not decreased rent for the land still in use, but the fact that less undesirable locations must be used, which brings the price reduction.

49. The ad valorem nature of the levy causes production to be carried on somewhat nearer the optimum.

50. Thus the assumption is implicitly made that there is no reduction in demand for goods as retail prices rise, or that a fall in employment and investment will not affect the interest rate or the wage level. The first possibility would involve a sharp fall in the volume of savings, which in classical analysis would affect prices, and is extremely unreal; the latter is simply inconsistent

with the system of theory on which the incidence analysis is based.

There is one exception to the statement in the context; in his recent *Journal of Political Economy* article ("General Sales Tax," *op. cit.*, 47: 254-262) H. G. Brown does consider this problem in relation to a retail sales tax.

51. Throughout this analysis the term "quality" will include all services, including advertising, provided in the transference of goods from wholesale seller to consumer. Advertising is included since, for purposes of the present analysis, the results are substantially the same as those of increase in other aspects of quality.
52. The terms " Quality-demand curve" and "Quality-supply curve" will be used throughout to distinguish them from the usual supply and demand curves.
53. The marginal curves are omitted from Chart 26 for purposes of simplification, since they are not essential for the analysis.
54. In an arithmetic sense.
55. This and the preceding express themselves primarily, as far as cost is concerned, through increased rates of turnover.
56. Thus, on Chart 26, QD turns downward sharply (QD") below the old quality, and comes to tangency with QS'.
57. In this case also, the point at which the quality demand curve increases sharply in slope is moved down on the chart.
58. The marginal curve, at each output level, is now lower than the old because the average curve is lower; thus the former must intersect the unchanged marginal quality supply curve nearer to the vertical axis, and thus the actual quality supplied is less.
59. Where neither price nor quality can be varied, with sufficiently great excess profit, the burden must rest entirely on the producer. Where no excess profit is earned, and no shifting of the tax to other lines is possible, the line will simply be dropped. This will certainly occur if special costs are no longer covered, and possibly even if they are, but less than usual contribution to common cost made. The remaining firms will experience increases in volume, and, with decreasing cost conditions, will, if the tax is not too great, be able to cover special costs again. If not, consumers will no longer be able to get the good. In any case the tax burden will rest upon producers or specialized factors; if the line is no longer carried at all, there will be indirect injury to consumers.
60. It might appear that a secondary fall in employment in production will occur because of the decreased purchasing power of those thrown out of work. This is not the case, in general, since the money spent by these groups is now spent by the government. The latter does not, however, serve to reemploy those losing their jobs in retailing. If the government spends the money for different purposes than individuals would have, modifications are introduced.
61. The decline in advertising display and convenience of location are of particular significance in this regard.
62. In 1937, six of the twenty-four state sales taxes exempted staple foods. See Institute of Distribution, *Manual of Taxes*, *op. cit.*, pp. 7-15.
63. For example, land rent of store sites.
64. In this case, as in others, separate charge provisions lessen greatly the likelihood of transfer of tax burden to untaxed lines.
65. When retail sales taxes are levied by only one or a few states within a country, modification of interest rates is very unlikely to occur.
66. The same considerations as to possible wage changes apply as in the preceding chapters.

APPENDIX I TO CHAPTER VII

1. *Mississippi's General Sales Tax*, *op. cit.*, pp.14-29.
2. *Ibid.*
3. *Ibid.*, p.64.
4. *Ibid.*, p.65.
5. *Ibid.*, p.67.
6. *Ibid.*, p.70.
7. *Ibid.*, p.75.
8. *Ibid.*, p.78.
9. "The Experiences of 2000 Retailers Under New York City's Sales Tax," *N.T.A.Bulletin*, 21:98-114, January, 1936.
10. *Ibid.*, p.100.
11. *Ibid.*, p.100.
12. *Ibid.*, p.114.

APPENDIX II TO CHAPTER VII

1. Lee, M.W., "Recent Trends in Chain Store Tax Legislation," *Journal of Business of the University of Chicago*, 13:259, July, 1940. One additional law has since been passed (Utah) but the operation has been suspended pending referendum. This levy is, of course, not a true sales tax.
2. The most complete analyses are to be found in Beckman, T.N., and Nolen, H.C., *The Chain Store Problem*, New York, 1938, pp.263-272; and Lee, M.W., "Anti-Chain-Store Tax Legislation," Chicago, 1939 (Published as *Studies in Business Administration*, University of Chicago, vol.9, number 1). Further references will be given on subsequent pages.
3. Note Morrill, A.H., "It's the Poor Who Pay a Sales Tax," *Nation's Business*, 20:46-51, February, 1932. The chain store argument on incidence usually ends at this point, the conclusion being reached that the consumers pay in full.
4. Beckman and Nolen, *Chain Store Problem*, *op. cit.*, pp.75-136. Some students of the problem believe, however, that this is not the case to nearly the extent that one would conclude from the material presented in Beckman and Nolen.
5. The fact that in many lines some independents meet chain store prices, of course, increases the elasticity of demand for the chain stores in situations of this sort and checks shifting.
6. Beckman and Nolen, *op. cit.*, p.136, take the position that since the tax is a relatively small part of the margin, it can be passed on to the consumers without substantial loss in volume. This does not necessarily follow. The latter fact is recognized by Lee, "Chain Store Tax," *Journal of Business*, *op. cit.*, 12:58-59, July, 1939.
7. Whether prices are increased or not, some reduction in investment in the chain field is inevitable, since marginal productivity of capital is reduced. Where prices are unchanged, the investment reduction will take the form of a reduction in the number of stores. Because the tax varies according to the number of units, some will no longer cover costs and will be closed, even though no price increase will be made in other stores. By eliminating the stores of smaller volume, costs can be cut more than proportionately to the sales volume loss; a reduction in volume of this nature will be profitable in many cases in which an ordinary reduction in output would not be. The reduction in number of stores involves in part an escape from the tax through quality reduction, in that less convenience of location is offered. This becomes profitable because a reduction in quality by this means is accompanied by very great cost reduction.
8. *Chain Store Problem*, *op. cit.*, p.151. The average earnings per dollar of net worth for twenty-six major chains in four lines for 1929 was 18.3%, for 1932, 10.8%, for 1936, 17.3%. The interesting problem of how limitation

of entry is maintained cannot be answered easily.

9. To simplify the exposition, the term "large chain" is used in the following paragraphs to refer to chains with a relatively large number of units.

10. Since the large chains lose what the small ones gain, the real burden is on the owners of the larger chains, if excess profits have been earned, or on the customers of this group, if prices are boosted further to compensate for the higher cost at reduced volume.

11. See Beckman and Nolen, *Chain Store Problem, op. cit.*, pp.110, 117. Larger-chain prices are in some cases, but not in all, lower than small-chain prices.

12. If the group of smaller chains is unable to raise, they will either bear the tax from excess profits, or go out of business, as described above. The larger chains will be forced to do likewise, unless they are able to obtain higher prices because of quality of service rendered, or possess sufficiently great initial price advantages. Shifting by the large firms is much more difficult in this case than would be the case if the small chains were able to shift.

13. If the systems were uneconomically large, cost will be reduced by the contraction, and consumer may gain; price will rise by less than the amount of the tax.

14. Beckman and Nolen, *The Chain Store Problem, op. cit.*, p.154.

15. Since grocery chains are characterized not only by large number of units but also by small volume per store, the tax is even more regressive than it otherwise would be.

16. As for example A.& P. in parts of the East.

17. For example, the super-market chains.

18. Again, mere price differences do not necessarily indicate the ability to raise prices by an amount greater than the increases made by the higher price stores; the latter may have important quality-service advantages.

19. That is, the elasticity of the portion of the demand curve above the old price is decreased for the price range up to or above the new chain price.

20. This is possible because of the use of average-cost instead of marginal-cost pricing methods.

21. The importance of the chain store argument that if chain prices are raised, prices in independent stores will be raised permanently in like manner, even though the latter are free of the tax, is apparently greatly exaggerated. See Sherrill, C.O., "Chain Store Taxes Hamper Distribution Efficiency," *Advertising and Selling*, 22:20, January, 1934.

22. The Federal Trade Commission *(Final Report on the Chain Store Investigation*, Senate Document 4, 74th Congress, 1st Session, Washington, 1935, p.82, concludes that chain store taxes, if substantial, will pass to consumers because of the increase in cost. Beckman and Nolen *(Chain Store Problem, op. cit.*, pp.263-268) grant that some shifting may occur, but maintain that under present competitive conditions in retailing, most of the tax must remain on the store. Lee concludes *(Chain Store Tax Legislation, op. cit.*, pp.65-66) that it will be doubtful, if not impossible, for the chains to shift the tax, because of competitive conditions. He indicates the possibility of backward shifting to the owners of the factors used by the chain stores. The typical chain store argument that the tax will pass in full to the consumer is presented by the Institute of Distribution, *Chain Store Manual, op. cit.*, pp.78-83; Morrill, A.H., "It's the Poor Who Pay a Sales Tax," *Nation's Business*, 20:46-51, February, 1932; Sherrill, C.O., "Chain Store Taxes Hamper Distribution Effi-

ciency," *Advertising and Selling*, 22: 20, January, 1934; Converse, Paul D., "Shall We Tax the Chains?" *N.T.A. Bulletin*, 22:88-94, December, 1936. Further references on this point of view are to be found in Institute of Distribution, *Chain Store Manual*, *op. cit.*, pp. 139-140. Buehler, A.G., "Chain Store Taxes," *Journal of Marketing*, 1: 177-188, January, 1937; Kreuger, L.B., "The Taxation of Chain Stores," *Tax Magazine*, 11:441, November, 1933; and Caverly, H.L., "State Sales Taxes," *N.T.A.Proceedings*, 1935, *op. cit.*, p. 160, agree that the tax may be shifted or not according to the particular conditions of the situation.

CHAPTER VIII

1. See Brown, "Incidence of General Sales Taxes," *Journal of Political Economy*, *op. cit.*, 47:254-262.
2. See *Colwyn Report*, *op. cit.*, pp. 108-169; Silverman, *Taxation*, *op. cit.*, pp. 127-181; Brown, *Taxation*, *op. cit.*, pp. 141-212; Dalton, *Public Finance*, *op. cit.*, pp. 103-129; Pigou, *Public Finance*, *op. cit.*, pp. 135-153; Black, *Income Taxes*, *op. cit.*
3. For a discussion of the incidence of a tax on sale of land, see Brown, *Taxation*, *op. cit.*, pp. 267-276. As far as a tax on sale of securities is concerned, the chief feature is the effect of such a levy in checking investment, since holdings could be disposed of only at reduced net proceeds. However, instability in security values and resulting disturbances to the economic system as a whole would be lessened. See Keynes, *General Theory*, *op. cit.*, p. 160.
4. The incidence of a tax on wholesalers alone is substantially the same as that of the retail sales tax, and is not of sufficient importance to warrant separate attention.
5. The peculiar problems of incidence of sales taxes levied upon the gross revenue of all enterprise rather than upon that of producers or retailers alone have received very little attention in the literature of incidence. Shoup, *Sales Tax in France*, *op. cit.*, pp. 315-327, indicates some of the problems involved, but provides no detailed analysis of their solution. Brief attention is also given by Buehler in *General Sales Taxation*, *op. cit.*, pp. 192-193, 199-211; Leroy-Beaulieu, *Sciences des Finances*, *op. cit.*, vol. 1, pp. 503-507; National Industrial Conference Board, *General Sales or Turnover Taxation*, *op. cit.*, pp. 8-55, and *The Tax Problem in West Virginia*, New York, 1925, pp. 173-177; and Seligman, *Studies in Public Finance*, *op. cit.*, p. 133. In general, however, these discussions confine their attention to only one problem, that of the effect of general levies in bringing about integration in production and distribution. As previously indicated, in economic theory in the past the problem of vertical price relationships has been almost entirely neglected, and any discussion of a general gross revenue levy has been accordingly rendered difficult.
6. The assumption is made throughout the first part of this chapter that the number of independent steps in the process of production and distribution of a commodity is determined independently of any forces subject to modification as a result of the tax. This assumption will be dropped at a later stage in the analysis.
7. In some cases, wholesale sales are taxed at lower rates than other sales because of the relatively low ratio of profit to turnover. See, for example, National Industrial Conference Board, *The Tax Problem in West Virginia*, *op. cit.*, pp. 161-162.
8. In this case, the entrepreneur is the specialized, non-mobile factor, since he can gain the excess return only in the line in question.
9. The study made by the Bureau of Agri-

cultural Economics on the incidence of the processing taxes indicates that the wholesalers and retailers passed forward the price increase made by the processors to cover the tax. The margins of the distributors on these products in all cases at least remained constant; in several cases they actually increased, as would be expected in the light of markup practices. See Bureau of Agricultural Economics, *Processing Taxes*, *op. cit.*, pp. 5, 32-33, 43, 64.

10. Thus, the conclusions of Adam Smith (*Wealth of Nation*, *op. cit.*, Book V, Chap. 2 (Rogers Edition, vol. 2, p. 467), J.S. Mill (*Principles*, *op. cit.*, V:IV:2, Ashley Edition, pp. 838-839), Cournot (*Mathematical Principles*, *op. cit.*, pp. 70-71), and Buehler (*General Sales Taxes*, *op. cit.*, p. 193), that dealers tend to increase prices by an amount greater than the tax, and so taxes imposed at earlier stages tend to pyramid, are accepted. However, the reason for this is only, ordinarily, to a minor extent the greater capital required for operation, but rather for the most part the ability of the same number of firms to continue in operation, at higher cost, as a result of common markup practices. Seligman's statement, as a part of his criticism of Cournot's position,

    The mere fact that the product passes through a number of hands cannot in itself raise the price by more than the exact cost of such transference. Cost, however, does not include profits; cost is the condition of profit. Otherwise, retail prices would increase geometrically according to the number of retailers--a conclusion which is obviously untrue. (*Incidence*, *op. cit.*, p. 353),

is not as obvious as he thinks it is under monopolistic competition. However, the position of the writers mentioned above ignores the fact that with a retail sales tax, the reduced demand at earlier stages may lead to similar increases in the strength of oliogopoly, though this is less likely than in the case of the tax levied on these earlier stages.

The whole problem of the shifting of taxes between links in the distribution system has received very little attention, apart from brief reference such as is given by Bastable:

    The diffusion of the burden may be still more complicated. . . . In modern society products pass through the hands of several distinct classes before reaching the consumer, and the struggle of buyer and seller will be repeated at each separate stage. The existence of monopoly or of some form of limitation at any point may prevent the shifting passing any further. An economically strong intermediate group may throw a charge back to the producer, send it forward to the consumer, or divide it between both. (*Public Finance*, *op. cit.*, p. 376).

Buehler (*General Sales Taxes*, *op. cit.*, pp. 193-194) and Seligman (*Incidence*, *op. cit.*, p. 351-354) give brief and inadequate analyses of the problem. Analysis which can be applied in this connection is to be found also in Nourse, *Agricultural Adjustment Administration*, *op. cit.*, pp. 518-520. See also Brown, "Incidence of General Sales Tax," *Journal of Political Economy*, *op. cit.*, 47: 260.

11. The same considerations as to wage reductions apply as in previous chapters.

12. Or, price increases by some may be absorbed by firms in subsequent stages.

13. See Shoup, *Sales Tax in France*, *op. cit.*, pp. 317-318; National Industrial Conference Board, *General Sales or Turnover Taxation*, *op. cit.*, pp. 18-19. Leroy-Beaulieu (*Sciences des Finances*,

op. cit., pp. 505-506), along with others, severely condemns the transactions tax as discriminating among commodities by imposing much more severe burdens on some than on others. It is beyond the purpose of this study to consider desirability of the various forms of taxes, but this particular problem will be considered briefly. It must not be forgotten that a producers' or retail sales tax likewise discriminates in similar manner, though less noticeably. The result of such discrimination is to burden particularly consumers of some groups of commodities in relation to those of others, and to redistribute production along certain lines. While it cannot be maintained that the present variety of output, and allocation thereof to consumers, is the most desirable and should not be disturbed by government, interference cannot well be justified unless it is aimed toward some particular purpose, as for example, redistribution of income in favor of the poorer groups. In this case, however, the discrimination is purely of a random nature. It is interesting to note that several countries, in order to check the effect of the general sales tax in aiding integration, have replaced such levies by a tax imposed on only one stage, the rate varying according to the number of times on the average the commodity changes hands. (See Buehler, *General Sales Taxes*, *op. cit.*, pp. 209-211.) It is hard to see how the latter provision can be justified on any accepted basis of allocation of tax burden.

14. In the case of a producers' sales tax, in contrast to the general sales tax, the entire burden passes forward in the form of increases in purchase prices of distributors. Accordingly, once the initial increase is made, there is greatest likelihood that the entire tax, plus an additional amount to maintain the original rate of profit, will pass to the consumer. In some cases, however, especially where pure competition exists in production, the initial increase will be less. Over a longer period, difference in incidence from this factor would disappear. Only where excess profits exist in production, with a situation of oligopoly such that little or no price increase is possible, will less price increase occur permanently with the producer levy. In general, once the increase comes at the production level, it will be carried forward, the increase at each successive step being greater than that at the preceding, resulting in a final increase in retail price by an amount considerably greater than the tax. Because the price increase is carried in full throughout the entire process of distribution, the need for cash for circulation is even greater than in the case of the other levies discussed, and the check on interest reduction still greater.
15. For consideration of this problem see Jensen, J.P., "General vs Selective Sales Taxes," *N.T.A. Proceedings*, 1929, pp. 409-411; National Industrial Conference Board, *General Sales or Turnover Taxation*, *op. cit.*, pp. 33-38; National Industrial Conference Board, *Tax Problem in West Virginia*, *op. cit.*, pp. 177-180; Shultz, *Public Finance*, *op. cit.*, pp. 384-385; Cole, S.T., in *N.T.A. Proceedings*, 1933, p. 237.
16. In the United States, the development of the use tax has served to check this tendency. See "Sales and Use Taxes," *N.T.A. Proceedings*, 1937, pp. 39-54.
17. See Brown, "Incidence of General Sales Tax," *Journal of Political Economy*, *op. cit.*, 47:258-259.
18. If the tax is levied by one state alone, possibility of interest and

wage reduction is less than otherwise; thus there is more assurance that the burden will remain on the consumer.

19. The significance of a general sales tax for integration is the only feature of this type of levy that has received fairly extensive treatment. See Shoup, *Sales Tax in France*, *op. cit.*, p.317; Buehler, *General Sales Taxes*, *op. cit.*, pp. 203-211; National Industrial Conference Board, *General Sales or Turnover Taxation*, *op. cit.*, pp. 23-29; National Industrial Conference Board, *Sales Taxes, General, Selective, and Retail*, New York, 1932, pp. 20-24; Shirras, *Public Finance*, *op. cit.*, p.613; Jensen, *Government Finance*, *op. cit.*, p.378; Leroy-Beaulieu, *Sciences des Finances*, *op. cit.*, pp. 506-507; Ballantine, A.A., "The General Sales Tax is Not the Way Out," in *Annals of the American Academy of Political and Social Sciences*, 95:218-219, May, 1921.
20. See Shoup, *Sales Tax in France*, *op. cit.*, pp. 315-316.
21. See Appendix II to Chapter VII.
22. It is difficult to see how this sort of discrimination can be justified. This problem, however, is beyond the scope of the present discussion.
23. There is one possible case in which the general levy would lower operating cost, whereas the latter would be unaffected by a retail levy. If integration had been delayed from mere inertia, or lack of knowledge or capital, the tax, by bringing about action, would reduce costs and cause part of the tax to be absorbed in this manner.

B I B L I O G R A P H Y

The first group of references is confined to those dealing, in part or in whole, specifically with sales tax incidence.* In the second part is included the principal books and articles on value theory, retail pricing, and distribution which have served as a basis for the analysis. The list is not to be considered at all a complete bibliography on these latter subjects.

I. INCIDENCE OF SALES TAXATION

BOOKS:

Adams, H.C., Science of Finance, New York, 1898.

Beckman, T. N., and Nolen, H. C., The Chain Store Problem, New York, 1938.

Brown, H. G., The Economics of Taxation, New York, 1924.

Buehler, Alfred G., General Sales Taxation, New York, 1932.

Buehler, Alfred G., Public Finance, New York, 1936.

Cournot, A., Recherches sur les Principes Mathématiques de la Théorie des Richesses, Paris, 1838.

Dalton, Hugh, Principles of Public Finance, Ninth Edition, London, 1936.

De Marco, Antonio, First Principles of Public Finance, New York, translation, 1936.

Edgeworth, F. Y., The Pure Theory of Monopoly, in Papers Relating to Political Economy, London, 1925.

Haig, Robert M., and Shoup, Carl, The Sales Tax in the American States, New York, 1934.

Jacoby, Neil H., Retail Sales Taxation, Chicago, 1938.

Jensen, J. P., Government Finance, New York, 1937.

Kendrick, M. S., Taxation Issues, New York, 1933.

Leroy-Beaulieu, Paul, Traité de la Science des Finances, Paris, 1912, Vol. I.

Lutz, H. L., Public Finance, New York, 1936.

Meyers, A. L., Modern Economic Problems, New York, 1939.

Mill, John Stuart, Principles of Political Economy, London, 1886, Book 5.

National Industrial Conference Board, General Sales or Turnover Taxation, New York, 1929.

*The references on chain store tax incidence are included, even though this levy is not a true sales tax.

National Industrial Conference Board, Sales Taxes, General, Selective, and Retail, New York, 1932.

National Industrial Conference Board, The Tax Problem in West Virginia, New York, 1925.

Nelson, C. I., Sales Taxes, Minneapolis, League of Minnesota Municipalities, 1935.

Nourse, E. G., Davis, J. S., and Black, J. D., Three Years of the Agricultural Adjustment Act, Washington, 1936.

Plehn, C. C., Introduction to Public Finance, New York, 1926.

Ricardo, D., Principles of Political Economy.

Robinson, M. E., Public Finance, Cambridge, 1922.

Seligman, E. R. A., The Shifting and Incidence of Taxation, New York, 2nd Ed., 1899; 3rd Ed., 1910; 5th Ed., 1927.

Seligman, E. R. A., Studies in Public Finance, New York, 1924.

Shirras, G. Findlay, Science of Public Finance, London, 1926.

Shoup, Carl, The Sales Tax in France, New York, 1930.

Shultz, W. J., American Public Finance and Taxation, New York, 1931.

Silverman, H. A., Taxation, Its Incidence and Effects, London, 1931.

Smith, Adam, The Wealth of Nations, London, 1776, Book 5.

Walker, Mabel, Where the Sales Tax Falls, New York, General Welfare Tax League, 1934.

Wicksell, Knut., Zur Lehre von der Steuerincidenz, Upsala Universität, Dissertations, Vol. 21, 1895.

JOURNAL ARTICLES:

Ballantine, A. A., "The General Sales Tax Is Not the Way Out," Annals of the American Academy of Political and Social Sciences, 95:218-19, May 1921.

Brown, H. G., "The Incidence of a General Sales Tax," Journal of Political Economy, 47:254-62, April 1939.

Brown, H. G., "The Incidence of a General Output or a General Sales Tax, A Correction," Journal of Political Economy, 47:418-20, June 1939.

Converse, Paul D., "Shall We Tax the Chains?", National Tax Association Bulletin, 22:88-94, December 1936.

Buehler, A. G., "Chain Store Taxes," Journal of Marketing, 1:177-88, January 1937.

Due, John F., "Ad Valorem and Specific Taxes," Quarterly Journal of Economics, 54:679-85, August 1940.

Due, John F., "The Incidence of Chain Store Taxation," Journal of Marketing, 5:128-36, October 1940.

Due, John F., "The Incidence of Retail Sales Taxes," National Tax Association Bulletin, 25:226-30, May 1940.

Edgeworth, F. Y., "Professor Graziani on the Mathematical Theory of Monopoly," Economic Journal, 8:234-39, June 1898.

Fagan, E. D., "Tax Shifting and the Laws of Cost," Quarterly Journal of Economics, 47:680-710, August 1933.

Fagan, E. D., and Jastram, R. W., "Tax Shifting in the Short Run," Quarterly Journal of Economics, 53:562-89, August 1939.

Fergen, Wirth F., "The Measurement of Tax Shifting; Economics and Law," Quarterly Journal of Economics, 54:429-54, May 1940.

Gilbert, D. W., "The Shifting of Sales Taxes," Quarterly Journal of Economics, 53:275-85, February 1939.

Gilbert, D. W., "Rejoinder" (on Ad Valorem and Specific Taxes), Quarterly Journal of Economics, 54:686-93, August 1940.

Hayes, Gordon, "The Incidence of a Sales Tax," Annals of the American Academy of Political and Social Sciences, 95:207-12, May 1921.

Higgins, Benjamin, "The Incidence of Sales Taxes," Quarterly Journal of Economics, 54:665-72, August 1940.

Holden, Grenville, "Incidence of Taxation as an Analytical Concept," American Economic Review, 30:774-86, December 1940.

Jastram, R. W., "The Shifting of Sales Taxes," Quarterly Journal of Economics, 54:673-78, August 1940.

Kendrick, M. S., "The Processing Taxes," Tax Magazine, 13:726-29, December 1935.

Kendrick, M. S., "The Processing Tax on Wheat," American Economic Review, 26:620-35, December 1936.

Kreuger, L. B., "The Taxation of Chain Stores," Tax Magazine, 11:441, November 1933.

Lee, M. W., "Anti-Chain Store Tax Legislation," Studies in Business Administration, Volume 9, Number 4, 1939, pp. 52-61.

Lord, Charles E., "Will the Sales Tax Solve the Problem?", Congressional Digest, 2:347, September 1923.

Lyle, Owen, "Who Pays the Taxes?", Tax Magazine, 15:83-4, February 1937.

Mangold, W. P., "Who Pays the Sales Tax?", Advertising and Selling, 18:24-5, March 16, 1932.

McEachern, Justin W., "A Retail Sales Tax and the Retail Merchant," National Tax Association Bulletin, 11:205-9, April 1926.

Morrill, A. H., "It's the Poor Who Pay a Sales Tax," Nation's Business, 20:46-51, February 1932.

Orcutt, B. S., "Why a Sales Tax?", Administration, 1:658-66, May 1921.

Paton, W. A., "The Pro and Con of a Sales Tax," Administration, 2:367-72, September 1921.

Riley, H. E., "State Sales Taxes and the Cost of Food," Monthly Labor Review, 44:241-45, January 1937.

Shoup, Carl, "The Sales Tax," Annals of the American Academy of Political and Social Sciences, 183:105-7, January 1936.

Shoup, Carl, "The Experience of 2000 Retailers under New York City's Sales Tax," National Tax Association Bulletin, 21:98-114, January 1936.

Sherrill, C. O., "Chain Store Taxes Hamper Distribution Efficiency," Advertising and Selling, 22:20, January 1934.

Webb, Ursula, "Taxation and Production," Review of Economic Studies, 2:18-30, October 1934.

Willemsen, A. C., "Operating Aspects of the Retail Sales Tax," Harvard Business Review, 11:107-14, October 1935.

GOVERNMENT REPORTS:

Great Britain, Treasury, Report of the Committee on National Debt and Taxation, London, 1927. (Colwyn Report.)

Kansas Legislative Council, Research Department, The Sales Tax, Topeka, 1934.

University of Mississippi School of Commerce and Business Administration, Mississippi's General Sales Tax, January 1933.

U. S. Federal Trade Commission, Chain Stores: Chain Store Price Policies, Washington, 1934.

U. S. Federal Trade Commission, Final Report on the Chain Store Investigation, Washington, 1935.

U. S. Treasury Department, Bureau of Internal Revenue (for Department of Agriculture, Bureau of Agricultural Economics), An Analysis of the Processing Taxes Levied Under the Agricultural Adjustment Act, Washington, 1937.

II. ECONOMIC THEORY AND PRICING PRACTICES

BOOKS:

Baker, H. S., Principles of Retail Merchandising, New York, 1939.

Barker, C. W., and Anderson, I. D., Principles of Retailing, New York, 1935.

Brisco, N. A., Retailing, New York, 1935.

Braithwaite, D., and Dobbs, S. P., The Distribution of Consumable Goods, London, 1932.

Burns, Arthur R., The Decline of Competition, New York, 1936.

Chamberlin, Edward, The Theory of Monopolistic Competition, Cambridge, 1936.

Clark, J. M., Studies in the Economics of Overhead Costs, Chicago, 1923.

Doubman, J. R., Principles of Retail Merchandising, New York, 1936.

Garver, F. B., and Hansen, A. H., Principles of Economics, Revised edition, New York, 1937.

Grether, Ewald T., Price Control Under Fair Trade Legislation, New York, 1939.

Keynes, John Maynard, The General Theory of Employment Interest and Money, London, 1936.

Marshall, Alfred, Principles of Economics, London, 1923.

Meyers, A. L., Elements of Modern Economics, New York, 1937.

Neal, L. E., Retailing and the Public, London, 1933.

Nystrom, Paul, Economics of Retailing, Third edition, New York, 1930, Vol. 2.

Pribram, Karl, Cartel Problems, Washington, 1935.

Robinson, Joan, The Economics of Imperfect Competition, London, 1933.

Sandage, C. H., Advertising Theory and Practice, Chicago, 1930.

Smith, Henry, Retail Distribution, London, 1937.

Von Haberler, Gottfried, Prosperity and Depression, Geneva, 1937.

Wicksell, K., Lectures on Political Economy, translation, New York, 1934.

JOURNAL ARTICLES:

Bronfenbrenner, M., "Applications of the Discontinuous Oligopoly Demand Curve," Journal of Political Economy, 48:420-33, June 1940.

Cassels, J. M., "Excess Capacity and Monopolistic Competition," Quarterly Journal of Economics, 51:426-43, May 1937.

Chamberlin, E. H., "Monopolistic or Imperfect Competition," Quarterly Journal of Economics, 51:557-80, August 1937.

Champernowne, D. G., "Unemployment Basic and Monetary," Review of Economic Studies, 3:201-16, June 1936.

Clark, J. M., "Toward A Concept of Workable Competition," American Economic Review, 30:241-56, June 1940.

Copeland, M. A., "Competing Products and Monopolistic Competition," Quarterly Journal of Economics, 55:1-35, November 1940.

Galbraith, J. K., "Monopoly and Price Rigidities," Quarterly Journal of Economics, 50:456-75, May 1936.

Hawkins, E. R., "Marketing and the Theory of Monopolistic Competition," Journal of Marketing, 4:382-87, April 1940.

Higgins, Benjamin, "Elements of Indeterminacy in the Theory of Non-Perfect Competition," American Economic Review, 29:468-79, September 1939.

Kaldor, Nicholas, "Professor Chamberlin on Monopolistic and Imperfect Competition," Quarterly Journal of Economics, 52:513-29, May 1938 and "Reply" by E. H. Chamberlin, pp. 531-38.

Lerner, A. P., "Concept of Monopoly and the Measurement of Monopoly Power," Review of Economic Studies, 1:173-75, June 1934.

Machlup, F., "Monopoly and Competition, a Classification," American Economic Review, 27:445-51, September 1937.

Machlup, F., "Theory of Monopolistic Competition," American Economic Review, 29:227-36, June 1939.

Pigou, A. C., "Money Wages in Relation to Unemployment," Economic Journal, 48:134-38, March 1938.

Pigou, A. C., "Real and Money Wage Rates in Relation to Unemployment," Economic Journal, 47:405-22, September 1937.

Robertson, D. H., Sraffa, P., and Shove, G. F., "Increasing Returns and the Representative Firm," Economic Journal, 40:78-116, March 1930.

Robinson, E. A. G., "Monopolistic and Imperfect Competition," Economic Journal, 47:169-72, March 1937.

Smith, H., "Advertising Costs and Equilibrium," Review of Economic Studies, 2:62-65, October 1934.

Smith, H., "The Imputation of Advertising Costs," Economic Journal, 45:684, December 1935.

Smithies, A., "Equilibrium in Monopolistic Competition," Quarterly Journal of Economics, 55:95-115, November 1940.

Sweezy, P. M., "Demand under Conditions of Oligopoly," Journal of Political Economy, 41:568-73, August 1939.

Sweezy, P. M., "On the Definition of Monopoly," Quarterly Journal of Economics, 51:362-63, February 1937.

I N D E X

A

Absence of price increase from tax, 37, 42, 131, 141, 143, 144, 171, 172, 219(10), 225(38), 229(26)
Adams, 218(2), 219(13)
Ad valorem taxes:
  nature, 88-89
  incidence of, 89-103
Advertising, 12-14, 57-61, 80, 99-100
Agricultural Economics, Bureau of 82-87, 226(1), 242(9)
Anderson, 233(3)
Average cost pricing, 15-16, 73-75, 80, 100-02, 103, 105, 123-26, 127-28, 132-33, 145, 146, 156, 182, 185, 225(36), 240(20)

B

Baker, 233(3), 235(16)
Ballantine, 244(19)
Barker, 233(3)
Bastable, 210(1), 218(2), 220(13), 222(1), 242(10)
Beckman, 170, 234(5), (12), 239(2), (3), (6), 240(11), (14), (22)
Black, D., 214(25), 241(2)
Black, J. D., 226(16)
Blakey, 233(2)
Bloomfield, 233(2)
Brisco, 233(3)
Bronfenbrenner, 207(6)
Brown, H. G., 210(1), 211(7), 212(12), 213(20), (22), 214(22), (29), 215(31), 218(2), (3), 219(10), (13), 226(1), 228(24), 229(26), 231(2), (3), (6), (7), 232(13), (16), 233(2), 238(50), 241(1), (2), (3), 242(10), 243(17)
Buehler, 210(1), 211(7), 214(22), (24), 218(2), 223(1), 230(1), (2), 233(2), 241(5), (22), 242(10), 244(19)
Bureau of Agricultural Economics, 82-87, 226(1), 242(9)
Bureau of Foreign and Domestic Commerce, 225(28)
Burns, 210(35), 225(28)

C

Carver, 233(2)
Cassel, 231(6), 237(43)
Cassels, 207(6)
Caverly, 233(2), 241(22)
Chain stores:
  general sales tax and, 192-94; literature, taxes, 239(2), 240(22); taxes on, 168-79
Chamberlin, 63,207(6), 209(26), 224(19), 234(8)
Champernowne, 216(32)
Chernin, 233(2)
Clark, F. E., 237(47)
Clark, J. M., 207(6), 221(1), 224(27), 232(14)
Class prices, 126, 139-40
Cole, 243(15)
Colwyn Report, 3, 207(3), 210(1), 216(35), 231(6), 233(2)
Common costs (overhead costs):
  meaning, 67, 224(24)
  significance for price determination and incidence, 16, 67, 68, 70, 73-75, 80, 100-01, 122, 123, 124, 125, 131, 132, 133, 163, 235(18), 236(33)
Constant cost:
  nature, 6, 7
  significance of, for incidence, 22, 34-37, 63, 73, 78, 89-90, 120
Converse, 241(22)
Copeland, 207(6)
Cost:
  accounting, 56, 68, 78, 82, 134, 136, 224(27)
  analysis, 5-6, 118-19, 146-47
  conditions - see increasing cost, decreasing cost, constant cost

Cournot, 217(2), 218(2), (6), 219(10), 224(20), 242(9)
Curtis, 216(34)
Customary prices, 140

D

Dalton, 210(1), 211(7), 214(24), 217(35), 218(2), 222(1), 241(2)
Davis, 226(16)
Decline in price, from tax, 57, 225(32)
Decreasing cost conditions:
 meaning, 7, 8, 22, 208(16), 209(18), 213(19)
 significance of, for incidence, 23, 24, 38-41, 54, 62, 90-92, 94, 95, 104, 137, 146, 150, 182, 213(21), (22), 219(13), 228(22), 238(59)
Demand:
 elasticity of, influence on incidence, 23, 35-37, 39-41, 41-43, 45-46, 55-56, 62, 65, 74, 76, 85, 86, 95, 104, 111-13, 131-32, 137, 143-44, 158, 169, 171, 178, 183, 214(22), (24), 218(6), 225(38), 240(19)
 shifts in, influence on incidence, 23-24, 47, 55, 75, 96, 111-13, 142, 160-61, 182, 214(25), 215(27)
Demand curves:
 diversity, see Diversity of cost and demand curves
 slope of, see Slope of demand curves
De Marco, Antonio, 215(27)
Diversity of cost and demand curves, 64, 128-29, 171-76
Doubman, 233(3)
Dynamic conditions, significance of for incidence, 28, 212(14)

E

Edgeworth, 217(2), 218(2), (6), 219(10), 220(13), 224(20), 225(32), 229(26)
Effects of tax, meaning, 3
Elasticity of demand, see Demand
Empirical studies, 83-87, 166-67, 233(2), 237(43), 242(9)
Employment, see Unemployment
Engle, 234(12)
Excess capacity, 109
Excess profits:
 definition, 209(29)
 significance for incidence, 37, 47, 60, 61-63, 66, 70, 72, 77, 78, 81, 97-99, 102, 104, 119, 120, 121, 128, 133, 135, 138, 146, 154, 155, 156, 170-71, 176, 178, 182, 184-85, 194, 240(10), (12), 243(14)
Exemption of certain lines, 113, 161-62
Exodus of firms, 20-21, 30, 53, 57, 60, 64, 68, 69, 70-71, 72, 73, 75, 85, 89, 96, 104, 119, 120-21, 132, 133, 134, 136, 138, 144-46, 153, 154, 155, 161, 163, 169, 170, 175, 176, 177, 181, 182, 191, 192
Expenditure of tax money, see Spending of tax money
Ezekiel, 221(1)

F

Factor prices - see Prices of factors
Fagan, 212(12), 221(1), 226(2), 229(26)
Fair trade laws, 129
Federal trade commission, 129, 225(28), 234(3), (6), 240(22)
Firm:
 definition, 3
 equilibrium of, monopolistic competition, 10-11
 pure competition, 8
Free entry, meaning, 11

G

Galbraith, 210(33), 225(27)
Garver, 231(5)
General equilibrium analysis, 232(23)

General producers sales taxes:
  incidence, 104-15
    comparison with that of retail sales tax, 134-36
  literature, 230(2)
  meaning, 3, 104
General sales tax:
  definition, 3, 180
  incidence, 180-97
  literature, 241(5), 242(10), 244(19)
Gilbert, 226(1), (2), 227(8), 228 (16), (18), (23), 230(26)
Graziani, 218(6)
Grether, 234(4), (7), 235(17), (21)
Gross income tax, 180

H

Haberler, 216(32)
Haig, 221(1), 233(2), 236(32), (34), 237(43)
Hansen, 231(5)
Hawkins, 234(4), (14), 235(19)
Hayes, 231(2)
Higgins, 207(6), 226(1)
Hobson, 216(35)
Hotelling, 225(32)

I

Imperfect competition, 207(6), 208(9)
Imperfect knowledge, 44, 56
Inadequacy of present theory of incidence, 1-2, 148, 211(7), 213(22), 221(1)
Incidence:
  definition, 2, 64-65
  inadequacy of theory of, see Theory of incidence
  of various taxes, see names of taxes
  of other types of cost increase, 33, 81
Increasing cost conditions:
  meaning, 6, 7
  significance of for incidence, 22, 23, 24, 41-45, 53, 63, 65, 92-93, 94-95, 104, 182, 185, 195, 213(22), 215(29), 228(22)
Industry:
  concept of, under monopolistic competition, 9-10
  definition, 3
  equilibrium of, in monopolistic competition, 10
    in pure competition, 8
Institute of distribution, 236(35) 238(62), 240(22), 241(22)
Integration, 192-93, 241(5), 243 (13), 244(19), (23)
Interest rate:
  classical theory, 26, 105-06, 148
  Keynesian theory, 26-27, 106-09, 216(34), 232(11)
  effect of tax on, 26, 27, 47, 105-09, 112, 113, 148, 161, 165, 185-86, 190, 192, 195

J

Jacoby, 233(2), 237(43)
Jastram, 212(12), 222(1), 226(1), 228(16), 229(26)
Jensen, 210(1), 213(22), 214(22), 218(2), (3), 231(2), 233(2), 237(43), 243(15), 244(19)
Joint costs (see also Overhead costs), 30, 234(13)

K

Kaldor, 207(6)
Kendrick, 214(25)
Keynes, 2, 26, 27, 106-09, 216(32), (33), (34), 232(8), (12), 241(3)
Kreuger, 241(22)

L

Labor unions, 26, 110, 232(18)
Laws requiring shifting, 138-39, 140-41, 142-43, 167, 237(43)
Leaders - see Loss leaders
Lee, 239(1), (2), (6), 240(22)
Lerner, 223(13)

Leroy-Beaulieu, 233(2), 241(5), 242(13), 244(19)
Limited entry, 11-12, 61-63, 77, 97-99, 102, 104, 119, 120-21, 128, 138, 154, 156, 170-71, 182, 187
Limited jurisdiction, significance of, for incidence, 28-29, 46, 191-92, 196, 217(39), 243(18)
Liquidity preference, 26, 106, 107, 216(34)
Long run:
  analysis of cost in, 6
  definition, 5
  equilibrium in, 8, 11
  incidence,
    chain store tax, 169-79
    general producers sales tax, 105-15
    general sales tax, 181-97
    retail sales tax, 119-20, 130-65
    special sales tax:
      ad valorem, 88-103
      specific:
        monopolistic competition, 53-82
        monopoly, 34-43, 44-50
        pure competition, 21-31
  supply curves in, 7
Lord, 231(2)
Loss leaders, 16, 131, 135, 136
Lutz, 210(1), 211(7), 214(22), 218 (2), 233(2), 237(43)

M

Machlup, 207(6)
Mangold, 233(2)
Manufacturers sales tax, see General producers sales tax
Marginal firm, 20, 64, 212(15), 220(13), 222(21), 224(21)
Marginal revenue-marginal cost pricing, 10, 11, 34-44, 45, 52-53, 58, 62, 67, 68, 70, 93-96, 98, 102, 118-19, 120, 123, 124, 125, 127, 128, 132, 137, 144, 146, 153, 154, 155, 157, 162, 224(27)
Markup system:
  development, 125, 235(15)
  nature, 125-29
  significance of, for incidence, 131, 132, 133, 134, 135, 136, 137, 138, 139, 147, 159, 162, 169, 184, 188, 195, 236(32)
Marshall, 4, 214(22), 231(6)
McEachern, 233(2)
Meyers, 208(6), 210(2), 214(22), 218(2), 222(1)
Mill, 216(35), 231(2), (3), (6), 242(9)
Monopolistic competition:
  incidence
    of special sales tax under, 51-82
    of ad valorem levies under, 96-103
    of retail sales taxes under, 100-64
    significance for, 1, 51-82, 86, 96-103, 104, 107, 109, 100-64, 169, 181, 183, 185, 187
  meaning, 8-10, 209(21), (25)
  neglect of, incidence analysis, 1, 221(1)
  price determination under, 10-16
  pricing practices, 14-16
  supply curves under, 7
  theory of, 3-5, 8-10
Monopoly:
  concept of, traditional analysis, 9
  nature, 9, 34
  significance of, for incidence, 34-50, 99, 93-96, 104, 105, 109, 121, 135, 143, 145, 181, 183, 185
Monopoly profit, see Excess profit
Morrill, 239(3), 240(22)
Multiple-line enterprise, 30-31, 66-75, 122-164, 236(40)

N

National Industrial Conference Board, 217(39), 230(1), (2), 232 (21), 241(5), (7), 242(17), 243 (15), 244(19)

Neal, 234(3)
Nelson, 218(2), 221(1), 230(2), 233(2)
Nolen, 171, 234(5), 239(2), (3), (6), 240(11), (14), (22)
Nourse, 226(16), 242(10)
Nystrom, 234(3)

O

Oligopoly:
  meaning, 8-9, 209(21)
  significance of, for incidence, 9, 11, 54-55, 56-57, 60, 63, 68, 75, 78, 79, 81, 82, 86, 100, 101, 104, 105, 109, 118, 119, 120, 123, 127, 133, 135, 136, 139, 143, 145, 147, 153, 162, 168, 181, 182, 183, 184, 185, 187, 188, 190, 191, 225 (30), (33), (38), 242(10), 243(14)
  significance of, for price determination, 10-12, 111-19
Orcutt, 231(2)
Overhead:
  meaning, 16, 224(44)
  significance for price determination and incidence, 16, 67, 68, 70, 73-75, 80, 100-01, 122, 123, 124, 125, 131, 132, 133, 163, 235(18), 236(33)
Owen, 231(2)

P

Paton, 231(2)
Perfect competition, 207(6), 208(9)
Pigou, 216(32), 231(6), 241(2)
Plehn, 210(1), 211(7), 218(2)
Pribram, 225(28)
Price cutting and price cutters, 53, 55, 56, 68, 124-26, 128, 141-43, 145, 158, 177, 224(27)
Price decline from tax, 57, 225(32)
Price discrimination, 15, 45-46, 95-96
Price lines, 126, 140-41
Price regulation, 44, 65, 129, 140-41
Prices of factors,
  effect of tax on, 25-27, 47, 75, 105-11, 146-47, 185-86, 215(31), 216(35), 240(22)
  (see also Interest rate changes and wage changes)
Processing taxes, 83-87, 242(9)
Process of readjustment from tax, 20-21, 52, 53, 104-05, 119-21, 129-40, 152-60, 168-77, 180-86
Producer, definition of, 3
Producers sales tax:
  definition, 3
  (see also General producers sales tax)
Production functions, 25, 47
Product differentiation, 10, 65
Product variation, 65-66, 149-60
Propensity to consume, 24, 47, 106, 160, 215(30), 236(42)
Pure competition:
  incidence
    of ad valorem levies under, 88-93
    of special sales taxes under, 17-33
    significance of, for incidence, 17-33, 73, 88-93, 99, 104, 105, 119, 135, 143, 183, 187, 189, 196
  meaning, 4-7
  price determination under, 7-8
  supply curves under, 6

Q

Quality:
  analysis of, 65, 149-52
  changes in, from tax, 65-66, 152-60, 164
Quality service difference, 65-66, 118, 134, 149-50, 158-59, 169-70, 171, 172, 174, 194

R

Readjustment from tax, process of, 20-21, 52-53, 104-05, 119-21, 129-48, 152-60, 168-77, 180-86, 207(2)

Reduction in price caused by tax, 57, 225(32)
Regulation of price, 44, 129, 140-41
Resale price maintenance, 16, 126-27, 140-41, 152, 157, 235(21)
Retail price determination:
  literature, 234(4)
  theory of, 116-19, 122-29
Retail sales tax:
  definition, 3
  incidence, 116-65
    comparison with general sales tax, 186-192
  literature, 233(2), 237(43)
  nature, 116-65
Ricardo, 216(35), 231(2)
Riley, 233(2), 237(43)
Robertson, 207(6)
Robinson, E. A. G., 208(6), 209 (25)
Robinson, Joan, 207(6), 208(7), (9), 217(2), 218(3), 219(8), (10), 220(14), 221(18)
Robinson, M. E., 210(1), 212(7)
Rolph, 215(31)

S

Sales policy, 12-14, 57-61, 80, 99-100
Sales tax, definition, 3
Sandage, 224(14)
Selling costs, 57-61, 99-100
Seligman, 207(1), 210(1), 214(22), 217(2), (35), 218(2), (16), 219 (10), 220(13), 229(26), 231(6), 241(5), 242(10)
Separate charge provisions, 138-39, 140-41, 142-43, 162, 167, 184, 189, 236(32), (42), 237(43)
Sherrill, 240(21)
Shifts in demand, see Demand
Shirras, 210(1), 218(2), 220(13), 233(2), 244(19)
Short run:
  analysis of cost in, 5
  definition, 5
  incidence in,
    chain store taxes, 168-70
    general producers sales tax, 104-05
    general sales tax, 179-80
    retail sales tax, 119-20, 130-34, 137-44
    special sales tax,
      monopolistic competition, 52-53, 58, 69, 71, 72, 75, 76, 82
      monopoly, 43-44, 49
      pure competition, 17-19, 212(12)
Shoup, 231(2), 233(2), 236(32), (35), 237(43), 241(5), 242(13), 244(19), (20)
Shove, 207(6)
Shultz, 210(1), 211(7), 214(22), 218(2), 231(2), 243(15)
Silverman, 3, 207(4), 210(1), 211 (7), 214(24), 218(2), 224(23), 226(1), 233(2), 241(2)
Slope of demand curve,
  effect of, on incidence, 23, 35-37, 39-41, 41-43, 45-46, 55-56, 62, 65, 74, 76, 85, 95, 104, 111-13, 131-32, 137, 143-44, 158, 169, 171, 178, 183, 214(22), (24), 218(6), 225(38), 240(19)
Smith, A., 216(35), 217(35), 242(9)
Smith, H., 210(31), 223(13), 234(4)
Smithies, 208(6)
Special sales tax:
  definition, 3
  incidence of, 17-103
  literature,
    ad valorem, 226(1), 229(26)
    monopolistic competition, 221(1)
    monopoly, 217(2), 218(3), 219 (13)
    pure competition, 210(1), 213 (22), 215(31), 216(35)
Specialty stores, 134, 161, 162, 236(40)
Spending of tax money, 23-24, 215 (30), 231(4), 238(60)
Sraffa, 207(6)
Supply curves, 6-7, 209(18), 211(5), 212(8),

Sweezy, 208(6), 234(7)

T

Taussig, 224(27)
Theory of monopolistic competition:
  analysis, 3-16
  development, 207(6)
  literature, 207(6)
  see also Monopolistic competition
Theory of incidence,
  inadequacy of, 1-2, 148, 211(7), 213(22), 221(1), 226(1), 233 (2)
  of various taxes, see names of taxes
Townshend, 216(34)
Trade associations, 68, 225(28)
Transactions tax, 180
Triffin, 208(6), 209(24)

U

Uncertainty, 44, 63
Unemployment, 2, 26-27, 108, 110-11, 148, 159, 161, 164, 185-86, 195, 215(30), 231(4), 232(19), 239(60)
Unions, see Labor unions
Use tax, 243(16)

V

Variations in constants, 23-28, 46-47, 75, 99, 105-13, 160-61, 185-86
Von Haberler, 216(32)

W

Wage changes, 26-27, 47, 107, 110-11, 112, 148, 164-65, 195, 232(18), (19), 238(66), 242(11)
Walker, 233(2), 237(43)
Webb, 232(23)
Wholesalers, reaction of, to tax, 120, 121, 147, 160, 181, 184, 186, 191-92, 193, 241(4), (7), 242(9)
Wicksell, 218(2), (3), 219(10), 221(16), 229(26)
Willemsen, 233(2), 235(28), 236(34), (35), (41)

Bei Fragen zur Produktsicherheit wenden Sie sich bitte an:
If you have any questions regarding product safety,
please contact:

Walter de Gruyter GmbH
Genthiner Straße 13
10785 Berlin
productsafety@degruyterbrill.com